Microsoft®
Office
Excel 2003:
Quick
Course 2 of 3

Microsoft Office Excel 2003: Quick Course 2 of 3

JUDY MARDAR
Community College Workforce Alliance

RUSSEL STOLINS
Santa Fe Community College

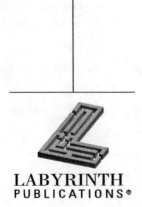

LABYRINTH
PUBLICATIONS®

Microsoft Office Excel 2003: Quick Course 2
by Judy Mardar and Russel Stolins

Copyright © 2004 by Labyrinth Publications

LABYRINTH
PUBLICATIONS®

Labyrinth Publications
3314 Morningside Drive
El Sobrante, California 94803
800.522.9746
On the Web at labpub.com

President and Publisher:
Brian Favro

Series Editor:
Russel Stolins

Managing Editor:
Laura A. Lionello

Production Manager:
Rad Proctor

Editorial/Production Team:
Holly Hammond, Nancy Logan,
Nancy Roberts

Indexing: Joanne Sprott

Cover and Interior Design:
Seventeenth Street Studios

ISBN 1-59136-037-4

Manufactured in the United States of America.

10 9 8 7 6 5 4 3   R

Microsoft Office Specialist Program

What Does This Logo Mean?

⚠ NOTE!

To be fully prepared for the Microsoft Office Excel 2003 and Microsoft Office Excel 2003 Expert exams, complete all three Quick Courses: Microsoft Office Excel 2003: Quick Course 1, Microsoft Office Excel 2003: Quick Course 2, and Microsoft Office Excel 2003: Quick Course 3.

It means this courseware has been approved by the Microsoft® Office Specialist program to be among the finest available for learning Excel 2003. It also means that upon completion of this courseware, you may be prepared to become a Microsoft Office Specialist.

What Is a Microsoft Office Specialist?

A Microsoft Office Specialist is an individual who has certified skills in one or more Microsoft Office desktop applications such as Microsoft Word, Microsoft Excel, Microsoft Outlook®, Microsoft PowerPoint®, or Microsoft Project. The Microsoft Office Specialist program typically offers certification exams at different skill levels.* The Microsoft Office Specialist program is the only Microsoft-approved program in the world for certifying proficiency in Microsoft Office desktop applications and Microsoft Project. This certification can be a valuable asset in any job search or career advancement.

Which Exam(s) Will This Publication Prepare You to Take?

Microsoft Office Excel 2003: Quick Course 1, *Microsoft Office Excel 2003: Quick Course 2*, and *Microsoft Office Excel 2003: Quick Course 3*, used in combination, have been approved by Microsoft as courseware for the Microsoft Office Specialist program. After completing a three-course sequence, students will be prepared to take the Microsoft Office Excel 2003 and the Microsoft Office Excel 2003 Expert exams.

For more information:

■ To learn more about becoming a Microsoft Office Specialist, visit www.microsoft.com/officespecialist/.

■ To purchase a Microsoft Office Specialist certification exam, visit www.microsoft.com/officespecialist/.

■ To learn about other Microsoft Office Specialist approved courseware from Labyrinth Publications, visit labpub.com/mos/.

---

* The availability of Microsoft Office Specialist certification exams varies by application, application version, and language. Visit www.microsoft.com/officespecialist/ for exam availability.

Microsoft Office Excel 2003 and Microsoft Office Excel 2003 Expert objectives covered in this book

Objective Number	Skill Sets and Skills	Concept Page References	Exercise Page References
XL03S-1-4	Insert, position, and size graphics	34–36	35–37
XL03S-2-2	Sort lists	4, 6	5–6
XL03S-2-4	Use statistical, date and time, financial, and logical functions	104	105–107
XL03S-3-2	Apply and modify cell styles	174–176, 178–179	176–180
XL03S-5-1	Create new workbooks from templates	32–33	33–34
XL03S-5-5	Preview data in other views	19–20	20
XL03S-5-6	Customize Window layout	7–8	7–10
XL03S-5-7	Setup pages for printing	10, 12–14, 16, 18–19	11–19
XL03E-1-1	Use subtotals	129–130	131–132
XL03E-1-2	Define and apply advanced filters	132–133	133–134
XL03E-1-3	Group and outline data	180–181, 183	182–184
XL03E-1-7	Perform data analysis using automated tools	108, 110, 112	108–113
XL03E-1-8	Create PivotTable and PivotChart reports	154–157, 159–161, 169–170	157–159, 161–164, 171
XL03E-1-10	Use Database functions	135–136	137
XL03E-1-14	Define, modify and use named ranges	72–75, 78	73–79
XL03E-2-3	Format and resize graphics	37–38	38–39
XL03E-3-1	Protect cells, worksheets, and workbooks	80–82	81–85
XL03E-3-2	Apply workbook security settings	85	86–87
XL03E-5-3	Modify Excel default settings	64	64–65

Contents in Brief

Contents

Index of Quick Reference Tables

Preface

Microsoft Office Excel 2003: Quick Course 2 enables students to master the fundamental skills required for effective use of Microsoft Excel 2003. When used as part of a three-book sequence with *Microsoft Office Excel 2003: Quick Course 1* and *Microsoft Office Excel 2003: Quick Course 3*, it also prepares students to pass either the Microsoft Office Excel 2003 exam or to master the more advanced skills required to pass the Microsoft Office Excel 2003 Expert exam.

The focus of *Microsoft Office Excel 2003: Quick Course 2* is to move beyond basic Excel skills. Students continue to apply the knowledge they gained in *Microsoft Office Excel 2003: Quick Course 1* as they are introduced to charting, financial functions, data analysis, and more. Upon completion of this course students will be prepared for the subject matter and challenges found in the Level 3 Quick Course. This book assumes students understand how to use a mouse and drop-down menus, save files to some type of storage media, and other basic skills required to run Windows programs.

Over the last 10 years of writing and publishing Microsoft Office courses, Labyrinth has developed a unique instructional design that makes learning faster and easier for students at all skill levels. Teachers have found that the Labyrinth model provides effective learning for students in both self-paced and instructor-led learning environments. The material is carefully written and built around compelling case studies that demonstrate the relevance of all subject matter. Mastery of subject matter is ensured through the use of multiple levels of carefully crafted exercises. The text includes Concepts Review questions and Hands-On, Skill Builder, Assessment, and Critical Thinking exercises.

The course is also supported on the Labyrinth Website with a comprehensive instructor support package that includes a printable solutions guide, detailed lecture notes, PowerPoint presentations, a course syllabus, extensive test banks, and more.

We are grateful to the many teachers who have used Labyrinth titles and suggested improvements to us during the 10 years we have been writing and publishing Office books.

About the Authors

Judy Mardar has been an independent computer trainer, technical writer, and consultant for many years. She teaches, writes, and consults at the Community College Workforce Alliance, as well as with private training companies, the state government, and small businesses. She is a certified Microsoft Office Expert and has trained thousands of people to use computers and business software over the last 10 years. Judy is coauthor of *Microsoft Office PowerPoint 2003: Essentials Course* and *Microsoft Office 2003: Essentials Course*.

Russel Stolins (MA, Educational Technology) teaches at Santa Fe Community College. He has been teaching adults about technology since 1982, including courses on desktop publishing, computer concepts, Microsoft Office applications, multimedia design, and the Internet. He is recognized nationwide as an expert in classroom teaching techniques and instructional technology, often being invited to present at education conferences throughout the U.S. In the fall of 2000, Russel developed his first Web-based course using the Blackboard Learning System in Georgia. The course has since been rolled out nationwide and new courses for the Blackboard Learning System and WebCT are currently under development. Russel's latest books, *Laying a Foundation with Windows XP* and *Welcome to the Internet*, were published by Labyrinth Publications in 2003. Russel is also a coauthor of *Microsoft Office 2003: Essentials Course*.

Introduction

Welcome to Labyrinth Publications, where you'll find your course to success. Our real world, project-based approach to education helps students grasp concepts, not just read about them, and prepares them for success in the workplace. Our straightforward, easy-to-follow language is ideal for both instructor-led classes and self-paced labs. At Labyrinth, we're dedicated to one purpose: delivering quality courseware that is comprehensive yet concise, effective, and affordable. It's no wonder that Labyrinth is a recognized leader in Microsoft Office and operating system courseware.

More than a million users have learned Office our way. At Labyrinth, we believe that successful teaching begins with exceptional courseware. That's why we've made it our goal to develop innovative texts that empower both teachers and students. We give educators the necessary resources to deliver clear, relevant instruction and students the power to take their new skills far beyond the classroom.

Labyrinth Series Give You More Choices

Labyrinth offers seven exceptionally priced series to meet your needs:

- Microsoft Office 2003 Series—These full-length, full-featured texts explore applications in the Office 2003 system. All application-specific books in this series are Microsoft Office Specialist approved for the Microsoft Office 2003 certification exams, and the Word and Excel books are also approved for the Microsoft Office 2003 Expert certification exams.

- Silver™ Series—Designed especially for adult learners, seniors, and non-native speakers, this series includes larger fonts and screens, our unmistakable straightforward design, and fun hands-on projects.

- ProStart Foundations™ Series—These full-length, full-featured texts for operating systems and applications include the new Microsoft Windows titles and are designed to lay a solid foundation for students.

- ProStart™ Series for Office XP—These full-length, full-featured texts walk students through the basic and advanced skills of the primary Office XP applications. Most are Microsoft Office Specialist approved. The Office XP Essentials and Comprehensive courses offer surveys of all the primary Office XP applications.

- Briefcase™ Series for Office XP—The popular and inexpensive choice for short classes, self-paced courses, and accelerated workshops (or mix and match for longer classes), these concise texts provide quick access to key concepts. Most are Microsoft Office Specialist approved.

- Off to Work™ Series for Office 2000—Full-length, full-featured texts set the standard for clarity and ease of use in this series. All books in this series are Microsoft Office Specialist approved.

- Briefcase Series for Office 2000—Designed for short classes, self-paced courses, and accelerated workshops, each lesson in this series is broken down into subtopics that provide quick access to key concepts. All books in this series are Microsoft Office Specialist approved.

Microsoft Office 2003 Series Teaching Resources

Instructor Support Material

To help you be more successful, Labyrinth provides a comprehensive instructor support package that includes the following:

Teaching Tools

- Detailed lecture notes, including a topic sequence and suggested classroom demonstrations

- PowerPoint presentations that give an overview of key concepts for each lesson (also available online for students)

- Answer keys for the Concepts Review questions in each lesson

- Comprehensive classroom setup instructions

- A customizable sample syllabus

- A teacher-customizable background knowledge survey to gather information on student needs and experience at the beginning of the course

Testing Tools

- Printer-friendly exercise solution guides and solution files for Hands-On, Skill Builder, Assessment, and Critical Thinking exercises

- Teacher-customizable, project-based Assessment exercises

- Teacher-customizable test banks of objective questions for each lesson and unit

- TestComposer™ test generator for editing test banks with Microsoft Word (and for creating new question banks and online tests)

These resources are available on our Website at labpub.com and on our instructor support CD, which you can obtain by calling our customer service staff at 800.522.9746.

Website

The Website labpub.com/learn/excel03/ features content designed to support the lessons and provide additional learning resources for this book. This main page contains links to individual lesson pages. Some of the items you will find at this site are described below.

PowerPoint Presentations The same presentations available to instructors are accessible online. They make excellent tools for review, particularly for students who miss a class session.

 Web-Based Simulations Some exercises contain topics that have Web-based simulations. These simulations can be accessed through the lesson pages.

Downloads Required course files can be downloaded on the lesson pages.

Student Exercise Files The student files needed to complete certain Hands-On, Skill Builder, Assessment, and Critical Thinking exercises are available for download at labpub.com/students/fdbc2003.asp.

Labyrinth's Successful Instructional Design

In conjunction with our straightforward writing style, Labyrinth books feature a proven instructional design. The following pages point out the carefully crafted design elements that build student confidence and ensure success.

Lesson introductions present clear learning objectives.

Case studies introduce a practical application that integrates topics presented in each lesson.

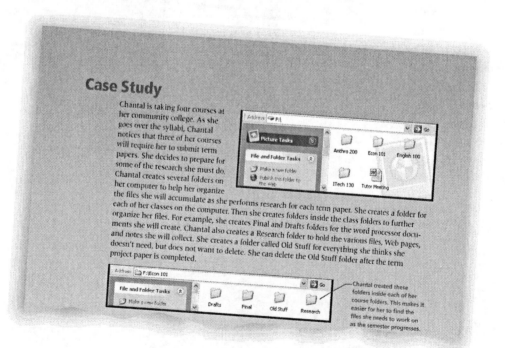

Concepts discussions are kept concise and use illustrations for added clarity and to help students understand the material introduced.

Quick Reference tables provide generic procedures for key tasks that work outside the context of the lesson.

Hands-On exercises are detailed tutorials that help students master the skills introduced in the concepts discussions. The illustrations provide clear instruction and allow unparalleled ease of use.

The Help Window Toolbar

You will encounter this toolbar when viewing Help topics in the Microsoft Word Help Window.

The Auto Tile button displays the Word window and the Help window tiled. If the window is already tiled, the button name changes to Untile. Clicking it causes the Help window to float over the Word window.

Move back one topic.

Move forward one topic.

Print the topic.

QR **QUICK REFERENCE: MOUSE MOTIONS**

Motion	How to Do It	This motion is used...
Click	Gently tap and immediately to release the left mouse button.	to "press" a button or select a menu option or object on the screen.
Double-click	Click twice in rapid succession.	as a shortcut for many types of common commands.
Drag	Press and hold down the left mouse button while sliding the mouse. Release the mouse button when you reach your destination.	to move an object, select several objects, draw lines, and select text.
Right-click	Gently tap and immediately release the right mouse button.	to display a context-sensitive menu for the object at which you are pointing.
Point	Slide the mouse without pressing a button until the pointer is in the desired location.	to position the pointer before using one of the four motions above, to select an object on the screen, or to get a menu to appear.

Hands-On 2.7 Move and Size the WordPad Window

In this exercise, you will move the WordPad window to a different location on the Desktop, then change the size of the window.

1. Follow these steps to move the WordPad window:

Click the Save in drop-down list, and choose the e 3½ Floppy (A:) drive.

Notice that WordPad proposes the name Document (or Document.doc) in the filename field.

The Hibernation option replaces Stand By in the Windows XP **shutdown** window when you press the (SHIFT) key.

Click the Save button. The light on your floppy drive will flash as the file is saved to your exercise diskette.

122 Lesson 2: Working with Windows Programs

The Concepts Review section at the end of each lesson includes both true/false and multiple choice questions.

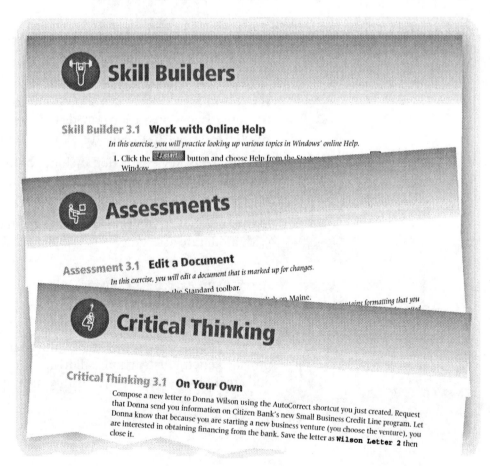

Concepts Review

True/False Questions

1. A Contents (or Home in Windows XP) search of online Help lets you locate Help topics by typing keywords.   TRUE   FALSE
2. A My Computer window lets you view the files and folders on the computer.   TRUE   FALSE
3. Windows organizes drives and folders in a hierarchy.   TRUE   FALSE
4. You can use the (CTRL) key to randomly select a group of files.   TRUE   FALSE
5. Folders can have subfolders within them.   TRUE   FALSE
6. You can use the Cut and Paste commands to move files.   TRUE   FALSE
7. Files are sent to the Recycle Bin when they are deleted from floppy disks.   TRUE   FALSE
8. The Properties command displays how much space is left on a floppy disk.   TRUE   FALSE
9. An Exploring window gives you a two-panel view of files and folder.   TRUE   FALSE
10. A quick way to open a file is to double-click on it in a My Computer windows.   TRUE   FALSE

Multiple Choice Questions

1. Which of the following methods would you use to view files and folders on the computer:
   a. Open a My Computer Window

3. Which command is used to create a new folder?
   a. File→Folder→Create
   b. File→New→Folder

Skill Builders, Assessments, and Critical Thinking exercises provide fun, hands-on projects with reduced levels of detailed instruction so students can develop and test their mastery of the material.

Skill Builders

Skill Builder 3.1   Work with Online Help

In this exercise, you will practice looking up various topics in Windows' online Help.

1. Click the [start] button and choose Help from the Start
   Window

Assessments

Assessment 3.1   Edit a Document

In this exercise, you will edit a document that is marked up for changes.

the Standard toolbar.

ck on Maine.

ntains formatting that you

Critical Thinking

Critical Thinking 3.1   On Your Own

Compose a new letter to Donna Wilson using the AutoCorrect shortcut you just created. Request that Donna send you information on Citizen Bank's new Small Business Credit Line program. Let Donna know that because you are starting a new business venture (you choose the venture), you are interested in obtaining financing from the bank. Save the letter as **Wilson Letter 2** then close it.

How This Book Is Organized

The information in this book is presented so that you master the fundamental skills first, and then build on those skills as you work with the more comprehensive topics.

Visual Conventions

This book uses many visual and typographic cues to guide you through the lessons. This page provides examples and describes the function of each cue.

Type this text   Anything you should type at the keyboard is printed in this typeface.

    Tips, Notes, and Warnings are used throughout the text to draw attention to certain topics.

Command→Command   This convention indicates multiple selections to be made from a menu bar. For example, File→Save means to select File then select Save.

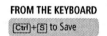   These margin notes indicate shortcut keys for executing a task described in the text.

    Quick Reference tables provide generic instructions for key tasks. Only perform these tasks if you are instructed to in an exercise.

    This icon indicates the availability of a Web-based simulation for an exercise. You may need to use a WebSim if your computer lab is not set up to support particular exercises.

    Hands-On exercises are introduced immediately after concept discussions. They provide detailed, step-by-step tutorials so you can master the skills presented.

    The Concepts Review section includes both true/false and multiple choice questions designed to gauge your understanding of concepts.

    Skill Builder exercises provide additional hands-on practice with moderate assistance.

    Assessment exercises test your skills by describing the correct results without providing specific instructions on how to achieve them.

    Critical Thinking exercises are the most challenging. They provide general instructions, allowing you to use your skills and creativity to achieve the result you envision.

Working with Large Worksheets

In this lesson, you will work with a large worksheet that tracks a personal budget and expenditures. You will sort the worksheet rows using various techniques. You will also learn commands that are particularly useful with large worksheets, including freezing rows and columns, splitting window panes, printing techniques, and inserting page breaks.

Microsoft Office Excel 2003 objectives covered in this lesson

Objective Number	Skill Sets and Skills	Concept Page References	Exercise Page References
XL03S-2-2	Sort lists	4, 6	5–6
XL03S-5-5	Preview data in other views	19–20	20
XL03S-5-6	Customize Window layout	7–8	7–10
XL03S-5-7	Setup pages for printing	10, 12–14, 16, 18–19	11–19

Case Study

Carla Adams has recently purchased a computer for home use. Carla has a flexible occupation that allows her to work out of her home two days a week. With her new Pentium computer, a high-speed Internet connection, and Office 2003, Carla can work as efficiently from home as she can in the office. Carla also uses Office 2003 for personal projects. Her most recent endeavor is to create a personal budget using Excel 2003. Carla likes Excel's flexibility and the sophisticated tools she can use with large worksheets like her home budget.

	A	B	C	D	E	F	G	H	I	J	K
1	2004 Home Budget										
2											
3		January		February		March		April		May	
4		Budget	Spent	Budget	Spent	Budget	Spent	Budget	Spent	Budget	Spent
5	Utilities	100	78	100	120	100	95	100	78	100	120
6	Mortgage	1000	1000	1000	1000	1000	1075	1075	1075	1075	1075
7	Insurance	200	200	0	0	0	0	200	200	0	0
8	Phone	60	75	60	80	60	145	60	75	60	80
9											
10											
11	Food	235	220	235	190	235	250	235	220	235	190
12	Entertainment	120	80	120	90	120	245	120	80	120	90
13	Clothing	100	54	100	0	100	234	100	54	100	0
14											
15											
16	Car Payment	400	400	400	400	400	400	400	400	400	400
17	Car Insurance	180	180	0	0	0	0	180	180	0	0
18	Car Maintenance	50	0	50	67	50	435	50	0	50	67
19											
20											
21	**Grand Total**										
22	**Differences**										

Managing Large Worksheets

Large worksheets can be difficult to work with. You may not be able to locate what you're looking for right away because the data is not organized well or you may have to constantly scroll to view different parts. Perhaps while scrolling, you lose the column or row headings. Perhaps the worksheet prints on multiple pages when you only expected it to print on one. This section contains topics to make all these headaches go away. You will learn how to sort data, make headings remain visible while you scroll, and view different parts of a worksheet at the same time.

Sorting Worksheets

Excel has powerful sorting capabilities that let you sort worksheet rows and columns. The most common type is when entire rows are sorted on the text or values in one column. However, using the Data→Sort command, you can sort by up to three columns. The sort is performed on all contiguous rows, although you can opt to select only certain rows to sort if you wish.

 NOTE!

Always save your worksheet prior to sorting. If you make a mistake while sorting you could render the worksheet useless.

Sorting by a Single Column

The Sort Ascending and Sort Descending buttons let you quickly sort by one column. Excel sorts all rows in the contiguous list unless it determines that the list has a header row. A header row is the row at the top of a list that contains column headings. To sort a list, click the column you want to use as the sort key then click either the Sort Ascending or Sort Descending button. You will learn about sorting by multiple columns in Hands-On 1.1.

Sorting Selected Rows

If the list contains rows you do not want included in the sort, you must select the rows you do want sorted before clicking one of the sort buttons. For example, if a list has a total row as its last row, you would not want that row sorted with all the others. By selecting the rows you do want to sort ahead of time, you instruct Excel to sort only those rows. It will use column A as the sort key by default.

If a sorting problem arises and you forget to use Undo, just close the worksheet without saving it. When you reopen the worksheet, it will be in the state it was prior to sorting.

Storing Your Exercise Files

Throughout this book you will be referred to files in your "file storage location." You can store your exercise files on various media such as a floppy disk, a USB flash drive, the My Documents folder, or on a network drive at a school or company. While many figures in exercises may display files in the 3½ Floppy (A:) drive, it is assumed that you will substitute your own location for that shown in the figure. See the appendix for additional information on alternative file storage media.

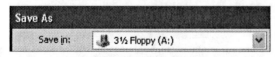

The Save In box as it appears in the book

The Save In box as it might appear if you are saving your files to a USB flash drive

Hands-On 1.1　Sort by One Column

In this exercise, you will use the sort buttons to sort several lists in a workbook.

Before You Begin: If you have not done so already, please turn to Downloading the Student Exercise Files section of the appendix (page 289) for instructions on how to retrieve the student exercise files for this book from the Labyrinth Website, and to copy the files to your file storage location for use in this and future lessons. See also pages 291–295 for additional details about using this book with a floppy disk, USB flash drive, the My Documents folder, and a folder on a network drive.

Sort Entire Lists

1. Open the workbook named Home Budget.

2. Take a few moments to browse through this worksheet.
   Notice that this worksheet is very large and contains budget data for all 12 months of the year. You will use this worksheet throughout this lesson.

3. Scroll to the top of the worksheet and click cell A5.
   In the next few steps, you will sort rows 5–8. When you do this, Excel will sort the entire rows. The rows will be sorted according to the text entries in column A because you selected a cell in this column. Keep in mind, however, that the entire rows will be sorted. Before you begin, notice that row 5 (the Utilities row) has the values 100, 78, 100, 120, etc., and row 6 (the Mortgage row) has either 1000 or 1075 in each column. Also notice that the rows are not in alphabetical order.

4. Click the Sort Ascending ![button] button.
   The Insurance row is now on top because it is the first row in alphabetical order. Also notice that the entire rows have been rearranged. For example, the Utilities row is now at the bottom of the list and the values 100, 78, 100, 120 are still part of that row. Finally, notice that the header rows 3 and 4 are not included in the sort.

5. Click the Sort Descending ![button] button to reverse the sort order.

6. Click cell B5.

7. Click the Sort Ascending ![button] button to sort the rows based on the numbers in column B.
   The Sort Ascending and Sort Descending buttons always sort rows based on the column that contains the highlight.

8. Click the Sort Descending ![button] button to sort in descending order based on the numbers in column B.

9. Click cell A5 then click the Sort Ascending ![button] button.

10. Click cell A11 then click the Sort Ascending ![button] button.
    The rows in the second list should now be in ascending order.

11. Sort the third list (rows 16–18) in ascending order based on column A.

Sort Selected Rows

12. Click cell A9 and enter the word **Subtotal**.

13. Enter **Subtotal** in cells A14 and A19.

14. Click cell A5 then click the Sort Descending ![button] button.
    Notice that Excel includes the Subtotal row in the sort. Excel usually does not include header rows and total rows in a sort. In this case, it could not determine that this was a subtotal row because formulas have not yet been used to compute the subtotals.

15. Click the Undo button to reverse the sort.

16. Select rows 5–8 by dragging the mouse pointer over the row headings.
If you need to select rows before sorting, be sure you select entire rows. If you select only certain cells in the rows, Excel will only sort those cells. This will render the entire worksheet useless. By dragging the row headings, you can be certain that you have selected entire rows.

17. Click the Sort Descending [A↓] button.
Excel should leave the Subtotal row out of the sort. Notice that Excel used column A as the sort key. Excel always uses column A as the sort key if you select rows prior to using the sort buttons, and you don't reposition the active cell.

18. Sort rows 11–13 and 16–18 in descending order (you need to select the rows before sorting).

19. Save the workbook and continue with the next topic.

Sorting by Multiple Columns

The Sort dialog box is used to specify multiple sort keys for multiple column sorts. For example, imagine you have a worksheet with last names in column A and first names in column B. Using the Sort dialog box, you can instruct Excel to first sort the rows by last name and then by first name. This way, all rows with the same last name will be grouped together. Then the rows would be sorted by first name within each group. You can sort by up to three columns. You display the Sort dialog box with the Data→Sort command.

Hands-On 1.2   Sort by Multiple Columns

In this exercise, you will use the Sort dialog box to perform a two-column sort.

1. Click the Addresses sheet tab at the bottom of the worksheet.

2. Click in any cell in the list then click Data→Sort.

3. Follow these steps to sort the address list by last name then by first name:

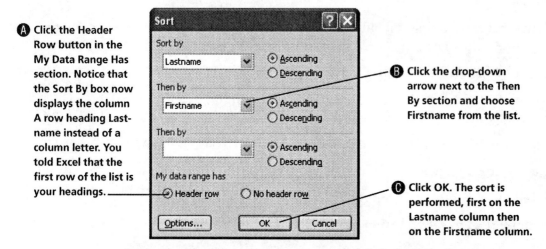

A Click the Header Row button in the My Data Range Has section. Notice that the Sort By box now displays the column A row heading Lastname instead of a column letter. You told Excel that the first row of the list is your headings.

B Click the drop-down arrow next to the Then By section and choose Firstname from the list.

C Click OK. The sort is performed, first on the Lastname column then on the Firstname column.

Notice that the Johnson entries are sorted alphabetically by first name.

4. Save the changes and continue with the next topic.

Freezing Header Rows and Columns

Freezing window panes is a useful technique when working with large worksheets. The Window→Freeze Panes command keeps header rows and columns in view while you scroll through a worksheet. When you issue this command, Excel freezes all rows above the selected cell and all columns to the left of the selected cell. For this reason, you must click the correct cell before issuing the command. You unfreeze the frozen rows and columns with the Window→ Unfreeze Panes command.

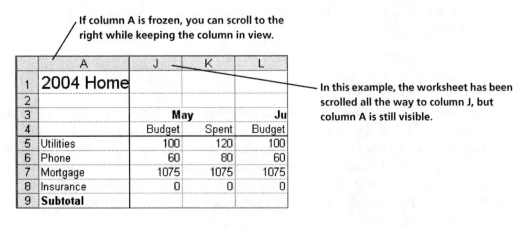

If column A is frozen, you can scroll to the right while keeping the column in view.

In this example, the worksheet has been scrolled all the way to column J, but column A is still visible.

 Hands-On 1.3   **Freeze and Unfreeze Rows and Columns**

In this exercise, you will freeze the row and column headings on the screen then scroll through the worksheet to test the results.

Freeze Panes

1. Display Sheet1 by clicking its worksheet tab.

2. Scroll through the worksheet until column Y is visible.

3. Scroll down until you cannot see rows 1–4.
    With the heading rows out of view, understanding the worksheet data is difficult.

4. Press ⌜Ctrl⌝+⌜Home⌝ to move the highlight to cell A1.
    This keystroke combination is quite useful when working with large worksheets.

5. Click cell B5.

6. Choose Window→Freeze Panes from the menu bar.

7. Scroll to column Y then scroll down to row 35.
    Notice that the headings in column A and rows 1–4 remain visible, allowing you to identify the contents of the worksheet cells.

Unfreeze Panes

8. Press Ctrl + Home and notice that the highlight moves to cell B5 instead of A1.
   Cell B5 is now the home cell because you froze the window panes at that location.

9. Click cell A5 and notice that you can edit this cell if desired.
   Frozen columns and rows are still available for editing.

10. Choose Window→Unfreeze Panes from the menu bar.

11. Feel free to experiment with freezing and unfreezing panes then continue with the next topic.

Splitting Window Panes

The Window→Split command lets you view different sections of a worksheet at the same time. This can be useful when comparing data in two different sections of a large worksheet. As with the Freeze Panes command, you should position the highlight in the desired cell before issuing the split command. You can remove the split with the Window→Remove Split command. When windows are split, they each have their own set of scroll bars. After the windows are split, you can drag any of the bars to change the split location.

The Split command lets you view two different parts of the worksheet. In this example, the January and February numbers can be compared to the October and November numbers.

	B	C	D	E	T	U	V	W
1	Budget							
2								
3	January		February		October		November	
4	Budget	Spent	Budget	Spent	Budget	Spent	Budget	Spent
3	January		February		October		November	
4	Budget	Spent	Budget	Spent	Budget	Spent	Budget	Spent
5	200	200	0	0	200	200	0	0
6	100	78	100	120	100	78	100	120
7	60	75	60	80	60	75	60	80
8	1000	1000	1000	1000	1075	1075	1075	1075

 ## Hands-On 1.4   Split Window Panes

In this exercise, you will split the window so you can compare data at the beginning of the year to data at the end of the year.

Split Window Panes

1. Click cell B5.

2. Choose the Window→Split command.
   Notice the thick border that separates the window into four panes.

3. Tap the ↑ key four times.
   Notice that the header rows are displayed in both the top and bottom panes. You can view any section of the worksheet in any pane. You can even view the same section in two or more panes.

4. Position the mouse pointer on the vertical split bar and drag to the right until it is in the middle of the window.

A Notice that this increases the amount of available space in the left panes, allowing you to compare two sections of the worksheet using the left and right panes.

	A	B	C	D	E
1	2004 Home	Budget			
2					
3			January		February
4		Budget	Spent	Budget	Spent
1	2004 Home	Budget			
2					

5. Use the scroll bar at the bottom of the fourth pane (the bottom-right pane) to make December visible.
Notice that the left panes remain stationary as you scroll through the right panes.

6. Use the scroll bar below the left panes to make December visible there.

7. Scroll through the right panes until January is visible.

8. Take a few minutes to experiment with the Window→Split Panes command.

9. When finished experimenting, use the Window→Remove Split command to remove the split from the panes.

10. Click cell B5 and use the Window→Freeze Panes command to freeze the panes.

Practice Navigation Techniques

11. Click on an open part of the horizontal scroll bar to scroll one screen.

12. Use the technique in step 11 to scroll one screen to the left.

13. Choose Edit→Go To from the menu bar.

FROM THE KEYBOARD
F5 to display the Go To box

14. Type **Y9** in the Reference box and click OK.
Excel will move the highlight to cell Y9. You can always use the Go To command to rapidly move to a specific cell.

15. Press Ctrl + Home to move the highlight to cell B5.

Special Selecting Techniques

16. Click cell B9.

17. Scroll to the right (using the mouse and scroll bar) until cell Y9 is visible.

18. Hold down the Shift key while clicking cell Y9.
This should select the range B9:Y9, which includes all the subtotal cells in row 9. This technique works better than the drag technique in large worksheets.

19. Click the AutoSum $\boxed{\Sigma}$ button to calculate the subtotals.
Notice the cells in row 21 and 22 update automatically. This happens because the cells have formulas in them already.

20. Use the preceding techniques to calculate the subtotals in rows 14 and 19.

21. Choose Window→Unfreeze Panes.

22. Save the changes to your workbook and continue with the next topic.

Setting Up Pages for Printing

Excel has a number of options to help you print large worksheets. The print options are accessed through the Page Setup dialog box. Using the Page Setup dialog box, you can adjust page orientation, margins, headers and footers, and many other options. The Page Setup dialog box is displayed with the File→Page Setup command.

Page Setup Options

The Page tab of the Page Setup dialog box lets you set various options. For example, you can choose Portrait or Landscape orientation to print your pages vertically or horizontally, respectively. Landscape orientation is useful with wide worksheets like 2004 Home Budget. The Page tab also provides automated scaling options to let you easily print large worksheets.

You can choose an orientation.

The Adjust To option compresses or expands all worksheet elements by the percentage you specify.

The Fit To option is convenient when a few rows or columns spill over to an extra page. Specify the number of pages you want and Excel will make the worksheet fit.

You can choose a paper size and print quality. Lowering the print quality can speed up printing and possibly save toner and ink.

You can change the starting first page number. For example, imagine that your Excel worksheet is part of a larger document, the first three pages of which are taken from a Word document. You can set the starting page number for the worksheet to 4 and it would bind the complete report in a logical numbering sequence.

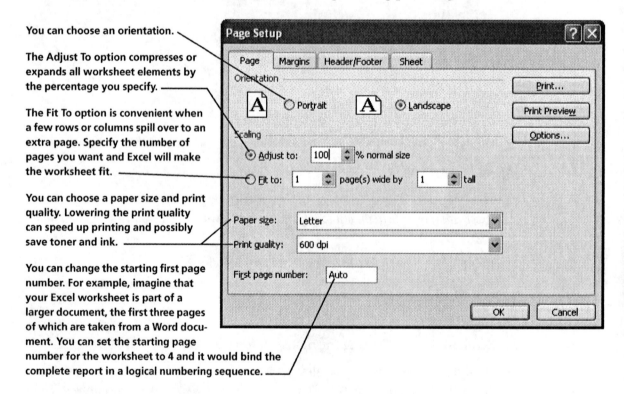

Hands-On 1.5   **Use the Page Options**

In this exercise, you will preview the worksheet, change the orientation, and work with the scaling option.

Use Print Preview

1. Zoom in on the page by clicking on the data near the top of the page.

2. If necessary, zoom in by clicking anywhere on the worksheet so the entire page is visible.
   Notice that Excel can only fit a portion of the worksheet on the page. Excel breaks up the worksheet over multiple pages if it is too large to fit on a single page. Also notice the header (Sheet1) at the top of the page and the footer (Page 1) at the bottom of the page. You will work with headers and footers later in this lesson.

3. Use the Next button on the Print Preview toolbar to view the next two pages.
   Your worksheet should have three pages.

4. Use the Previous button to move back to the first page.

5. Click the Close button to exit Print Preview.

6. Scroll to the right and notice the vertical dashed lines between columns I and J and columns R and S.
   These lines represent page breaks. They indicate where one page ends and another begins.

Switch to Landscape Orientation

7. Choose File→Page Setup from the menu bar.

8. Be sure the Page tab is active then choose Landscape orientation.

9. Click the Print Preview button on the right side of the dialog box.

10. If necessary, zoom in by clicking on the worksheet.
    Print Preview and Page Setup are designed to work together, so Excel lets you access Print Preview from Page Setup and vice versa. Notice the landscape (horizontal) orientation of the page.

11. Use the Next button to view the second page.
    Your worksheet should now fit on two pages.

Use the Scaling Options

12. Click the Setup button to display the Page Setup dialog box.

13. Choose the Fit To option and make sure the pages are set to one page wide by one page tall, as shown to the right.

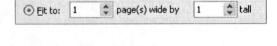

14. Click OK and notice that Excel compresses the worksheet to fit on one page.
    As you can see, it wasn't such a good idea to compress a two-page worksheet onto one page. The printed worksheet will be unreadable. The Fit To option is most convenient when you have a few columns or rows that spill over to an extra page and in long worksheets that are just slightly wider than the page. You can specify the pages wide as 1 and the pages tall setting as say, 100. Excel will reduce the width of the worksheet to fit on the page and print as many pages as necessary to complete the worksheet.

15. Click the Setup button.

16. Choose the Adjust To option button and set the percentage to 100% as shown to the right.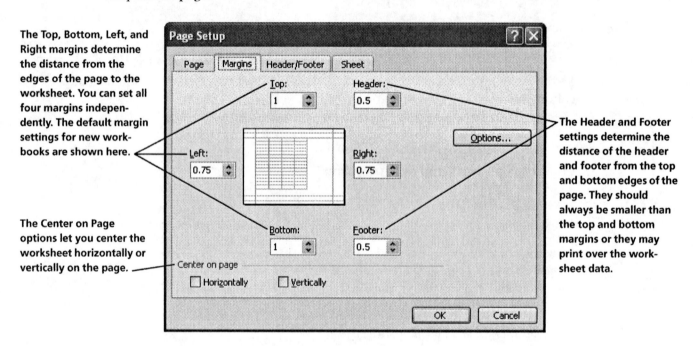
Setting the Adjust To percentage back to 100% effectively turns off the Fit To option.

⊙ Adjust to: 100 ⬍ % normal size

17. Click OK to display the worksheet in Print Preview.
Continue with the next topic, in which you will work with margin options.

Margin Options

The Margins tab of the Page Setup dialog box lets you adjust the margins and the header and footer position. You can also use the Margins tab to center the worksheet horizontally or vertically on the page.

The Top, Bottom, Left, and Right margins determine the distance from the edges of the page to the worksheet. You can set all four margins independently. The default margin settings for new workbooks are shown here.

The Center on Page options let you center the worksheet horizontally or vertically on the page.

The Header and Footer settings determine the distance of the header and footer from the top and bottom edges of the page. They should always be smaller than the top and bottom margins or they may print over the worksheet data.

Page Setup

| Page | Margins | Header/Footer | Sheet |

Top: 1
Header: 0.5
Left: 0.75
Right: 0.75
Options...
Bottom: 1
Footer: 0.5

Center on page
☐ Horizontally   ☐ Vertically

OK   Cancel

 Hands-On 1.6   Use the Margin Options

In this exercise, you will change the margins, center the worksheet vertically on the page, and adjust the header and footer positions.

The worksheet should still be in Print Preview mode from the previous exercise.

Set the Margins with Page Setup

1. If necessary, use the Previous button to move back to the first page.
The last visible column on your worksheet will most likely be the June Budget column. The June Spent column is probably on the second page and the word June may be cut off and split between the two pages. You can bring the June Spent column back to the first page by reducing the left and right margins. This will create more room on the page.

2. Click the Setup button.

3. Click the Margins tab in the Page Setup dialog box.

4. Set the left and right margins to 0.5 (that's 0.5, not 5).

5. Click the Vertically checkbox at the bottom of the dialog box.

6. Click OK to complete the changes.
   The June Spent column should be on the first page and the worksheet should be centered vertically between the top and bottom margins.

7. Click the Setup button.

8. Remove the checkmark from the Vertically checkbox.

9. Change the Header and Footer settings to 1 and click OK.
   Now both the worksheet and the header (Sheet 1) are positioned one inch from the top of the page. You should always make the header and footer settings smaller than the top and bottom margins so they print in the margin area.

10. Click the Setup button.

11. Change the Header and Footer settings to 0.5 and click OK.

Header and Footer Options

Headers print at the top of every page and footers print at the bottom of every page. You can include page numbers, dates, the workbook name, and other text in a header or footer. Excel provides a variety of built-in headers and footers from which you can choose. You can even create customized headers and footers to suit your particular needs.

Header and Footer Sections

Excel divides headers and footers into left, center, and right sections. The left section prints on the left side of the page, the center section prints in the center, and the right section prints on the right side of the page. You can instruct Excel to insert the current date, page number, or time in any section. You can also format customized headers and footers by changing the font size and typeface.

You use the Custom Header and Custom Footer buttons to create custom headers and footers. Custom headers and footers appear on the same drop-down lists as the built-in headers and footers.

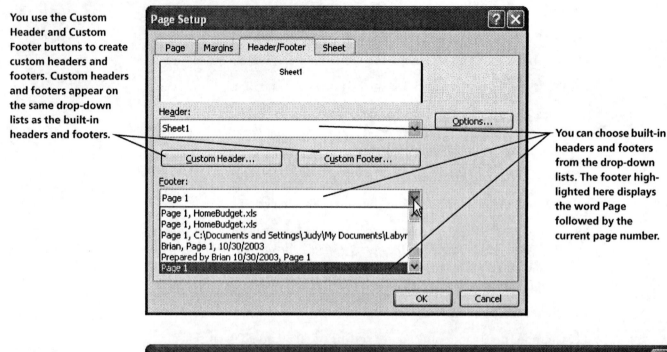

You can choose built-in headers and footers from the drop-down lists. The footer highlighted here displays the word Page followed by the current page number.

The Left Section of this customized header has a simple text label.

The Center Section contains text and fields. The fields are preceded by & symbols. The &[Page] field inserts the current page number and the &[Pages] field inserts the total number of pages in the worksheet.

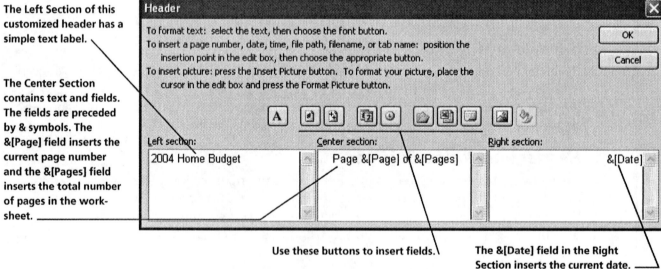

Use these buttons to insert fields.

The &[Date] field in the Right Section inserts the current date.

 ## Hands-On 1.7   Headers and Footers

In this exercise, you will work with both built-in and custom headers and footers. The worksheet should still be displayed in Print Preview from the previous exercise.

Use Built-In Headers and Footers

1. Click the Setup button then click the Header/Footer tab.

   Notice that the header is currently set to Sheet1 and the footer to Page 1. These are built-in headers and footers. The header and footer will print at the top and bottom of each page, respectively. The page number is updated on every page. For example, the footer will appear as Page 2 on the second page.

2. Follow these steps to remove the header and choose a different footer:

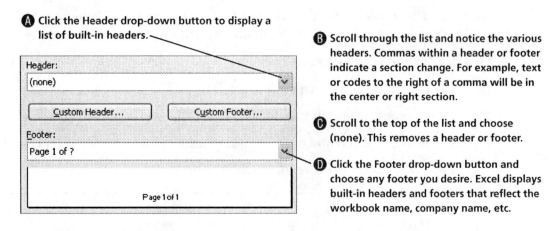

Ⓐ Click the Header drop-down button to display a list of built-in headers.

Ⓑ Scroll through the list and notice the various headers. Commas within a header or footer indicate a section change. For example, text or codes to the right of a comma will be in the center or right section.

Ⓒ Scroll to the top of the list and choose (none). This removes a header or footer.

Ⓓ Click the Footer drop-down button and choose any footer you desire. Excel displays built-in headers and footers that reflect the workbook name, company name, etc.

3. Click OK and the new footer appears in Print Preview. *The header will not be displayed because you chose (none).*

4. Take a few minutes to experiment with different built-in headers and footers. You will need to click the Setup button to return to the Page Setup dialog box. Be adventurous and choose any built-in headers or footers you desire.

Use Customized Headers and Footers

5. Display the Page Setup dialog box and make sure the Header/Footer tab is active.

6. Click the Custom Header button.

7. Follow these steps to begin creating a custom header:

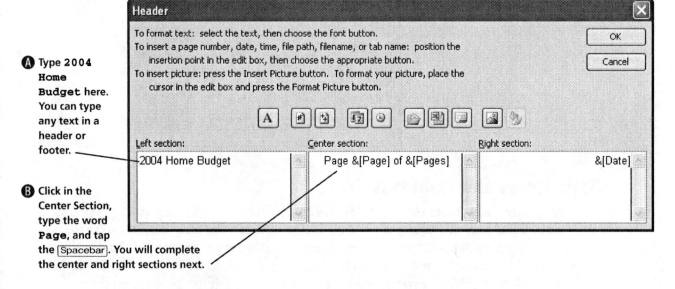

Ⓐ Type **2004 Home Budget** here. You can type any text in a header or footer.

Ⓑ Click in the Center Section, type the word **Page**, and tap the [Spacebar]. You will complete the center and right sections next.

8. Follow these steps to complete the center section:

- Click the Page Number button to insert the &[Page] code.
- Tap the [Spacebar], type **of**, and tap the [Spacebar] again.
- Click the Total Pages button to insert the &[Pages] code.

9. Click in the Right Section then click the Date button to insert the &[Date] code.

10. Take a few moments to study the header you just created. It should match the one shown in the preceding illustration. Try to understand the significance of the text and codes.

11. Click OK and your customized header will be displayed in the Page Setup dialog box.

12. Click the Footer drop-down button, scroll to the top of the list, and choose (none).

13. Click OK on the Page Setup dialog box to see the new header displayed in Print Preview.

14. Click the Next button and notice that the header is also displayed on Page 2.

15. Take a few minutes to experiment with the header and footer options.

Sheet Options

The Sheet tab of the Page Setup dialog box contains options that affect all pages in the worksheet. For example, the Gridlines option, which surrounds every cell in a printed worksheet with dotted lines, lets you turn gridlines on and off.

The Print Area option lets you specify a range of cells to print.

You set print titles here. The Print Titles option is discussed in detail in the next topic.

You can turn these options on and off.

Change the order in which pages are printed in a multiple-page worksheet.

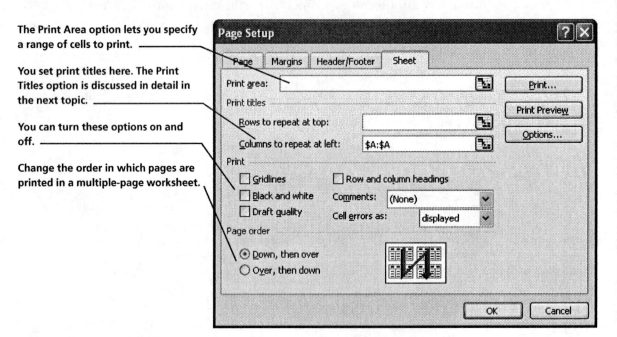

Title Rows and Columns

You can specify one or more rows as title rows and one or more columns as title columns. Title rows and columns are printed on every page of a worksheet. For example, the 2004 Home Budget worksheet will print on two pages. It may be difficult to understand the data on the second page because column A contains the headings that describe the content of the various rows. This can be resolved by specifying column A as a title column so it appears on both pages.

TIP! *The Title Rows and Title Columns options are not available if you display the Page Setup dialog box from Print Preview. To use these options, you must display the Page Setup dialog box from the worksheet with the File→Page Setup command.*

Hands-On 1.8 **Use the Sheet Options**

In this exercise, you will set options to print the gridlines and column and row headings in black and white. You will all have the column A headings print on each page.

Use Print Options

1. Display the Page Setup dialog box from Print Preview and click the Sheet tab.

2. Follow these steps to set gridlines and the row and column headings options:

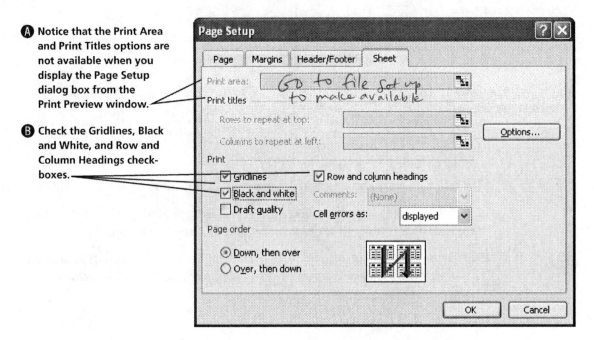

Ⓐ Notice that the Print Area and Print Titles options are not available when you display the Page Setup dialog box from the Print Preview window.

Ⓑ Check the Gridlines, Black and White, and Row and Column Headings checkboxes.

3. Click OK and examine the results in the Print Preview window.

4. Click the Close button to exit Print Preview.

Set a Title Column

5. If necessary, choose Window→Unfreeze Panes to unfreeze the panes.

6. If necessary, scroll up or down until cells A1:A22 are visible.

7. Choose File→Page Setup from the menu bar.

8. Make sure the Sheet tab is active.

9. If necessary, drag the Page Setup dialog box to the side until column A is visible.

10. Follow these steps to set the title column and adjust other options:

Ⓐ Click the Columns to Repeat at Left box.

Ⓑ Click any cell in column A. Notice that the symbols $A:$A appear in the Columns to Repeat at Left box. If you had selected columns A and B, the symbols would read $A:$B, etc.

Ⓒ Uncheck the Gridlines, Black and White, and Row and Column Headings checkboxes.

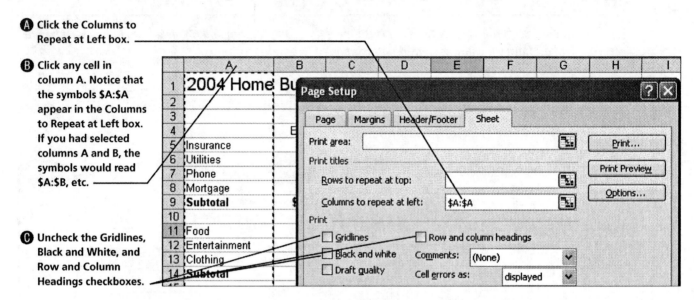

11. Click the Print Preview button and notice column A on the left side of the page.

12. Click the Next button and column A will be repeated on the second page.
It is now easy to identify the rows on both the first and second pages.

13. Click the Setup button and notice that the Print Titles section is unavailable.
The Page Setup dialog box must be displayed through the File→Page Setup command if you want to set print titles.

14. Click OK to close the Page Setup dialog box.

15. Take a few minutes to experiment with the Page Setup options.

16. Close Print Preview when you are finished experimenting.

Working with Page Breaks

Excel formats most printed worksheets by inserting automatic page breaks when necessary. However, you may want to force a page break at times. For example, in the budget worksheet, Excel may split a month by printing the budget column on the first page and the spent column on the second page. The budget and spent columns for a given month should really be printed side by side. You can insert a manual page break with the Insert→Page Break command. Manual page breaks appear as dashed lines, where the dashes are slightly longer than the automatic page breaks.

Location of Manual Page Breaks

The Insert→Page Break command inserts page breaks to the left of and above the highlight. For this reason, you must position the highlight in the desired cell before issuing the command.

Removing Page Breaks

To remove a page break, position the highlight just below or to the left of the desired break. The Insert→Remove Page Break command will then remove the desired page break(s). If necessary, Excel will insert automatic page breaks after you remove manual page breaks.

 Hands-On 1.9   Work with Page Breaks

In this exercise, you will experiment with page breaks.

Restore Print Options

1. Choose File→Page Setup from the menu bar.

2. Click the Margins tab and set all four margins to 1".

3. Click the Sheet tab and delete any codes or text in the Columns to Repeat at Left box.

4. Click OK to return to the worksheet.

Insert and Remove a Page Break

5. Notice the vertical dashed line between columns L and M.
   This automatic page break broke the page after the June Budget column.

6. Click cell L1.
   In the next step, you will insert a manual page break. This will cause the automatic page break between columns L and M to vanish. Also, the page break will be inserted to the left of the column with the highlight. The highlight is positioned in row 1 because you only need to break the page horizontally. If the highlight is in row 1, no page break will be inserted above the highlight (only to the left of the highlight). Your worksheet will print on several pages if you insert the break further down the column.

7. Choose Insert→Page Break from the menu bar.
   The vertical dashed line should now be to the left of column L.

8. Choose Insert→Remove Page Break.
   The automatic page break should return between columns L and M.

Page Break Preview

Page Break Preview shows where page breaks occur on a worksheet and which part of the worksheet will be printed. In Page Break Preview, printable areas of the worksheet appear in white while nonprintable areas appear in gray. You can adjust the location of page breaks by dragging them in Page Break Preview. When you adjust page breaks using Page Break Preview, Excel automatically sets the Scaling percentage in the Page Setup dialog box to fit the worksheet within the page break boundaries you specify. You use the View→Page Break Preview command to switch to Page Break Preview. You return to the normal view mode with the View→Normal command.

In Page Break Preview, you can drag the page break lines to change the page breaks. Excel scales the worksheet to fit within the boundaries you specify.

	A	B	C	D	E	F	G	H	I	J	K	L	M	N	O	P	Q	R	S
1	2004 Home Budget																		
2																			
3		January		February		March		April		May		June		July		August		September	
4		Budget	Spent	Budget	Spent	Budget	Spent	Budget	Spent	Budget	Spent	Budget	Spent	Budget	Spent	Budget	Spent	Budget	Spent
5	Insurance	200	200	0	0	0	0	200	200	0	0	0	0	200	200	0	0	0	0
6	Utilities	100	78	100	120	100	95	100	78	100	120	100	95	100	78	100	120	100	95
7	Phone	60	75	60	80	60	145	60	75	60	80	60	145	60	75	60	80	60	145
8	Mortgage	1000	1000	1000	1000	1000	1000	1075	1075					1075	1075	1075	1075	1075	1075
9	Subtotal	$1,360	$1,353	$1,160	$1,200	$1,160	$1,315	$1,435						28	$1,235	$1,275	$1,235	$1,315
10																			
11	Food	235	220	235	190	235	250	235						220	235	190	235	250
12	Entertainment	120	80	120	30	120	245	120						80	120	30	120	245
13	Clothing	100	54	100	0	100	234	100						54	100	0	100	234
14	Subtotal	$455	$354	$455	$280	$455	$729	$455						54	$455	$280	$455	$729
15																			
16	Car Payment	400	400	400	400	400	400	400						400	400	400	400	400
17	Car Insurance	180	180	0	0	0	0	180						180	0	0	0	0
18	Car Maintenance	50	0	50	0	50	435	50						0	50	67	50	435
19	Subtotal	$630	$580	$450	$467	$450	$835	$630						80	$450	$467	$450	$835
20																			
21	Grand Total	$2,445	$2,287	$2,065	$1,347	$2,065	$2,879	$2,520						62	$2,140	$2,022	$2,140	$2,879
22	Differences	$158		$118		-$814		$158								$118		-$739	

(Dialog box overlaying worksheet: **Welcome to Page Break Preview** — "You can adjust where the page breaks are by clicking and dragging them with your mouse." ☐ Do not show this dialog again. [OK])

(Watermark text: Page 1 ... Page 2)

 ## Hands-On 1.10 Use Page Break Preview

In this exercise, you will explore the Page Break Preview feature.

1. Choose View→Page Break Preview from the menu bar.

2. If the Welcome to Page Break Preview dialog box appears, click the OK button to close the dialog box.
   You should see a vertical, dark blue page break line near the middle of the worksheet.

3. Try dragging the blue page break line to the left or right.
   Notice that Excel shows you exactly which part of the worksheet will be printed on pages 1 and 2.

4. Drag the blue page break line until it is positioned between columns O and P.

5. Click anywhere on Page 1 then click the Print Preview 🔍 button.
   The worksheet has been scaled to fit within the page break boundaries you specified.

6. Click the Setup button on the Print Preview toolbar then click the Page tab in the Page Setup dialog box.
   The Adjust To percentage has been reduced to make the page fit within the boundaries you specified.

7. Click Cancel to close the Page Setup dialog box.

8. Close the Print Preview window and choose View→Normal to return to the Normal view.

9. Scroll to the right in your worksheet and notice that a page break is positioned between columns O and P.
   This is the page break you inserted by dragging the page break in Page Break Preview.

10. Click in column P and choose Insert→Remove Page Break.
    The appearance of the page break line will change slightly.

11. Save and close the workbook.

Concepts Review

True/False Questions

1. Sorting may damage worksheets so you should always save before sorting.   TRUE   FALSE

2. The Sort Ascending ![icon] button can only be used if you first select the desired rows.   TRUE   FALSE

3. The Sort dialog box lets you specify more than one sort key.   TRUE   FALSE

4. The Window→Freeze Panes command lets you view two sections of the worksheet at the same time.   TRUE   FALSE

5. Freezing the panes makes identifying data in large worksheets easier.   TRUE   FALSE

6. The Page Setup dialog box provides access to many features useful when printing large worksheets.   TRUE   FALSE

7. Headers and footers have three sections.   TRUE   FALSE

8. Page Break Preview can be used to view page breaks, but you cannot change page breaks in this view.   TRUE   FALSE

9. You can perform sorts on up to three columns.   TRUE   FALSE

10. The Fit To feature compresses worksheet data.   TRUE   FALSE

Multiple Choice Questions

1. Which columns and rows are frozen when you issue the Window→Freeze Panes command?
   a. Columns to the left of and rows above the highlight
   b. Columns to the left of and rows below the highlight
   c. Columns to the right of and rows below the highlight
   d. Columns to the right of and rows above the highlight

2. Which tab in the Page Setup dialog box lets you set Landscape orientation?
   a. Page
   b. Margins
   c. Header/Footer
   d. Sheet

3. Assuming the current page is 1, how will the header Page &[Page] be printed?
   a. Page 1 of 1
   b. Page 1 of 2
   c. Page 1
   d. Page 1, Current Date

4. Which command is used to insert a manual page break?
   a. Format→Page Break
   b. Insert→Page Break
   c. Ctrl + Enter
   d. None of the above

Skill Builders

Skill Builder 1.1   Insert Formulas and Sort rows

In this exercise, you will open a workbook that contains an accounts receivable aging report. You will use a formula to calculate the number of days the accounts are past due and sort the rows. You will also use the TODAY function.

Create the Formulas

1. Open the Aging Report workbook.

2. Use the TODAY function to insert the current date in cell C2.

3. Click cell E5 and enter the formula **=TODAY()-C5**.

4. Use the Format Painter ✐ button to copy the General Style number format from a blank cell to cell E5.
   A whole number should be displayed in the cell.

5. Use the fill handle to copy the formula down the column.

6. Click cell F5 and enter the formula **=E5-30**.

7. Use the fill handle to copy the formula down the column.

Sort the Rows

8. Notice that the rows are currently sorted by invoice number in column B.

9. Click cell A5.

10. Click the Sort Ascending ⬇ button to sort the rows by the names in column A.

11. Click cell B5 and click the Sort Descending ⬇ button.
    The rows should be sorted in descending order by invoice number.

12. Sort the rows in descending order by the invoice amount. When you have finished, the largest invoice amount should be at the top of the list.

13. Save the changes and close the workbook.

Skill Builder 1.2   Use Multiple Sort Keys

In this exercise, you will use the Sort dialog box to sort worksheet rows using two sort keys.

1. Open the Balance Due Report workbook.
   Notice that the list is currently sorted by the Outstanding Balance column.

2. Click anywhere in the Lastname column and choose Data→Sort from the menu bar.
   Excel will identify the list and select the correct rows. The header row will not be selected. Notice that Lastname is already in the first Sort By box and set to Ascending order.

3. Set the first Then By key to Firstname in Ascending order and click OK.
   Take a moment to study the results. Notice that rows with the same last names are grouped together. Those groups are then sorted by the first names.

4. Choose Data→Sort from the menu bar.
   Now you will change the sort order. First you will sort the list by the Lastname column. Then you will sort those groups by the Outstanding Balance column.

5. Use the following guidelines to change the sort order:
   - Use the Lastname column in ascending order for the Sort By box.
   - Use the Outstanding Balance column in ascending order for the first Then By box, and then click OK.

   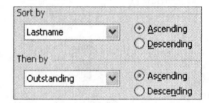

   Notice that the rows with the same last names are still grouped together. Notice also that the groups are sorted by the Outstanding Balance column. You will perform one more sort in the next step.

6. Sort the rows in ascending order using only the Outstanding Balance column.
   You don't have to use the Sort dialog box because you are using just one sort key. Just click on any item in column D and click the Sort Ascending button. All rows with an Outstanding Balance code of N should move to the top of the list.

7. Save the changes and close the workbook.

■

Skill Builder 1.3   Create a Customized Footer

In this exercise, you will remove a header and create a custom footer. You will also preview and print the worksheet.

1. Open the Home Budget workbook that you used throughout the Hands-On exercises in this lesson.

2. Choose File→Page Setup and click the Header/Footer tab.

3. Remove the header by clicking the header drop-down button and choosing (none) from the top of the list.

4. Click the Custom Footer button.

5. Follow these steps to create a customized footer and format the footer:

Ⓐ Enter the text and codes in the left, center, and right sections shown here. Use the toolbar buttons to enter the codes.

Ⓑ Select the Page &[Page] text and code in the left section by dragging the mouse over them.

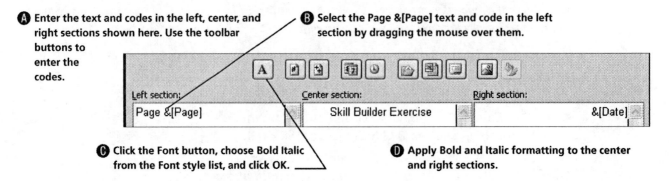

Ⓒ Click the Font button, choose Bold Italic from the Font style list, and click OK.

Ⓓ Apply Bold and Italic formatting to the center and right sections.

6. Click OK and the customized footer should be displayed in the Page Setup dialog box.

7. Click the Print Preview button on the dialog box.

8. Use the Next button to browse though the worksheet and check out the footer.

9. Close Print Preview, save the changes, and close the workbook.

Skill Builder 1.4   Print a Large Worksheet on One Page

In this exercise, you will set a worksheet to print on a single page. You will accomplish this by using landscape orientation and the Fit To options. You will also add a header and footer.

1. Open the Volume Comparison workbook.

2. Click the Print Preview ⬚ button.
   Notice that the worksheet currently is in Portrait (vertical) orientation.

3. Use the Next button to browse though worksheet and notice that it is three pages long.
   In the remainder of this exercise, you will adjust settings in the Page Setup dialog box so this worksheet prints on a single page.

4. Use the Previous button to go to page 1.

5. Click the Setup button on the Print Preview toolbar.

6. Make sure the Page tab is active and set the orientation to Landscape.

7. Click the Fit To button and make sure the Fit To option is set to 1 Pages Wide by 1 Pages Tall.

8. Click the Header/Footer tab.

9. Choose the built-in footer Page 1 of ?.

10. Click OK and the worksheet should fit on one page.

11. Close Print Preview, save the changes, and close the workbook.

Assessments

Assessment 1.1   Use Multiple Sort Keys

In this exercise, you will sort the rows in a worksheet using three sort keys.

1. Open the workbook named 2004 Orders.
   Notice that the rows are currently sorted by 2004 Sales Volume in column D.

2. Use the Sort dialog box to sort the rows using three sort keys as follows:
   - Key 1—Customer in Ascending order
   - Key 2—Division in Ascending order
   - Key 3—Key Contact in Ascending order

3. Format the numbers in column D as Comma style with no decimals.

4. AutoFit all column widths.
   Your completed worksheet should match the following example.

	A	B	C	D
1	2004 Orders			
2				
3	Customer	Division	Key Contact	2004 Sales Volume
4	Alexis	Battery Division	Frank Jordan	3,303,336
5	Alexis	Battery Division	Richard Warren	1,605,476
6	Alexis	Battery Division	Susan Christopher	1,775,262
7	Alexis	Battery Division	William J. Pinckerton	4,831,410
8	Dimension Systems	Automotive	Michael Chricton	2,624,192
9	Dimension Systems	Automotive	Michael Wilson	3,473,122
10	Dimension Systems	Automotive	Stephen Crane	2,963,764
11	Dimension Systems	Large Vehicle	Bill Clayton	2,114,834
12	Dimension Systems	Large Vehicle	Carl Bartholomew	4,152,266
13	Dimension Systems	Large Vehicle	Larry Alexander	4,661,624
14	Qualtron	Computer Technology	Bill Thompson	2,454,406
15	Qualtron	Computer Technology	Dick Morris	1,435,690
16	Qualtron	Computer Technology	Sandy Princeton	2,793,978
17	Qualtron	Medical Techologies	Joe Gecko	3,133,550
18	Qualtron	Space Systems	Bill Rogers	1,945,048
19	Qualtron	Space Systems	Stacey Crawford	4,322,052
20	Qualtron	Space Systems	Stan Barnes	1,265,904
21	Qualtron	Space Systems	Wanda Wilson	3,812,694
22	Zenex	CAD	Alice Senton	4,491,838
23	Zenex	CAD	Joseph Harding	3,982,480
24	Zenex	Semiconductor	Ben Warren	3,642,908
25	Zenex	Semiconductor	Lois Lane	2,284,620

5. Print the worksheet, save the changes, and close the workbook.

Assessment 1.2   Print a Large Worksheet on One Page

In this exercise, you will use the Page Setup dialog box to format the worksheet so it prints on one page. You will also include a header and footer.

1. Open the Mary Cook Expenses workbook.

2. Use the Page Setup dialog box to format the worksheet to print on one page. You will need to change the orientation, add a header and footer, and change the margins or use the Fit To option.

3. Use Print Preview to review the worksheet prior to printing.

4. Print the worksheet, save the changes, and close the workbook.

Mary Cook 2004 Expenses

2004 Expenses for Mary Cook

	January	February	March	April	May	June	July	August	September	October	November	December
Cell Phone	245	270	295	320	345	370	205	220	235	250	265	280
Automobile	325	345	365	385	405	425	205	240	275	310	345	380
Entertainment	150	170	190	210	230	250	15	70	125	180	235	290
Miscellaneous	105	115	125	135	145	160	165	170	175	180	185	190

Selmar Systems   Page 1 of 1   10/30/2003

Critical Thinking

Critical Thinking 1.1   On Your Own

Carmen Brandow is an administrative assistant at Fremont Pet Supplies, a wholesale distributor of pet supplies to companies in Northern California. Carmen asks you to set up a worksheet to track the number of orders and their total dollar value for Fremont's six largest customers. She tells you to record the information on a monthly basis for each month of the year. Carmen provides you with the following data for January orders.

Customer	# of Orders	Total Dollar Value
Northern California Pet Care	12	$ 2,568
My Pet Stores	16	$ 4,568
John Adams Pet Stores	23	$ 6,870
Pinnacle Pet Care	10	$ 1,250
West Side Pet Care	6	$ 5,900
Perfect Pets	52	$19,900

Set up a worksheet using this data. Format the entries using the formats shown in the preceding table; that is, center and bold the column headings, center the values in the # of Orders column, and use currency with no decimals for the dollar values. Set up the worksheet for all 12 months of the year but only add numeric data for January, February, and March (you determine the numbers used for February and March). Center the month headings above the # of Orders and Total Dollar Value columns. Save the workbook as **Customer Orders**.

Critical Thinking 1.2   On Your Own

Open the Customer Orders workbook and save it as **Qtrly Orders**. Insert a row above the row with the months. Use the Merge and Center option to center the headings Quarter 1, Quarter 2, Quarter 3, and Quarter 4 above the corresponding months. For example, Quarter 1 should be centered above the January–March headings. Copy the Quarter 1 data and paste the duplicate data into the new quarters (columns H–Y). Add a totals row that calculates the total number of orders and total dollar value of orders for each month. Make the worksheet print on four pages in portrait orientation. Each page should include the headings and data for one quarter. For example, all of the Quarter 1 information will print on the first page, Quarter 2 will print on the second page, etc. Make sure the customer names in column A are repeated on every printed page. Format the worksheet as desired and save it when you are finished.

Critical Thinking 1.3   On Your Own

Brittany Barton is the manager of the accounting department of Kids in Cloth, a provider of reusable cloth baby diapers. Some aspects of Kids in Cloth's business can be quite messy, but not Brittany's accounting department. Brittany asks you to prepare a worksheet that lists each customer account and the number of diapers used on a weekly basis. Set up a worksheet to track this information. Use customer numbers beginning with the number 100 and continuing sequentially through 200. Use the headings Week 1 through Week 52. This may seem like a lot of data entry but you can do this very rapidly using the fill handle. Also, enter a number in the first cell requiring a number and copy the number to all other cells in the worksheet. Each cell will have the same number, but this is a quick way to fill the sheet with data. Set up the worksheet to print in portrait orientation two pages high by five pages wide. Make sure the customer numbers and the weeks will print on every page. Don't print the worksheet but use Print Preview to review your work. Save the workbook as **Diaper Usage**.

Critical Thinking 1.4   Web Research

Open the Qtrly Orders workbook and save it as **Potential Custs**. Use Internet Explorer and a search engine of your choice to locate potential customers for Fremont Pet Supplies in Northern California. Enter the customer names, location (city), Website URLs, and telephone numbers in Sheet2 of the workbook. Also include any information that may be useful to the sales force at Fremont Pet Supplies, such as the size of the potential customer and the types of pets to which they cater. Include as many potential customers as you can find. When you have finished, format the worksheet to print on a single page. You can use either portrait or landscape orientation. Save the worksheet when you are finished.

Critical Thinking 1.5   Web Research

Martha Robinson is the owner of Martha's Books. In recent years, Martha's business has come under intense competitive pressure from online booksellers. Martha hires you to conduct a research project to help her analyze the threat posed by her deep-pocketed competitors. Locate three online booksellers and visit their Websites to get pricing information on six different book titles. You choose the book titles or use titles you find on the sites. Set up a worksheet with the three online bookseller's names and URLs, the six titles you have chosen, ISBNs of the titles, suggested retail prices, actual selling prices, freight charges, and Martha's price for the same titles (you determine Martha's prices). Use a formula to calculate the total price of the online sellers' books, which includes the selling price plus freight. Format all total cells with a blue color. For each title, use a formula to calculate the difference between Martha's price and the average price of the three online booksellers. Format all different cells with a distinctive color. Set up the worksheet to print on a single page in landscape orientation. Save the workbook as **Competition Research**.

LESSON 2

Introducing Templates and Graphics

As Excel becomes an integral part of your business toolkit, you may find a need to use certain workbooks over and over again. For example, many sales people need to fill out monthly expense reports, sales forecasts, and call reports. You can use Excel templates as the basis for these and other frequently used workbooks. You may also want to enhance your workbooks with pictures, drawing objects, and special effects like WordArt. This lesson will introduce you to templates and a variety of graphic tools. You will learn how to create custom templates in *Microsoft Office Excel 2003: Quick Course 3.*

Microsoft Office Excel 2003 and Microsoft Excel 2003 Expert objectives covered in this lesson

Objective Number	Skill Sets and Skills	Concept Page References	Exercise Page References
XL03S-1-4	Insert, position, and size graphics	34–36	35–37
XL03S-5-1	Create new workbooks from templates	32–33	33–34
XL03E-2-3	Format and resize graphics	37–38	38–39

Additional learning resources are available at labpub.com/learn/excel03/

Case Study

Megan Shepherd is a manager for Trade Winds Sailing Club. The sailing club sponsors frequent sailing events for club members and Megan is responsible for organizing these events. She wants a tool that will allow her to report event results consistently. She decides that Excel is the right tool for the job. With Excel, Megan can set up a template that is used as the basis for new workbooks. Megan also gives her staff the freedom to add pictures, graphics, and other enhancements to new workbooks generated from the template. In this lesson, you will use a template as the basis for a new workbook. You will add the picture and graphics shown in the following illustration to the workbook.

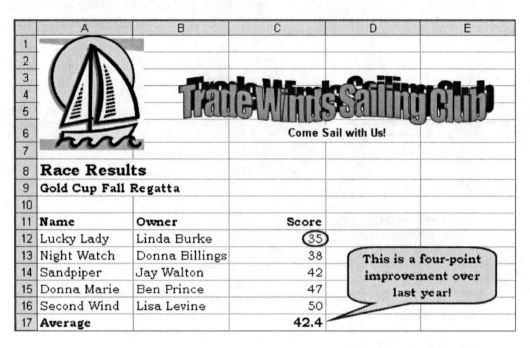

Creating Workbooks from Templates

You can use templates as the basis for new workbooks. Templates can include any type of cell entries, formatting, pictures, drawing objects, and any other objects and formats available in Excel. The benefit of templates is that they do not change when workbooks based on them change. This lets you use templates over and over as the basis for new workbooks.

The New Workbook Task Pane

The File→New command displays the New Workbook task pane, which can be used to open existing workbooks, create new blank workbooks, and create new workbooks based on templates. The following illustration describes the options available through the New Workbook task pane.

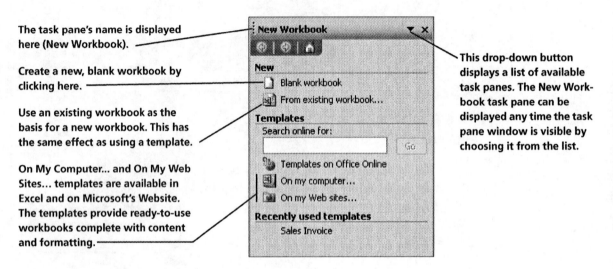

The task pane's name is displayed here (New Workbook).

Create a new, blank workbook by clicking here.

Use an existing workbook as the basis for a new workbook. This has the same effect as using a template.

On My Computer... and On My Web Sites... templates are available in Excel and on Microsoft's Website. The templates provide ready-to-use workbooks complete with content and formatting.

This drop-down button displays a list of available task panes. The New Workbook task pane can be displayed any time the task pane window is visible by choosing it from the list.

Using Templates

The On My Computer… option on the New Workbook task pane displays the Templates box. The Templates box displays built-in Spreadsheet Solutions templates and custom templates. You can base a new workbook on a template by double-clicking the desired template or choosing it and clicking OK. The new workbook can then be developed and saved to any storage location. The underlying template remains unchanged.

You can also base a workbook on a template by navigating to the location in which the template is stored and double-clicking the template. This is the technique you will use in the Hands-On exercises throughout this lesson. The following illustration describes options available through the Templates box.

The General tab is where custom templates are stored by default.

The Spreadsheet Solutions tab displays sophisticated templates installed with Excel.

The Template on Office Online button displays Microsoft's Website, from where you can download additional templates.

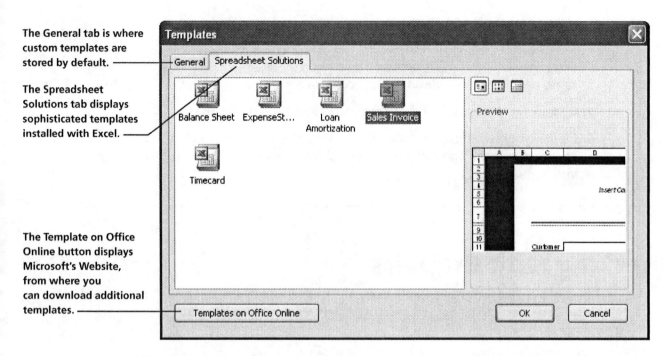

You can also base one workbook on another using the From Existing Workbook link on the New Workbook task pane. *Microsoft Office Excel 2003: Quick Course 3* teaches you how to create custom templates, edit existing templates, and change the default location for templates.

 Hands-On 2.1   Use a Template

In this exercise, you will base a new workbook on a template. You will use Window's Explorer tool to display the template.

Use the Template

1. Right-click the Start button and choose Explore from the context menu.

2. Use Windows Explorer to navigate to your file storage location.

3. Double-click the Race Results (Template) file.
   A new workbook based on the template will appear. Notice that the workbook contains formatted text entries. In addition, the column widths are wider here and the row heights are higher than Excel's standards. The new workbook is set up exactly like the underlying template.

IMPORTANT!   *Use the preceding steps to access templates stored in locations (such as a floppy disk) other than the Templates box.*

Save the Workbook

4. Click the Save ![save icon] button to display the Save As box.

   Notice that the Save As Type option at the bottom of the box is set to Microsoft Excel Workbook. Once again, you are working with a workbook based on the underlying template.

5. Change the name in the File Name box to **Fall Gold Results**.

6. Choose your file storage location in the Save In box, and then click Save.

   You will modify this workbook throughout this lesson though the underlying template will remain unchanged.

Working with Graphics

You can dress up your worksheets using the professionally designed clip art provided with Office 2003. You can also insert your own pictures, such as a company logo or a scanned picture.

The Insert Clip Art Task Pane

The Insert Clip Art ![clip art icon] button on the Drawing toolbar and the Insert→Picture→Clip Art command display the Clip Art task pane. The Clip Art task pane lets you search for clip art using keywords. Every clip art image provided with Office 2003 has a number of keywords associated with it that describe the image. For example, the image shown to the right can be located using keywords such as boats, sailboats, and sailing. The following illustrations describe the Clip Art task pane.

You search for clip art by entering one or more keywords in the Search For text box.

The Search In and Results Should Be lists let you narrow your search to include only certain clip art categories or media types. The Clip Art task pane also lets you search for movies, sound files, and pictures.

Access the Microsoft Clip Organizer here. The Clip Organizer has a Windows Explorer-like interface, letting you locate clip art by browsing categorized folders.

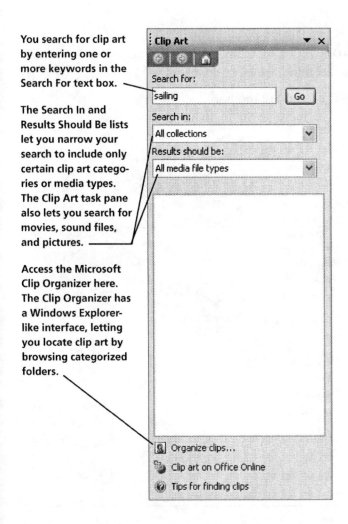

The search displays all images containing the keyword(s) you enter. An image can be inserted by simply choosing it from the list.

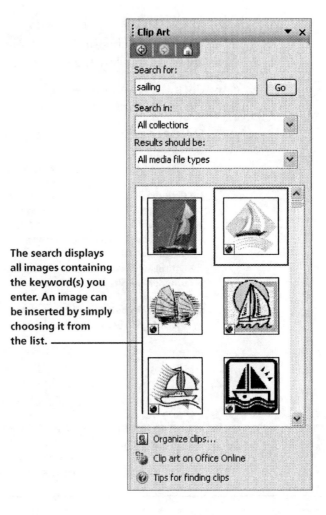

 Hands-On 2.2   Insert Clip Art

In this exercise, you will modify the worksheet you created from the template. You will insert rows to create space for a clip art image at the top of the worksheet.

Modify the Worksheet

1. If necessary, click cell A1 and tap [Delete] to remove the title.

2. Select rows 1–5 by dragging the mouse pointer over the row headings.

3. Choose Insert→Rows to insert five blank rows at the top of the worksheet.

4. Click cell A1.
   When the clip art image is inserted in the next section of this exercise, it will be positioned in the top-left corner of the worksheet. Images are inserted at the location of the current cell.

Insert Clip Art

5. If necessary, choose View→Toolbars→Drawing to display the Drawing toolbar. It should appear just below the worksheet at the bottom of the Excel window.

6. Click the Insert Clip Art  button on the Drawing toolbar.
   The Clip Art task pane appears.

7. Follow these steps to conduct a search:

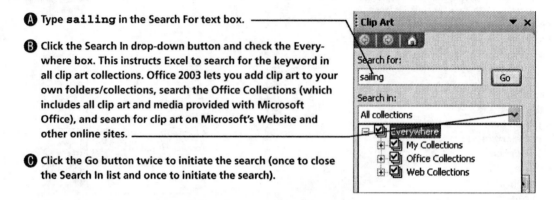

Ⓐ Type **sailing** in the Search For text box.

Ⓑ Click the Search In drop-down button and check the Everywhere box. This instructs Excel to search for the keyword in all clip art collections. Office 2003 lets you add clip art to your own folders/collections, search the Office Collections (which includes all clip art and media provided with Microsoft Office), and search for clip art on Microsoft's Website and other online sites.

Ⓒ Click the Go button twice to initiate the search (once to close the Search In list and once to initiate the search).

8. Scroll through the clips that appear and click the one shown at right. (If this image is not available, choose one you like.)

9. Feel free to experiment with the Clip Art task pane and close it when you are finished.

10. Save the changes to your worksheet.

Moving, Sizing, and Rotating Objects

When you click an object (such as a clip art image), sizing handles and a rotate handle appear. You can easily move, size, and rotate a selected object as described in the following illustration.

Drag the green rotate handle to rotate an object.

Sizing handles appear on the sides and corners of a selected object. You can adjust either the width or height by dragging the side-, top-, or bottom-sizing handles. Or, you can adjust both the width and height proportionately by dragging a corner handle.

The move pointer appears when you point on an object. You can move an object by dragging it while the move pointer is visible.

Hands-On 2.3   Move, Rotate, and Size the Image

In this exercise, you will modify the appearance of the clip art image you have selected.

1. Follow these steps to move, rotate, and size the image:

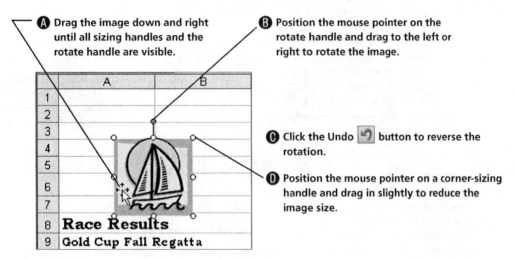

Ⓐ Drag the image down and right until all sizing handles and the rotate handle are visible.

Ⓑ Position the mouse pointer on the rotate handle and drag to the left or right to rotate the image.

Ⓒ Click the Undo button to reverse the rotation.

Ⓓ Position the mouse pointer on a corner-sizing handle and drag in slightly to reduce the image size.

2. Now adjust the size and position of the picture so it fits in the top-left corner of the worksheet, as shown to the right.

3. Click outside the picture to deselect it.

4. Save the changes to your worksheet.

Cropping and Scaling Graphics

You can make many formatting changes to a graphic once it is inserted. You can crop part of the picture or, if you prefer to leave all the background. If the picture is just too big and you don't want to crop it, you can scale it instead.

You use the Crop 🖟 button on the Picture toolbar to cut out a portion of the picture. The Format→Picture dialog box also contains a crop feature, from where you specify an amount in inches to crop. Since figuring out just how much to specify is so difficult, most users prefer the button on the Picture toolbar.

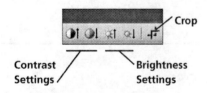

Crop

Contrast Settings

Brightness Settings

Scaling a picture reduces its overall size to a percentage of its original size. You can scale precisely by using the Size page in the Format Picture dialog box.

Hands-On 2.4   Crop and Scale a Graphic

In this exercise, you will crop part of the background of the sailboat picture then scale the entire picture to 90% of its original size.

1. Follow these steps to crop the sailboat picture:

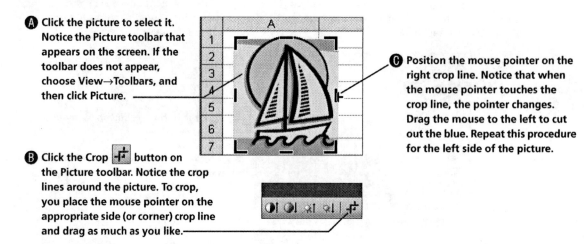

A Click the picture to select it. Notice the Picture toolbar that appears on the screen. If the toolbar does not appear, choose View→Toolbars, and then click Picture.

B Click the Crop button on the Picture toolbar. Notice the crop lines around the picture. To crop, you place the mouse pointer on the appropriate side (or corner) crop line and drag as much as you like.

C Position the mouse pointer on the right crop line. Notice that when the mouse pointer touches the crop line, the pointer changes. Drag the mouse to the left to cut out the blue. Repeat this procedure for the left side of the picture.

2. Click outside the graphic to deselect it and end the crop command.

3. Select the graphic again then choose Format→Picture and click the Size tab.

4. Follow these steps in the Scale section of the dialog box to scale the sailboat picture:

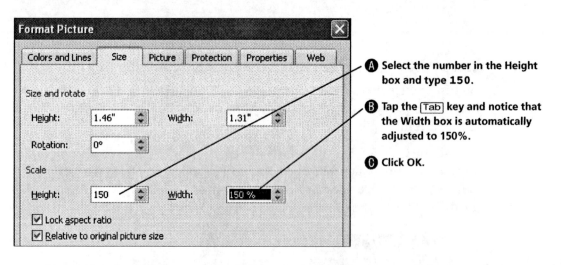

A Select the number in the Height box and type 150.

B Tap the Tab key and notice that the Width box is automatically adjusted to 150%.

C Click OK.

Controlling Contrast and Brightness

You can adjust the contrast and brightness of inserted clip art images. Like cropping, you adjust the contrast and brightness using buttons on the Picture toolbar or in the Format→ Picture dialog box. Using the toolbar for this feature is usually easier since you can see the adjustments as they are being made.

Hands-On 2.5 **Set the Contrast and Brightness of a Graphic**

In this exercise, you will change the contrast and brightness of the sailboat graphic.

1. Click the picture to select it.

2. Follow these steps to change the contrast and brightness of the graphic:

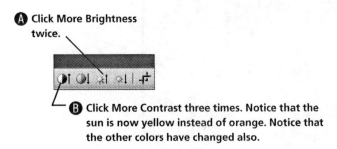

Ⓐ **Click More Brightness twice.**

Ⓑ **Click More Contrast three times. Notice that the sun is now yellow instead of orange. Notice that the other colors have changed also.**

3. Feel free to experiment with the contrast and brightness features.

Drawing Objects

Office 2003 has an excellent set of drawing tools that let you draw lines, arrows, rectangles, callouts, WordArt, and many other objects. Drawing objects are easy to work with and a lot of fun! Lines and callouts are drawing objects particularly useful for emphasizing areas of interest on worksheets and charts. You insert a drawing object by choosing the desired object from the Drawing toolbar then dragging or clicking in the worksheet.

The Drawing 🔄 button on the Standard toolbar is used to display and hide the Drawing toolbar. The Drawing toolbar is usually located at the bottom of the Excel window. You can also display or hide the Drawing toolbar with the View→Toolbars→Drawing command. The following illustration highlights the buttons on the Drawing toolbar.

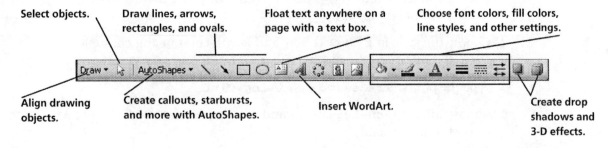

Select objects.

Draw lines, arrows, rectangles, and ovals.

Float text anywhere on a page with a text box.

Choose font colors, fill colors, line styles, and other settings.

Align drawing objects.

Create callouts, starbursts, and more with AutoShapes.

Insert WordArt.

Create drop shadows and 3-D effects.

WordArt

The WordArt button on the Drawing toolbar displays the WordArt Gallery. You can add special text effects by choosing a style from the gallery. Once you choose a style, Excel displays a dialog box in which you enter the text and choose the font and font size for your stylized WordArt text. The WordArt gallery is shown in the following illustration.

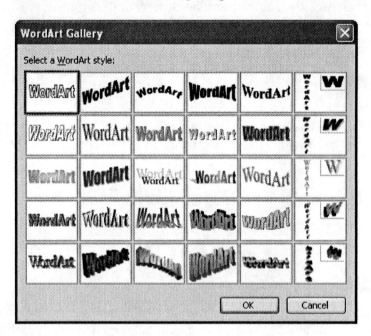

Hands-On 2.6   Insert WordArt and Format the Worksheet

In this exercise, you will insert a WordArt object for the title of the worksheet. You will also reformat the object.

Insert and Edit a WordArt Object

1. Click the Insert WordArt button on the Drawing toolbar.
   The WordArt Gallery appears.

2. Choose the style in the fourth row and fourth column and click OK.
   The Edit WordArt Text box appears. This is where you enter your WordArt text.

3. Type the phrase **Tradewinds Sailing Club**.

4. Choose Impact from the Font list and set the font size to 24. Choose Arial as the font if Impact is not available.

5. Click OK to insert the WordArt object in the worksheet.
   The WordArt toolbar appears. The WordArt toolbar lets you edit the WordArt text and object.

6. Click the Edit Text button on the WordArt toolbar.

7. Edit the word Tradewinds by breaking it into the two words: **Trade** and **Winds**.

8. Change the font size to 28 and click OK.

9. Follow these steps to reposition the WordArt object:

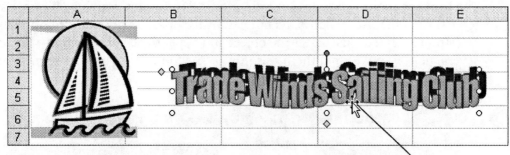

A Position the mouse pointer on the object and a cross hair pointer will appear.

B Drag the object to the right of the picture.

10. Save your worksheet and continue with the next topic.

AutoShapes and Other Shapes

You can use AutoShapes to add a variety of shapes to your worksheets. AutoShapes are predefined shapes organized into the categories Stars and Banners, Callouts, FlowChart, and more. You choose AutoShapes by clicking the AutoShapes button on the Drawing toolbar. You can also draw lines, arrows, rectangles, and ovals to bring attention to areas on the worksheet. To draw a shape, click the desired button on the Drawing toolbar then either click or drag in the document.

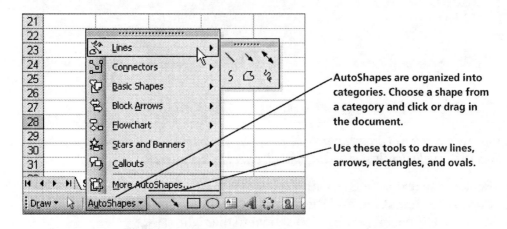

AutoShapes are organized into categories. Choose a shape from a category and click or drag in the document.

Use these tools to draw lines, arrows, rectangles, and ovals.

Formatting Buttons on the Drawing Toolbar

The Drawing toolbar includes several buttons that format drawing objects. Use the Drawing toolbar to format AutoShapes, rectangles, ovals, lines, text boxes, and other drawing objects. To format an object, just select the object and apply the desired format(s). You can also select several objects and format them as a group. The following Quick Reference table discusses the formatting buttons on the Drawing toolbar.

 QUICK REFERENCE: FORMATTING BUTTONS ON THE DRAWING TOOLBAR

Button	Function
Select Objects	Encloses objects in a selection box (click and drag the Select Objects mouse pointer) or press [Shift] while clicking the desired objects
Fill Color	Fills the background of an object with a solid color, pattern, gradient, or other fill effects
Line Color	Changes the color of lines or applies a line pattern
Font Color	Changes the font color of text in a text box or other object
Line Style	Changes the thickness and style of lines and object borders
Dash Style	Formats lines and borders with various dash styles
Arrow Style	Applies arrowheads to lines and changes the arrowhead style
Shadow	Applies a shadow effect to objects
3-D	Applies a 3-D effect to objects

 Hands-On 2.7   Draw and Format Objects

In this exercise, you will draw standard objects from the Drawing toolbar and objects from the AutoShapes collection. You will also change the line and fill color of the drawn objects.

1. Replace the text in cell A9 with the subtitle **Gold Cup Fall Regatta**. Add the text, numbers, and AVERAGE function (in cell C17) shown to the right into rows 12–17.
Format the entries with the color and formatting options of your choice.

8	Race Results		
9	Gold Cup Fall Regatta		
10			
11	Name	Owner	Score
12	Lucky Lady	Linda Burke	35
13	Night Watch	Donna Billings	38
14	Sandpiper	Jay Walton	42
15	Donna Marie	Ben Prince	47
16	Second Wind	Lisa Levine	50
17	Average		42.4

Draw and Format an Oval

2. Click the Oval ⬭ button on the Drawing toolbar.

3. Follow these steps to draw an oval in cell C12:

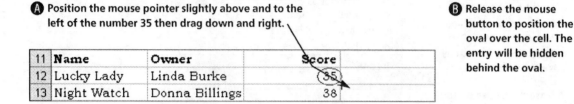

Ⓐ Position the mouse pointer slightly above and to the left of the number 35 then drag down and right.

Ⓑ Release the mouse button to position the oval over the cell. The entry will be hidden behind the oval.

11	Name	Owner	Score	
12	Lucky Lady	Linda Burke	35	
13	Night Watch	Donna Billings	38	

4. With the oval selected, click the Fill Color drop-down 🎨 ▾ button.
   You can use the Fill Color button on either the Formatting or the Drawing toolbar.

5. Choose No Fill from the top of the color palette.
   The oval should now have a transparent fill.

6. Use the Line Color 🖌 ▾ button on the Drawing toolbar to change the line color of the oval. Use the same color you used for the text entries.

7. Click the Line Style ≡ button on the Drawing toolbar and choose $1\frac{1}{2}$ pt.
   The oval line should now be much thicker.

Draw and Format a Callout AutoShape

8. Click the AutoShapes ▾ button on the Drawing toolbar.

9. Follow these steps to choose the Rounded Rectangular Callout shape:

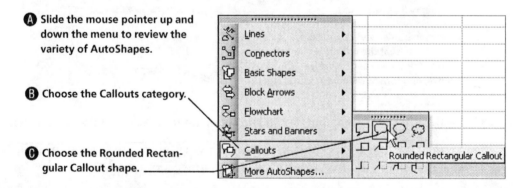

Ⓐ Slide the mouse pointer up and down the menu to review the variety of AutoShapes.

Ⓑ Choose the Callouts category.

Ⓒ Choose the Rounded Rectangular Callout shape.

Lines ▸
Connectors ▸
Basic Shapes ▸
Block Arrows ▸
Flowchart ▸
Stars and Banners ▸
Callouts ▸
More AutoShapes...

Rounded Rectangular Callout

10. Follow these steps to draw the callout:

A Position the mouse pointer to the right of the 42.4 average and drag up and to the right until the callout has approximately this shape and size. ———

B Release the mouse button to complete the callout.

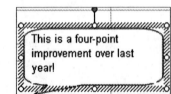

11	**Name**	**Owner**	**Score**		
12	Lucky Lady	Linda Burke	35		
13	Night Watch	Donna Billings	38		
14	Sandpiper	Jay Walton	42		
15	Donna Marie	Ben Prince	47		
16	Second Wind	Lisa Levine	50		
17	**Average**		**42.4**		
18					

11. Now type the text shown to the right into the callout. Don't be concerned if your text wraps differently than what is shown here.

This is a four-point improvement over last year!

12. Select the callout text by dragging the mouse over it.

13. Format the text with a Bookman Old Style 11 pt Bold font.

14. Apply the same color to the text that you used for the cell entries and the oval border.

15. Click the Center ☰ button to center the lines within the callout.

16. Click anywhere in the worksheet to deselect the callout.

17. Follow these steps to select the callout:

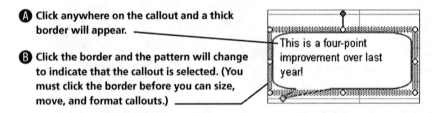

A Click anywhere on the callout and a thick border will appear. ———

B Click the border and the pattern will change to indicate that the callout is selected. (You must click the border before you can size, move, and format callouts.) ———

This is a four-point improvement over last year!

18. Use the Fill Color 🖋 ▾ button on the Drawing toolbar to fill the callout with a light color.

19. Use the Line Color 🖋 ▾ button on the Drawing toolbar to format the callout with the same line color you used for the text inside the callout.

20. Use the Line Style ☰ button on the Drawing toolbar to set the line weight to 1½ pt.

21. Follow these steps to move and size the callout until it matches the example shown here:

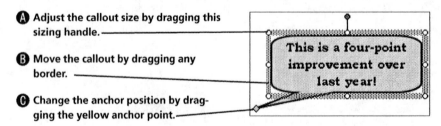

A Adjust the callout size by dragging this sizing handle. ———

B Move the callout by dragging any border. ———

C Change the anchor position by dragging the yellow anchor point. ———

This is a four-point improvement over last year!

22. If necessary, continue to format your callout until it has the shape and position shown in the following worksheet.

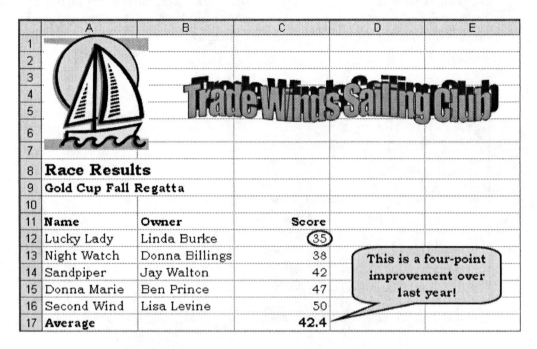

23. Save the changes to your workbook and continue with the next topic.

Special Drawing Techniques

Thus far, you have learned the basic techniques for working with drawing tools. In the following topics we continue our discussion by introducing a few more important drawing tools and drawing techniques. Upon completion of this lesson, you will have enough knowledge so you can use all drawing tools effectively.

Constraining Objects

You can constrain objects to specific shapes or angles as you draw. These techniques are outlined in the following Quick Reference table.

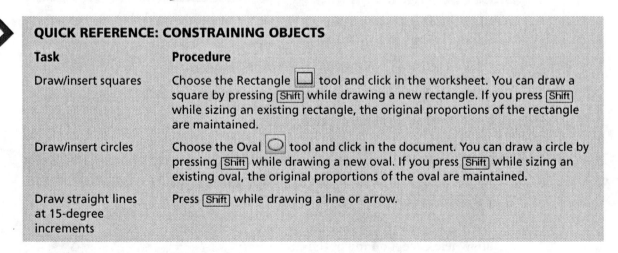

QUICK REFERENCE: CONSTRAINING OBJECTS

Task	Procedure
Draw/insert squares	Choose the Rectangle ☐ tool and click in the worksheet. You can draw a square by pressing [Shift] while drawing a new rectangle. If you press [Shift] while sizing an existing rectangle, the original proportions of the rectangle are maintained.
Draw/insert circles	Choose the Oval ○ tool and click in the document. You can draw a circle by pressing [Shift] while drawing a new oval. If you press [Shift] while sizing an existing oval, the original proportions of the oval are maintained.
Draw straight lines at 15-degree increments	Press [Shift] while drawing a line or arrow.

Layering Objects

Drawing objects reside on layers above the worksheet. Each drawing object is placed on a new layer, and the layers are stacked on top of one another. You can change the layering of drawing objects by clicking the Draw button on the Drawing toolbar and choosing layering options from the Order menu.

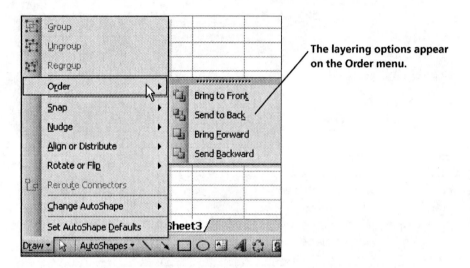

The layering options appear on the Order menu.

Text Boxes

 Text boxes are one of the most useful drawing objects. Text boxes look like rectangles when they are inserted. However, unlike rectangles, you can type text inside a text box. Click the Text Box button to insert a text box, click in the box, and type. The text automatically wraps. Text boxes let you position text anywhere on a worksheet. You can use text boxes to superimpose text on worksheet entries, pictures, and other graphics.

Hands-On 2.8   Use Special Drawing Techniques

In this exercise, you will draw perfect circles and squares, use the Order commands, and add a text box.

Draw Circles and a Square

1. Click the Sheet2 worksheet tab.
   You will experiment in this clean worksheet.

2. Click the Oval ⬭ button on the Drawing toolbar.

3. Click anywhere in the worksheet to create a perfect circle.

4. Click the Oval ⬭ button again.

5. Press the Shift key and drag in the worksheet to create another perfect circle on top of the first circle, as shown to the right.
   Notice that you can draw the circle to any size using the Shift key. When you simply click to create a circle, as you did in step 3, you cannot.

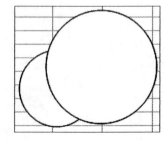

6. Use the Rectangle ⬜ tool and the Shift key to draw a square anywhere except on top of the circles.

Layering Objects

7. Follow these steps to change the order objects are layered on top of each other:

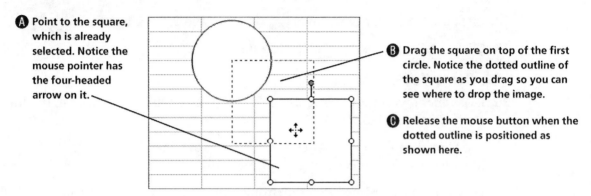

A Point to the square, which is already selected. Notice the mouse pointer has the four-headed arrow on it.

B Drag the square on top of the first circle. Notice the dotted outline of the square as you drag so you can see where to drop the image.

C Release the mouse button when the dotted outline is positioned as shown here.

8. Now drag the other circle on top of the square.
Notice that when you release the mouse button, the circle is positioned behind the square but still on top of the first circle. This happens because of the order in which the objects were drawn: first a circle, then another circle, and finally the square. The first circle is the bottom layer because it was the first object drawn and the square is the top layer because it was the last object drawn. In the next few steps, you will change the order of the layers.

9. Select the square by clicking anywhere on it.

10. Click the Draw▾ button on the left end of the Drawing toolbar and choose Order→Send to Back.
The square is now behind the circles.

11. Now choose Draw→Order→Bring to Front to move the square to the front of the stack.

12. Take a few moments to experiment with the various order options.

Add a Text Box

13. Click the Sheet1 worksheet tab.

14. Click the Text Box ▣ button.

15. Follow these steps to add a text box under the WordArt object:

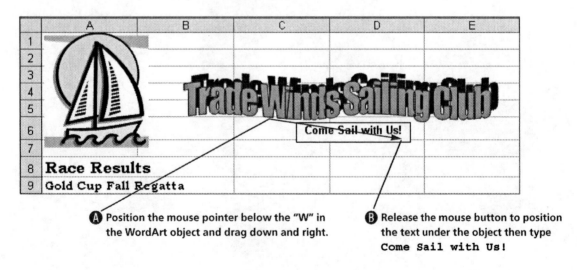

A Position the mouse pointer below the "W" in the WordArt object and drag down and right.

B Release the mouse button to position the text under the object then type
`Come Sail with Us!`

16. Select the text you just typed by dragging the mouse over it.

17. Apply the same font color you used for the cell entries and center the text within the box.

18. Click the Line Color drop-down ![button] button and select No Line.

19. Click outside the text box to deselect it.

Use Other Tools

20. Experiment with the other tools on the Drawing toolbar. In particular, try drawing lines, arrows, and text boxes.

21. Try using the [Shift] key technique while you draw lines.
    You will notice the lines are completely straight.

22. When you have finished experimenting, save and close the workbook.

Concepts Review

True/False Questions

1. A template is updated whenever you save a workbook based on the template. TRUE FALSE
2. You can change the size of pictures after they have been inserted. TRUE FALSE
3. The Clip Organizer is accessed through the Template box. TRUE FALSE
4. The Drawing ⏣ button displays and hides the Drawing toolbar. TRUE FALSE
5. You cannot format text within a callout box. TRUE FALSE
6. The Select Objects ⏣ tool is used to select multiple drawing objects. TRUE FALSE
7. You press the ⌷Ctrl⌷ key while using the Oval tool to draw a perfect circle. TRUE FALSE
8. The WordArt ⏣ button displays the Clip Gallery. TRUE FALSE
9. You cannot change the layering order of objects. TRUE FALSE
10. Text will not wrap in a text box. TRUE FALSE

Multiple Choice Questions

1. Which command displays the New Workbook task pane?
   a. Format→Template
   b. File→New
   c. Insert→Template
   d. None of the above

2. When you use Windows Explorer to navigate to a template then double-click the template, _____ .
   a. Excel creates a new workbook based on the template
   b. the template is opened for editing
   c. the Template box is displayed
   d. None of the above

3. Which key is used to draw perfect squares?
   a. ⌷Shift⌷
   b. ⌷Alt⌷
   c. ⌷Ctrl⌷
   d. ⌷Enter⌷

4. Which keyboard key is used to draw horizontal, vertical, and 45-degree lines?
   a. ⌷Shift⌷
   b. ⌷Alt⌷
   c. ⌷Ctrl⌷
   d. None of the above

Skill Builders

Skill Builder 2.1   Use a Workbook as a Template

In this exercise, you will use the Fall Gold Results workbook as the basis of a new workbook. To accomplish this, you will use the New from Existing Workbook option on the New Workbook task pane.

Create the New Workbook

1. Choose File→New to display the New Workbook task pane.

2. Click the From Existing Workbook link in the task pane.
   The New from Existing Workbook box appears. This box lets you locate an existing workbook to be used as the basis of a new workbook.

3. Navigate to your file storage location.

4. Choose the Fall Gold Results workbook and click the Create New button.
   A new workbook identical to the Fall Gold Results workbook will appear.

Modify the Workbook

5. Click in cell A9 and change the word Gold to **Silver**.

6. Change the scores in column C as follows:

Change	To
35	38
38	41
42	45
47	45
50	53

   The Average function in cell C17 will recalculate the average based on the new numbers.

7. Now click in the callout and change the phrase to **seven-point**.
   The text wrapping within the callout will change to accommodate the longer phrase. If necessary, adjust the dimensions of the callout so the text fits on three lines.

Save the Workbook

8. Click the Save ![save icon] button.
   The Save As box appears, allowing you to save the workbook with a new name. The From Existing Workbook option on the task pane allows you to use an existing workbook just like you use a template.

9. Save the workbook as **Fall Silver Results**.

10. Close the workbook and continue with the next exercise.

Skill Builder 2.2   Insert Clip Art and Draw and Copy Objects

In this exercise, you will insert a picture and use and copy drawing objects.

Insert and Size a Picture

1. Click the New ⬜ button to start a new workbook.

2. Click cell D10.
   When you insert a clip in the next few steps, it will be positioned near cell D10.

3. Click the Insert Clip Art 🖼 button on the Drawing toolbar to display the Clip Art task pane.

4. Follow these steps to conduct a search for bird clips:

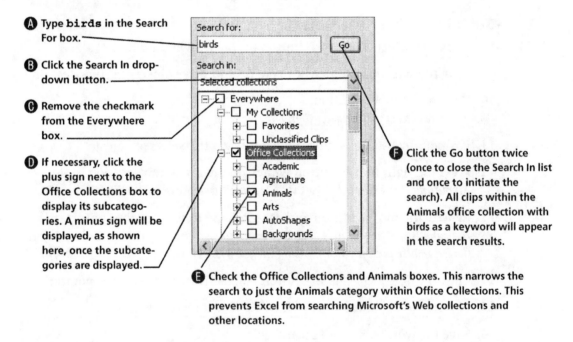

Ⓐ Type **birds** in the Search For box.

Ⓑ Click the Search In drop-down button.

Ⓒ Remove the checkmark from the Everywhere box.

Ⓓ If necessary, click the plus sign next to the Office Collections box to display its subcategories. A minus sign will be displayed, as shown here, once the subcategories are displayed.

Ⓕ Click the Go button twice (once to close the Search In list and once to initiate the search). All clips within the Animals office collection with birds as a keyword will appear in the search results.

Ⓔ Check the Office Collections and Animals boxes. This narrows the search to just the Animals category within Office Collections. This prevents Excel from searching Microsoft's Web collections and other locations.

5. Insert any bird clip by choosing it from the list.

6. Resize the clip to approximately 1 inch by 1 inch by dragging one of the corner-sizing handles.

Draw a Text Box and Arrow

7. Follow these steps to draw a text box and a horizontal arrow:

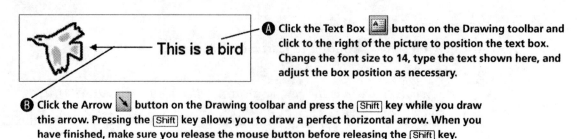

This is a bird

A Click the Text Box button on the Drawing toolbar and click to the right of the picture to position the text box. Change the font size to 14, type the text shown here, and adjust the box position as necessary.

B Click the Arrow button on the Drawing toolbar and press the [Shift] key while you draw this arrow. Pressing the [Shift] key allows you to draw a perfect horizontal arrow. When you have finished, make sure you release the mouse button before releasing the [Shift] key.

Text boxes let you float text anywhere over a worksheet.

Select and Copy the Objects

8. Click the Select Objects button on the Drawing toolbar.

9. Drag the selection pointer to enclose all three objects in the selection box.

10. Release the mouse button.
    All three objects will be selected and display sizing handles.

11. Position the mouse pointer anywhere over the selected objects.

12. Press the right mouse button while you drag to a new location in the worksheet.
    An outline of the selected objects will be attached to the mouse pointer.

13. Release the mouse button and choose Copy Here from the context menu.
    You can always copy groups of objects using this technique. You can also copy objects by dragging with the left mouse button while pressing the [Ctrl] key. However, this can be a little tricky.

14. Click the Select Objects button to deactivate the selection pointer.

15. Feel free to experiment with drawing object techniques.

16. Save the workbook as **Bird** and close it.

Skill Builder 2.3   Use a Template

In this exercise, you will update a template to be used as the basis for later workbooks.

1. Choose From Existing Workbook in the New Workbook task pane.

2. Double-click the Sales Forecast (Template) file.
   A new workbook based on the Sales Forecast (Template) file will appear. Notice that no data is currently in cells B10:C13.

3. Click the Revenue Forecast and Revenue Breakdown sheet tabs.
   Notice that these chart sheets do not currently display charts. This is because no data is in the range C10:C13 of the Data Sheet. The charts will be generated when you enter data in the next step.

4. Enter the numbers shown to the right into columns B and C of the Data Sheet. The text should already be entered in column A.
   The Total should be calculated as $457,500. The data will also be formatted with the Comma Style and Currency Style formats already set in the template.

	A	B	C
9	Product	Forecast Units	Forecast Dollars
10	Cell Phones	100	12,500
11	Pagers	200	10,000
12	GPS Systems	450	85,000
13	PCs	250	350,000

5. Click the Revenue Forecast and Revenue Breakdown sheet tabs.
   Notice that the charts have been generated.

6. Click the Save 🖫 button to display the Save As box.

7. Choose your file storage location from the Save In list.

8. Change the name to **Wilsons Forecast** and save the workbook.
   The workbook has been saved and the template is ready to be used again.

Close the Workbook and Review the Template

9. Choose File→Close to close the workbook.

10. Use Windows Explorer to navigate to your file storage location then double-click the Sales Forecast (Template) file.

11. Click the various sheet tabs to examine the workbook.
    Notice that the template is unchanged. As you can see, this powerful template contains text, formatting, formulas, and charts. This type of template is especially useful for inexperienced users who are interested only in entering data.

12. Close the workbook without saving.

Skill Builder 2.4   Use the Clip Organizer

In this exercise, you will work with the Clip Organizer. The Clip Organizer is a powerful tool for managing clip art and other media files in Office 2003.

1. Click the New ▢ button to display a blank workbook.

2. Display the Clip Art task pane and choose the Organize Clips link near the bottom of the task pane.
   The Clip Organizer window appears. You may be prompted to organize if this is the first time the Clip Organizer is being used. The Clip Organizer arranges clips in a hierarchical folder structure. It uses a Windows Explorer-like interface to locate clips.

3. Follow these steps to explore the Clip Organizer window:

A Click the Search button. The window transforms, allowing you to search for clips using the same techniques used in the Clip Art task pane.

B Click the Collection List... button.

C Notice the Copy, Paste, and Delete buttons on the toolbar. You can move, copy, and delete clips within the folder structure.

D The Clip Organizer even has its own help system.

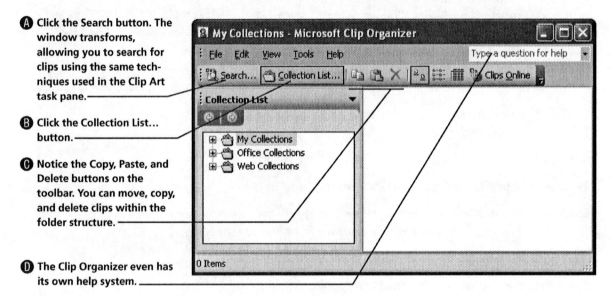

4. Follow these steps to navigate the folder structure and view clips:

Ⓐ If necessary, click the plus sign on the Office Collections folder to display its subfolder list.

Ⓑ Click the plus sign on a subfolder, and then click a folder in the list to display the clips in the folder.

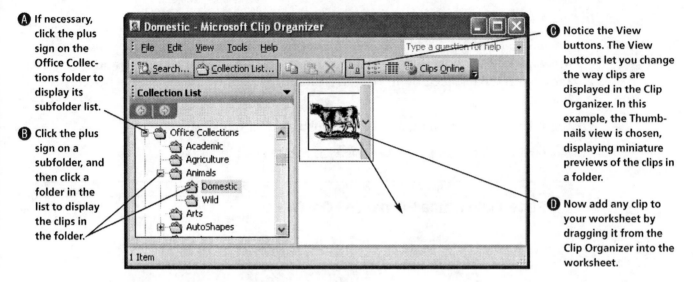

Ⓒ Notice the View buttons. The View buttons let you change the way clips are displayed in the Clip Organizer. In this example, the Thumbnails view is chosen, displaying miniature previews of the clips in a folder.

Ⓓ Now add any clip to your worksheet by dragging it from the Clip Organizer into the worksheet.

5. If necessary, click the Clip Organizer button on the Windows taskbar to redisplay the Clip Organizer.

6. Click the Clips Online button on the right end of the Clip Organizer toolbar.
This launches an Internet Explorer window and displays Microsoft's Office Clip Art and Media Web page. This is an excellent online site that provides access to a variety of high-quality clips. This page will only display if you have access to an Internet connection on your computer.

7. Feel free to explore the Clip Art and Media site. When you have finished, close the Internet Explorer window.

8. Feel free to explore the Clip Organizer. Close the Clip Organizer when you have finished.

9. Close the workbook without saving it.

# Assessments

Assessment 2.1 Use Drawing Objects

In this exercise, you will create a workbook that includes a chart and a text box.

1. Create the following workbook. You will need to create the chart as shown and use the drawing tools to create the text box and arrow. Use the chart style shown and notice that the chart has data labels on top of each column. Also, draw the arrow as a perfect horizontal line.

2. Print the worksheet, chart, and drawing objects on a single page.

3. Save the workbook as **Q1 Sales Graphic** and close it.

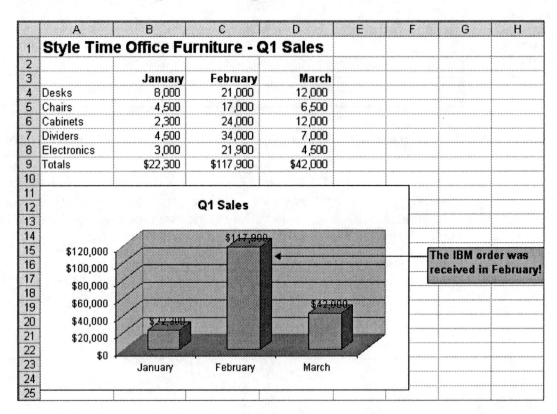

Assessment 2.2   Create a Workbook with a Chart

In this exercise, you will create a workbook for the Redmont School District. Each school within the district will use the workbook to create a budget workbook and accompanying chart. They will use the New from Existing Workbook option on the New Workbook task pane to base their new workbooks on the workbook you create.

1. Click the New [ ] button to display a blank workbook.

2. Create the following worksheet and embedded pie chart. Notice that the elevation has been increased using the 3-D View option.

3. Create a footer that displays only the filename in the center section of the footer.

4. Delete the dummy data in cells B4:B8 and save the workbook as **Budget Allocation (Template)**.

5. Close the workbook.

6. Use the From Existing Workbook option on the New Workbook task pane to create a new workbook based on the Budget Allocation (Template) file.

7. Add the phrase **(Barrett School)** to the end of the title in cell A1 and enter the data shown in the following illustration to cells B4:B8. The chart in your new workbook should display the new percentages.

	A	B	C	D	E	F
1	Redmont School District (Barrett School)					
2						
3	Item	Budget				
4	Facilities	$2,000,000				
5	Employee Costs	$1,500,000				
6	Transportation	$200,000				
7	Students	$1,500,000				
8	Equipment	$700,000				
9						

2004 Budget Allocation

Equipment 12%
Facilities 35%
Students 25%
Transportation 3%
Employee Costs 25%

8. Save the new workbook as **Barrett Budget** and close it.

Assessment 2.3   Add Clip Art and Drawing Objects

In this exercise, you will create insert clip art image and add a drawing object to the Q1 Sales workbook you created in Assessment 2.1.

1. Open the Q1 Sales workbook.

2. Use these guidelines to add clip art and drawing objects to the workbook:
   - Insert four blank rows above row 6.
   - Modify the Search In box to look Everywhere and search for desks in the Clip Art task pane. (Choose the one displayed or another one that you like.)
   - Make the image brighter and add more contrast to it.
   - Crop away any shadows around the desk.

- Delete the text box containing the sentence, The IBM order was received in February!
- Draw a 16-point start shape and type **Wow! What a Month!**
- Change the font to 12pt Red, Bold.
- Change the fill color to light yellow and remove the line from the star.

3. Save the changes and close the workbook.

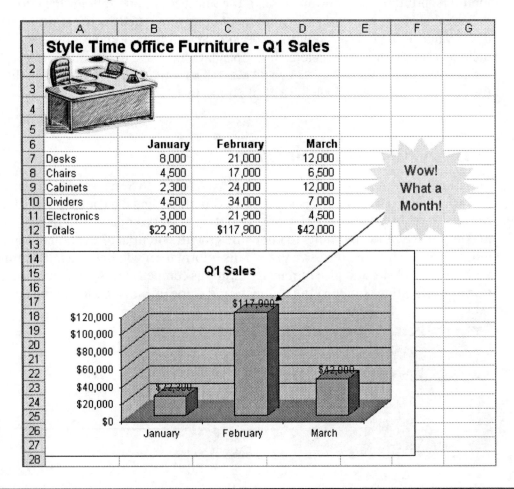

Critical Thinking

Critical Thinking 2.1   On Your Own

Jeff Adams is the sales manager for Performance Office Systems, a company that distributes high-end computer systems, monitors, printers, and copy machines. Jeff manages three sales people, each with a monthly quota of $100,000. He asks you to set up a workbook that can be distributed to each sales person. The workbook must include a row for each item (computers, monitors, printers, and copy machines), the number of units sold for the current month, the dollar value of the units sold, the number of units forecasted for the next month, and the dollar value of the forecasted units to be sold. Set up the workbook with sample data and include a Totals row. Then, delete all sample data but leave the formulas in the Totals row intact. Save the workbook as **Sales (Template)** and close it. You will use the workbook as the basis for a new workbook in Critical Thinking 2.3.

Critical Thinking 2.2   On Your Own

Christina Giamo is the founder and CEO of Web Research Services, which conducts research for companies on a contract basis. Recently, Christina signed a contract with Jack Norton of Norton Travel Alternatives. Jack wants to put his travel company on the Web. However, before making such a move, he wants to know the growth potential of the online travel services industry for each of the next five years. This information will help Jack determine the budget for his new Website and give him insight into his competition. After conducting the necessary research, Christina crunched the numbers and came up with the following data:

Year	Estimated Revenues for Online Travel Services
FY 2005	$1.1 Billion
FY 2006	$2.5 Billion
FY 2007	$3.7 Billion
FY 2008	$6.2 Billion
FY 2009	$7.5 Billion

Using this data, set up a worksheet and embedded column chart that depicts the growth of the online travel services industry. Use the years as the x-axis labels and the dollar amounts as the y-axis labels. Indicate in one of the chart titles that the numbers are in billions of dollars. Remove the legend from the chart.

Using the AutoShapes button, insert this callout pointing to the last column in the chart that reads **This represents nearly 700% growth over a five year period**. Format the callout with an attractive color and apply a fill color to the callout. Save the workbook as **Estimated Revenue**.

Critical Thinking 2.3   Web Research

Create a new workbook based on the one you created in Critical Thinking 2.1. Use Internet Explorer and a search engine of your choice to locate Websites of companies that sell personal computers, monitors, printers, and copy machines. Choose a typical top-of-the-line personal computer, a 1200 dpi laser printer, a 17" monitor, and a copy machine. Record the model numbers and prices in the new workbook. Choose any models you desire but you need only choose one computer, printer, monitor, and copy machine.

Include the name of each item in the item column of the workbook. For example, use **Printers (HP LaserJet)** if you chose an HP LaserJet. Insert a new column in the worksheet in front of the Dollar Value column. Enter the prices of each item you researched into the new column and label the column **Unit Price**.

Enter a formula in the **Dollar Value** column to calculate the dollar value as the **Units Sold** multiplied by the **Unit Price**. Your dollar value numbers will definitely increase or decrease depending on the items you chose. Use formulas in the **Forecasted Dollar Value** column to calculate the Forecasted Dollar Value as the Unit Price multiplied by the Units Forecasted. Save your workbook as **Comp Research (Template)**.

LESSON 3

Working with Multiple-Sheet Workbooks

As you continue to work with Excel, you may find your worksheets growing in size and complexity. Often breaking up a worksheet into several smaller worksheets is better than having one large document. For example, many Excel workbooks are organized with a master sheet and two or more detail sheets. Summary information from the detail sheets is often reflected on the master sheet. In this lesson, you will set up a workbook with a master sheet and detail sheets. You will also learn how to efficiently print multiple-sheet workbooks, copy worksheets, and protect workbooks. In *Microsoft Office Excel 2003: Quick Course 3*, you will expand your knowledge of multiple worksheets by working with them as a group.

Microsoft Office Excel 2003 Expert objectives covered in this lesson

Objective Number	Skill Sets and Skills	Concept Page References	Exercise Page References
XL03E-1-14	Define, modify and use named ranges	72–75, 78	73–79
XL03E-3-1	Protect cells, worksheets, and workbooks	80–82	81–85
XL03E-3-2	Apply workbook security settings	85	86–87
XL03E-5-3	Modify Excel default settings	64	64–65

Case Study

Folsom Technical College has just received its 2004 Federal grant. Brittany Stevens, the budgeting department's director, needs to allocate the grant to various budget categories. Brittany needs a workbook that tracks the year-to-date expenditures and consolidates the information on a master worksheet. The master sheet will provide summary information and give Brittany an instant overview of how their expenditures compare to their budget allocations. The workbook will be dynamic. The master sheet will be linked to detail sheets, where all the necessary detail information will be stored. These illustrations show the master sheet and three detail sheets that you will create in this lesson.

	A	B	C
1	**Postage Tracking Sheet**		
2			
3		**Amount Spent**	
4	September	300	
5	October	350	
6	November	325	
7	December	400	
8	January	800	
9	February		
10	March		
11	April		
12	May		
13	June		
14	July		
15	August		
16	**Total**	$2,175	

	A	B	C
1	**Equipment Tracking Sheet**		
2			
3		**Amount Spent**	
4	September	3,000	
5	October	2,500	
6	November	4,000	
7	December	1,000	
8	January		
9	February		
10	March		
11	April		
12	May		
13	June		
14	July		
15	August		
16	**Total**	$10,500	

	A	B	C
1	**Folsom Technical College**		
2	**2004 - 2005 Federal Grant and Budget Tra**		
3			
4	**Grant Amount**	$300,000	
5	**Today's Date**	3/15/2004	
6			
7	**Category**	**Budget Allocation**	**Year-to-Date Spent**
8	Postage	5,000	2,175
9	Equipment	40,000	10,500
10	Instructional Materials	50,000	40,500

	A	B	C
1	**Instructional Materials Trackin**		
2			
3		**Amount Spent**	
4	September	25,000	
5	October	10,000	
6	November	5,000	
7	December	500	
8	January		
9	February		
10	March		
11	April		
12	May		
13	June		
14	July		
15	August		
16	**Total**	$40,500	

Using Multiple Worksheets

Most workbooks you create will use only one worksheet. However, as you learned in *Microsoft Office Excel 2003: Quick Course 1*, you can have multiple worksheets in a workbook, limited only to the amount of available memory on your computer. The default number of sheets can be changed using the Tools→Options dialog box. Multiple worksheets can be connected with a linking formula, thereby creating a dynamic multiple-sheet workbook.

Modifying the Default Number of Sheets

Each new workbook contains three worksheets. When you change the default number of sheets in a workbook, each new workbook after the change will contain that number of sheets. Changing the default number can be a valuable time saver if your workbooks typically contain more than three sheets. For example, if you track quarterly data for each department and also need to summarize the data for all departments, you may want to set the default number of worksheets to five. Then you can create a separate sheet for each quarter and one for the summary.

 Hands-On 3.1   Change the Default Sheets in Workbook

In this exercise, you will change the number of sheets in new workbooks, test the change, and change it back to three.

1. Open Excel then click Tools→Options from the menu bar.

2. Follow these steps to change the default number of sheets in a workbook:

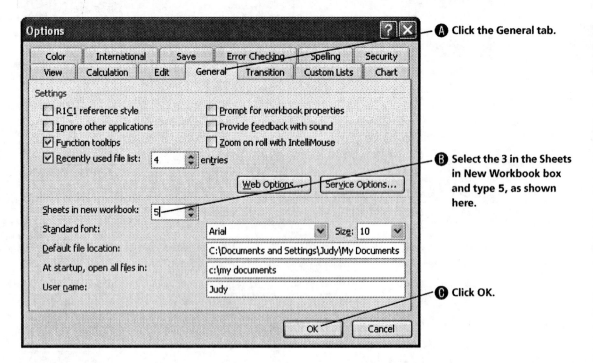

Ⓐ Click the General tab.

Ⓑ Select the 3 in the Sheets in New Workbook box and type 5, as shown here.

Ⓒ Click OK.

3. Click the New ⬜ button.
   Notice the five sheet tabs at the bottom of the worksheet window.

4. Display the Options dialog box again.

5. Change the default number of sheets back to **3** and click OK.

6. Click the New ⬜ button to verify that the number of sheets is again three.

7. Close all open workbooks.

Linking Cells

Excel lets you link cells from different worksheets and different workbooks. Linking lets you reflect values from a source worksheet into a destination worksheet. This powerful capability is the glue that binds worksheets together.

Why Link?

Linking is often used to make totals from detail worksheets appear in summary or master worksheets. This lets you keep detailed information in the detail sheets and see the totals or big picture in the summary sheet. This capability reflects the needs of many organizations. For example, top-level managers are usually interested in seeing the big picture, whereas detailed information is needed at the departmental level. The illustration on page 63 shows data from three detail sheets appearing in a master sheet. Notice that the totals on the detail sheets are also visible in the master sheet.

Linking Formulas

You link cells by inserting linking formulas in the destination worksheet. Linking formulas specify the cells in the source worksheet, from which the data originates. You must use the correct syntax when creating linking formulas. The following illustrations show examples of linking formulas between cells in the same workbook and between cells in different workbooks.

This formula is inserted into a cell in a destination worksheet. The exclamation point separates the sheet name Postage from the cell name B16. The number in cell B16 of the Postage sheet will appear in the cell in the destination sheet that contains this formula.

=Postage!B16

This formula also specifies a filename (surrounded by square brackets). This type of formula lets you link cells between different workbooks.

=[FederalGrant.xls]Postage!B17

Creating Linking Formulas

The syntax of linking formulas is quite simple. A linking formula specifies the sheet name and cell name of the source cell. Like all formulas, you begin a linking formula with an equals sign. Then you include the sheet name of the source cell followed by an exclamation point. Finally, you include the cell reference of the source cell. If the source cell is in a different workbook, you must include the workbook name in square brackets, as shown in the second example of the preceding illustration. You can type linking formulas or use the mouse to create them in point mode. You will use both techniques in this lesson.

 ## Hands-On 3.2   Create a Linking Formula

In this exercise, you will create a formula to link the Postage sheet to the Master sheet.

Check Out the Workbook

1. Open the Federal Grant workbook.

2. Click cell B4 and notice that it contains the number $300,000.
   This is the amount of the grant Folsom Technical College was awarded for the 2004–2005 school year.

3. Click cell B5 and notice that this cell contains the TODAY function.
   This cell will always display the current date.

4. Notice the categories in column A and the budget allocations in column B.
   The budget allocations add up to $300,000, as shown in cell B19. As you can see, the budgets are equal to the total grant of $300,000.

5. Notice that the cells in column C will contain the Year-to-Date Spent numbers.
   The detail sheets (Postage, plus others you will add) will track the year-to-date expenditures for each category. The cells in column C will be linked to the year-to-date expenditure totals in the detail sheets.

6. Notice column D.
   The Available Balance in column D will be the difference between the Budget Allocation in column B and the Year-to-Date Spent numbers in column C. Column D will show how much of the budget remains for each category.

7. Click the Postage sheet tab.
   Each month the total amount spent on postage will be entered into a cell in column B. Cell B16 will contain a SUM function that will add all cells in the column. Cell B16 will be linked to cell C8 in the Master sheet.

8. Click the Master sheet tab.
   Notice that cell C8 will contain the Year-to-Date Spent amount for postage. Once again, this cell will be linked to cell B16 in the Postage sheet.

Create a Link to the Postage Sheet

9. Click the Postage sheet tab.

10. Enter the three numbers shown in the following illustration into column B:

	A	B
1	Postage Tracking Sheet	
2		
3		Amount Spent
4	September	300
5	October	350
6	November	325

11. Click cell B16 and use AutoSum $\boxed{\Sigma \; \cdot}$ to calculate the column total.
    The total should equal 975. Notice that AutoSum summed the entire range B4:B15. This is desirable because AutoSum will keep a running total as you enter data throughout the year.

12. Click the Master sheet tab.

13. Click cell C8, enter the formula **=Postage!B16**, and tap $\boxed{\text{Enter}}$.
    Make sure to type the formula exactly as shown, including the exclamation point. The number 975 should appear in cell C8. Notice that the formula instructs Excel to link to cell B16 in the Postage sheet. The exclamation point separates the two arguments (information that tells formulas what to work with).

14. Click the Postage sheet tab.

15. Click cell B7 and enter the number **400**.
    The SUM formula in cell B16 should display the number 1375.

16. Click the Master sheet tab and cell C8 should now display 1375.
    This link is dynamic, always reflecting the current value in the source cell.

Delete the Link and Re-create It Using Point Mode

17. Click cell C8 and tap the $\boxed{\text{Delete}}$ key to remove the linking formula.
    You can delete linking formulas just as you delete any other formula.

18. Make sure the highlight is in cell C8 and type an equals (**=**) sign.
    Excel will display the equals sign in the Formula bar.

19. Click the Postage sheet tab.
    Excel will display the Postage sheet. The sheet name Postage will appear in the Formula bar followed by an exclamation point.

20. Click cell B16 and the linking formula =Postage!B16 will appear in the Formula bar.

21. Complete the formula by clicking the Enter $\boxed{\checkmark}$ button on the Formula bar.
    Excel will display the Master sheet with the completed link in cell C8. Once again, the result should equal 1375. Notice that point mode works the same with linking formulas as it does with other formulas.

Calculate the Available Balance in Cell D8

22. Click cell D8 and enter the formula **=B8-C8**.
    The result should equal 3,625.

23. Click cell B8 and use the Format Painter $\boxed{\mathcal{J}}$ button to copy the Comma Style to cell C8.

24. Save the changes and continue with the next topic.

Copying Worksheets

In *Microsoft Office Excel 2003: Quick Course 1*, we touched on copying entire worksheets. Now we will go into more detail. The Folsom grant and budget workbook will eventually contain several worksheets with the same structure as the Postage sheet. For example, each sheet will have a title in cell A1 and the monthly totals for September through August will be entered in column B. Rather than recreate each sheet, you can use the Edit→Move or Copy Sheet command to copy the desired sheet. A new sheet created with the Move or Copy Sheet command is an exact duplicate of the original sheet. The data, structure, print settings, and page setup settings are identical to the original sheet.

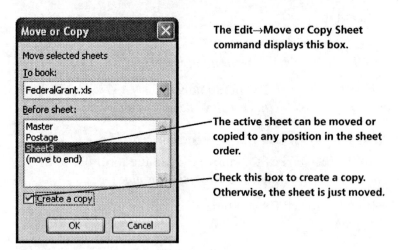

The Edit→Move or Copy Sheet command displays this box.

The active sheet can be moved or copied to any position in the sheet order.

Check this box to create a copy. Otherwise, the sheet is just moved.

 Hands-On 3.3   Make Two Copies of the Postage Sheet

In this exercise, you will make two copies of the Postage worksheet. The copies will become two new sheets named Equipment and Instructional_Materials.

Create the Equipment Sheet

1. Click the Postage sheet tab.
   The active sheet is always the sheet that is copied.

2. Choose Edit→Move or Copy Sheet from the menu bar.

3. Choose Sheet3 from the Before Sheet list.

4. Check the Create a Copy box and click OK.
   Excel positions the new sheet before Sheet3 and names it Postage (2).

5. Double-click the Postage (2) worksheet tab.

6. Type the new name, **Equipment**, and tap Enter to rename the sheet.

Edit the Title and Number Entries in the Equipment Sheet

7. Double-click cell A1 to position the insertion point in the cell.

8. Double-click again on the word Postage to select it.

9. Type the word **Equipment** and complete the entry.
   The title should now read Equipment Tracking Sheet.

10. Change the numbers in the range B4:B7 as shown in the following illustration:

	A	B
1	Equipment Tracking Sheet	
2		
3		Amount Spent
4	September	3,000
5	October	2,500
6	November	4,000
7	December	1,000

Create the Instructional Materials Sheet

11. Click the Postage sheet tab.

12. Use the technique outlined in the previous steps to create a copy of the Postage sheet. Position the new sheet before Sheet3.

13. Change the name of the new sheet to **Instructional Materials**.

14. Edit the title in cell A1 of the new sheet and change the numbers in the B4:B7 range as shown in the following illustration:

	A	B
1	Instructional Materials Track	
2		
3		Amount Spent
4	September	25,000
5	October	10,000
6	November	5,000
7	December	500

15. Save the changes to your workbook and continue with the next topic.

A Quick Copying Technique

The Select All [ ] button is located at the top-left corner of the worksheet area. You can use the Select All button and Copy and Paste to copy the data and structure of one worksheet to another worksheet. This technique is a fast way to copy a worksheet without inserting a new sheet into the workbook. This technique produces a duplicate worksheet except that the Page Setup settings (for example, margin settings, page orientation, and so forth) are not copied to the new sheet.

FROM THE KEYBOARD
Ctrl + A to select all

Hands-On 3.4   Create a Mileage Tracking Sheet

In this exercise, you will copy the Postage sheet to create a new sheet named Mileage.

1. Click the Postage sheet tab.

2. Click the Select All ☐ button at the top-left corner of the Postage sheet.

3. Click the Copy 🖹 button on the Standard toolbar.

4. Click the Sheet3 sheet tab.

5. Make sure the highlight is in cell A1 and click the Paste 🖹 button.

6. Click anywhere in the worksheet to deselect it.
   Notice that the data, column widths, and other formats were copied.

7. Change the name of the sheet to **Mileage**.

8. Edit the title in cell A1 of the new sheet and change the numbers in the B4:B7 range as shown in the following illustration.

	A	B
1	Mileage Tracking Sheet	
2		
3		Amount Spent
4	September	300
5	October	350
6	November	325
7	December	400

9. Save the changes to your workbook and continue with the next topic.

Copying Formats between Worksheets

✓ The Format Painter can be used to copy text and number formats between worksheets. This technique can help you create consistent formatting between worksheets. You can copy the formats from one cell or a range of cells. You can also use the Select All button to copy the formats of an entire worksheet. This technique is useful, provided that the sheets have the same structure.

 Hands-On 3.5   Copy Formats

In this exercise, you will format the text and number entries in the Postage sheet. You will use the Format Painter to copy the formats to the three worksheets you just created.

Copy Formats from the Master Sheet to the Postage Sheet

1. Click the Master sheet tab and click cell A2.
   You will copy the text formats from this subheading to the heading in the Postage sheet.

2. Click the Format Painter ✓ button.

3. Click the Postage sheet tab.

4. Click cell A1 and the formats will be copied to that cell.
   Cell A1 should have the same dark blue color and size as the subheading in the Master sheet. Notice that you can switch to any sheet after the Format Painter has been activated.

5. Click the Master sheet tab and click cell A4.

6. Click the Format Painter button, and then click the Postage sheet tab.

7. Click cell B3 to copy the formats to that cell.

8. Click the Master sheet tab and select cells A19 and B19 (the cells in the Total row).

9. Click the Format Painter button.

10. Click the Postage sheet tab and select cells A16 and B16 (the cells in the Total row).
    The Bold formatting and the Currency Style number format should be copied to the cells.

Copy all Formats to another Sheet

The Postage, Equipment, Instructional Materials, and Mileage sheets have identical structure and format. This enables you to use the Format Painter to copy all formats from one sheet to another. The Format Painter will copy all text and number formats—and will even copy column widths and row heights—to the other sheets.

11. With the Postage sheet active, click the Select All button.
    The entire Postage sheet should be selected.

12. Click the Format Painter button, and then click the Equipment sheet tab.

13. Click the Select All button.

14. Click anywhere in the worksheet to deselect it.
    The entire sheet should have the same formatting as the Postage sheet. Notice that this technique creates consistent formatting between worksheets (provided they have an identical structure).

15. Click the Select All button on the Equipment sheet.

16. Double-click the Format Painter button.
    Double-clicking the Format Painter button lets you copy the formats as many times as desired.

17. Click the Instructional Materials sheet tab, and then click the Select All button.
    Notice that the Format Painter is still active.

18. Click the Mileage sheet tab, and then click the Select All button.

19. Click the Format Painter button to deactivate it.

20. Click anywhere in the worksheet to deselect it.
    Take a few moments to review the various sheets. The formatting should be consistent.

Edit the Mileage Sheet

21. Click the Mileage sheet tab.

22. Click cell B3, change the heading to **Mileage**, and click the Align Right button.
    The numbers in column B are the number of miles driven in a given month. You will add another column to calculate the actual mileage expense. The mileage expense is calculated as the number of miles multiplied by a cost of 32¢ per mile.

23. Click cell C3 and enter the heading **Mileage Expense**.

24. Click cell C4 and enter the formula **=B4*.32**.
The result should equal 640.

25. Use the fill handle to copy the formula down the column to row 15.
Some of the cells will display zeros or dashes (depending on the default settings on your computer) because column B is not yet complete.

26. Use the AutoSum **Σ ▾** button to calculate the total mileage expense in cell C16.

Format the Mileage Sheet

27. Use the Format Painter **✓** button to copy the formats from cell B3 to C3 and from B16 to C16.

28. Autofit column C to make the heading in cell C3 visible.

29. Use the Format Painter **✓** button to copy the Comma Style format from cell B4 to cell B16.
The Total should not have a Currency Style format.

30. Now apply Bold **B** formatting to cell B16.

Using Named Ranges

You can define cell names and use them in formulas in place of cell references. For example, cell C8 in the Master sheet contains the linking formula =Postage!B16, where Postage is the sheet name and B16 is the cell reference. If you assign the name PostageTotal to cell B16 in the Postage sheet you can use the linking formula =PostageTotal in the Master sheet instead of the more abstract formula =Postage!B16. Cell names are also a valuable time saver when working with multiple-worksheets and large worksheets because once the name is created, you can simply click the name in the Name box and Excel immediately navigates to the cell(s).

Name Rules

Cell names can have up to 255 characters (although you should keep names much shorter than this). Also, names cannot contain spaces. If necessary, use the underscore (_) character as a substitute for spaces. For example, use Instructional_Materials instead of Instructional Materials.

Creating Cell Names

You can assign a name to any cell or range of cells. Cell names are available throughout a workbook. This is convenient because you can assign a name in one sheet then reference that name in any other sheet. Three ways to create cell names are: type in the Name box, use Insert→Name→Define, or use Insert→Name→Create.

The Name box is located on the left end of the Formula bar. When a cell or range of cells has been assigned a name, however, the name is displayed in the Name box. You can easily name a cell by clicking in the Name box and typing the desired name. The name is assigned when you tap [Enter]. To name a range, select the desired range, click in the Name box, type the desired name, and tap [Enter].

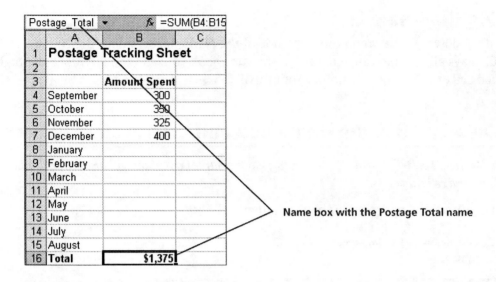

 Hands-On 3.6 Create Cell Names

In this exercise, you will create descriptive names for the totals in the detail sheets.

1. Click the Equipment sheet tab then click cell B16.

2. Follow these steps to name the cell:

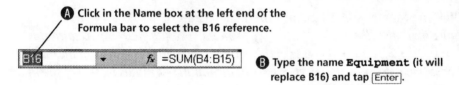

A Click in the Name box at the left end of the Formula bar to select the B16 reference.

B Type the name **Equipment** (it will replace B16) and tap Enter.

⚠WARNING! *You must tap Enter after typing the name. If you simply click outside the Name box, the name will not be created.*

3. Click anywhere in the worksheet (other than cell B16).

4. Click cell B16 and the name Equipment will appear in the Name box.
   The Name box displays the cell name or reference of the current cell.

5. Click the Instructional Materials sheet tab then click cell B16.

6. Click in the Name box.

7. Type **Instructional_Materials** (be careful not to use a space) and tap Enter.
   The underscore character is inserted by pressing Shift and tapping the hyphen key. Don't use a blank space because Excel won't accept it.

8. Click the Mileage sheet tab, and then click cell C16.

9. Click in the Name box and enter the name **Mileage**.

Using the Name List

The drop-down button on the right side of the Name box displays the Name list. The Name list displays all cell and range names in the workbook. You can rapidly move the highlight to a named cell or range by choosing it from the list.

Hands-On 3.7   Use the Name Box and Create Linking Formulas

In this exercise, you will use the Name box to go to the named cells. You will also create linking formulas using named cell ranges.

1. Follow these steps to go to the Equipment cell:

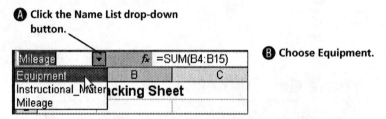

Ⓐ **Click the Name List drop-down button.**

Ⓑ **Choose Equipment.**

Notice that Excel displays the Equipment sheet and positions the highlight in the Equipment cell.

2. Use the technique described in step 1 to go to the Instructional_Materials cell.

Create a Linking Formula Using the Keyboard

3. Click the Master sheet tab, and then click cell C8.
   Notice that this cell contains the linking formula =Postage!B16. You created this link in Hands-On 3.2. In the remainder of this exercise, you will create links to the totals in the other three sheets. However, you will use cell names in the linking formulas instead of sheet names and cell references as you did in cell C8.

4. Click cell C9 and enter the linking formula **=Equipment**.
   The number 10500 should appear. This is the total from cell B16 of the Equipment sheet.

5. Click the Name box drop-down button and choose Equipment.
   Excel will position the highlight in cell B16 of the Equipment sheet. Notice that the total equals 10500.

Create a Linking Formula Using Point Mode

6. Click the Master sheet tab, and then click cell C10 if necessary.

7. Type an equals (**=**) sign.

8. Click the Instructional_Materials sheet tab.

9. Click cell B16, and then click the Enter ✓ button to complete the entry.
   The formula =Instructional_Materials appears in the Formula bar. The result should equal 40500.

Create the Last Linking Formula, Format Cells, and Copy a Formula

10. Click cell C11.

11. Type **=Mileage** and complete the entry.

The result should equal 1913.6. Keep in mind that these links are dynamic. If the totals change in the detail sheets, the Master sheet will change as well.

12. Click cell C8, and then click the Format Painter ✓ button.

13. Select cells C9:C11 to copy the Comma Style to those cells.

14. Use the fill handle to copy the Available Balance formula from cell D8 to cells D9:D11.

15. Save the changes to your workbook and continue with the next topic.

Modifying and Deleting Cell Names

You can change and delete cell names and range names after they have been created. However, formulas that use the names will not work after the names have been changed or deleted. You will need to recreate any linking formulas that used the changed or deleted names. For this reason, you should choose names carefully when you create them. You change and delete names with the Insert→Name→Define command.

 Hands-On 3.8   Modify a Cell Name

In this exercise, you will change the Instructional_Materials cell name to Instructional. You will also insert a new worksheet and recreate the linking formula that used the Instructional_Materials cell name.

Rename the Instructional_Materials Cell

1. Click the Name box drop-down ▾ button and choose Instructional_Materials.

2. Choose Insert→Name→Define from the menu bar.

3. Follow these steps to add one name and delete another name:

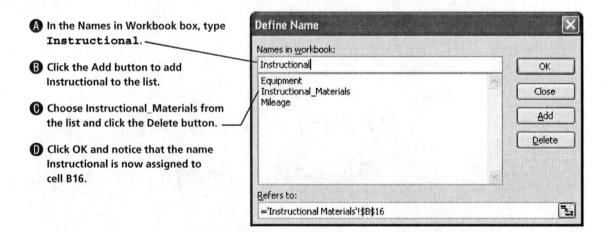

Ⓐ In the Names in Workbook box, type **Instructional**.

Ⓑ Click the Add button to add Instructional to the list.

Ⓒ Choose Instructional_Materials from the list and click the Delete button.

Ⓓ Click OK and notice that the name Instructional is now assigned to cell B16.

4. Click the Name box drop-down ▾ button and notice that the name Instructional_Materials is no longer available.

Repair the Formula in the Master Sheet

5. Tap the [Esc] key and click the Master sheet tab.
   Notice that a #NAME? message appears in cells C10 and D10. This message indicates that a formula is referencing a cell name that no longer exists. You will correct this by replacing the formula in cell C10.

6. Click cell C10 and enter the formula **=Instructional**.
   The result should once again equal 40500. The formula in D10 is dependent on C10 so it will return the correct result (9500) once the formula in C10 is corrected.

Insert a New Worksheet

7. Choose Insert→Worksheet from the menu bar.
   A new worksheet will be inserted to the left of the current sheet.

8. Drag the new worksheet tab to the right so it is last in the order.

9. Double-click the new sheet tab and change the sheet name to **Salaries**.

10. Click the Postage sheet tab.
    In the next few steps, you will copy the data and structure of the Postage sheet to the Salaries sheet.

11. If necessary, click the Select All ☐ button to select the Postage sheet.

12. Click the Copy ☐ button.

13. Click the Salaries sheet tab and make sure the highlight is in cell A1.
    The highlight must be in cell A1 if you wish to paste an entire sheet.

14. Click the Paste ☐ button to paste the Postage sheet.

15. Click anywhere in the sheet to deselect it.

16. Follow these steps to edit the Salaries sheet as shown in the following illustration:
    - Add the names and numbers shown in columns B–F. Also, edit the title in cell A1 as shown.
    - Copy the SUM formula from cell B16 across the row to cells C16:F16.
    - Use the Format→Column→Width command to widen columns B–F to 10.
    - Use the Format Painter to copy the text and comma formats from column B to columns C–F.

Insert, Name, Define to add, change, or delete

	A	B	C	D	E	F
1	**Salaries Tracking Sheet**					
2						
3		Connie	Alicia	Thomas	Mildred	Burt
4	September	3,500	2,750	3,400	4,250	4,200
5	October	3,750	3,250	3,450	3,850	3,450
6	November	4,200	3,800	3,400	2,900	3,480
7	December	4,000	3,750	3,400	3,450	3,490
8	January					
9	February					
10	March					
11	April					
12	May					
13	June					
14	July					
15	August					
16	**Total**	**$15,450**	**$13,550**	**$13,650**	**$14,450**	**$14,620**

Name the Cells in the Salaries Sheet

17. With the Salaries sheet active, click cell B16.

18. Follow these steps to name cell B16:

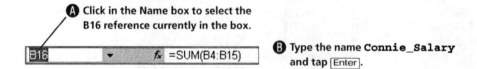

Ⓐ Click in the Name box to select the B16 reference currently in the box.

Ⓑ Type the name **Connie_Salary** and tap ⌷Enter⌷.

19. Name cells C16–F16 as shown in the following table:

Cell	Use This Name
C16	Alicia_Salary
D16	Thomas_Salary
E16	Mildred_Salary
F16	Burt_Salary

Click after naming each cell

Create Links in the Master Sheet

20. Click the Master sheet tab, and then click cell C14.
   Cell C14 needs to be linked to the Connie_Salary cell.

21. Enter the formula **=Connie_Salary** and the result should equal 15450.

!TIP! *Names are not case sensitive; therefore, you can type formula names in all lowercase letters.*

22. Use the names you just created to link cells C15, C16, C17, and C18 to the Salaries sheet.

23. Use the Format Painter 🖌 button to copy the Comma Style format from cell C11 to cells C14–C18.

Copy the Available Balance Formula to Rows 14–18

24. Click cell D11 and click the Copy ⊞ button.

25. Select cells D14:D18 and click the Paste ⊞ button.

26. Now use the fill handle to copy the total formula from cell B19 to cells C19 and D19. *The completed Master sheet should match the following example.*

	A	B	C	D
1	**Folsom Technical College**			
2	**2004 - 2005 Federal Grant and Budget Tracking**			
3				
4	Grant Amount	$300,000		
5	Today's Date	3/15/2004		
6				
7	Category	Budget Allocation	Year-to-Date Spent	Available Balance
8	Postage	5,000	1,375	3,625
9	Equipment	40,000	10,500	29,500
10	Instructional Materials	50,000	40,500	9,500
11	Mileage	5,000	1,914	3,086
12				
13	**Salaries**			
14	Connie	42,000	15450	26,550
15	Alicia	40,000	13550	26,450
16	Thomas	40,000	13650	26,350
17	Mildred	38,000	14450	23,550
18	Burt	40,000	14620	25,380
19	Total	$300,000	$126,009	$173,991

Take a few minutes to study the work you have completed thus far in this lesson. In particular, try to understand how the Master sheet functions. The number in cell C19 reflects the total year-to-date expenditures. The number in cell D19 shows how much of the $300,000 grant is still available. All of the numbers in the Year-to-Date Spent column are linked to the detail sheets.

Creating Cell Names from Row and Column Headings

You can rapidly name a group of cells using existing row or column titles. You accomplish this by selecting both the titles and the cells to which you wish to assign the names. These cells will normally be adjacent to the title cells. You then use the Insert→Name→Create command to create the names.

Hands-On 3.9   Assign Names Using Column Headings

In this exercise, you will assign names to each of the budgeted amounts for the employees in column B of the Master sheet. You will use these names to create linking formulas in the Salaries sheet. The linking formulas will reflect the budgets from column B of the Master sheet.

Create Names for the Employee Budgets

1. Be sure the Master sheet is active.

2. Select the range A14:B18, as shown to the right.
   You will use the Insert→Name→Create command to assign the employee names to cells B14:B18.

14	Connie	42,000
15	Alicia	40,000
16	Thomas	40,000
17	Mildred	38,000
18	Burt	40,000

3. Choose Insert→Name→Create from the menu bar.
   The Create Names box appears. The checkboxes let you specify which cells should be used for the names. In this example, the cells in the left column (column A) will be used to name the cells in column B. For this reason, the Left Column box should be checked.

4. With the Left Column box checked, click OK.

5. Click cell B14 and notice that the word Connie appears in the Name box.
   This cell was assigned the name Connie.

6. Click the Name box drop-down [▾] button and scroll up and down the list of names. Notice that the names Connie, Alicia, Thomas, Mildred, and Burt now appear on the list.

7. Click cell B15 and notice that this cell has been assigned the name Alicia.

Insert Links in the Salaries Sheet

8. Click the Salaries sheet tab.

9. Click cell A17 and enter the word **Budget**.

10. Click cell B17 and enter the formula **=Connie**.
    The number 42000 should appear. This is the budget amount for Connie from the Master sheet.

11. Enter the formula **=Alicia** in cell C17.

12. Create the same type of linking formulas in cells D17, E17, and F17.

13. Save the changes and continue with the next topic.

Using Protection Options

Excel lets you protect the structure of workbooks and the contents of worksheets. The protection options prevent your workbooks and worksheets from being accidentally or intentionally modified. Protection is often used to prevent inexperienced users from damaging workbooks.

Protecting Workbooks

Protecting a workbook prevents structural changes from being made to the workbook. For example, you cannot delete, rename, copy, or move worksheets in a protected workbook. You can also protect a workbook window to prevent users from changing the appearance of the window. You use the Tools→Protection→Protect Workbook command to protect a workbook. You use the Tools→Protection→Unprotect Workbook command to unprotect a workbook. The following illustration highlights the options available in the Protect Workbook dialog box.

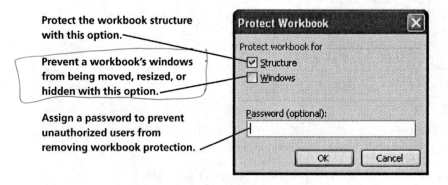

Protect the workbook structure with this option.

Prevent a workbook's windows from being moved, resized, or hidden with this option.

Assign a password to prevent unauthorized users from removing workbook protection.

WARNING! *If you forget your password, you will have to recreate the workbook, as you will not be able to get into the file. You will not assign passwords during this course.*

Protecting Worksheets

The Tools→Protection→Protect Sheet command lets you protect individual worksheets within a workbook. You can specify the types of items you wish to protect. Protected items cannot be modified. You use the Tools→Protection→Unprotect Sheet command to unprotect a protected sheet. The following illustration describes the options available in the Protect Sheet box.

and

must be done for each worksheet.

This checkbox instructs Excel to protect the entire worksheet and the contents of locked cells. By default, all cells in a worksheet are locked when the worksheet is protected unless you first unlock the cells. You will learn how to unlock cells in the next topic.

The same password entered here will be required to remove protection from the sheet at a later time. Passwords are case sensitive so be sure to enter the correct case.

You can also select additional protections to the sheet.

Protect Sheet

☑ Protect worksheet and contents of locked cells

Password to unprotect sheet:

Allow all users of this worksheet to:

☑ Select locked cells
☑ Select unlocked cells
☐ Format cells
☐ Format columns
☐ Format rows
☐ Insert columns
☐ Insert rows
☐ Insert hyperlinks
☐ Delete columns
☐ Delete rows

[OK]   [Cancel]

 ## Hands-On 3.10   Protect the Workbook and the Master Sheet

In this exercise, you will protect the workbook and the Master sheet. The Master sheet can be protected because you will not have to modify it or enter data into it. The Master sheet also contains important data and formulas, such as the grant numbers and the budget numbers. These data should be protected to prevent unauthorized users from modifying it.

Protect an Entire Workbook

1. Be sure the Excel window is maximized.

2. Notice the two sets of quick-sizing buttons at the top-right corner of the Excel window.
   The top buttons size the program window and the bottom buttons size the worksheets within the program window. The bottom buttons will disappear once you protect the windows on the sheet.

3. Choose Tools→Protection→Protect Workbook from the menu bar.

4. Check both the Structure and Windows boxes and click OK.
   Notice that the bottom set of quick-sizing buttons has been removed from the window. The Windows protection option prevents you from sizing, deleting, copying, and moving the worksheet windows within the program window. If desired, you can still size and move the program window.

5. Try dragging the Master sheet tab to a different position in the worksheet order.
   An icon will appear to tell you that you cannot change the worksheet position.

6. Double-click the Master worksheet tab and Excel will display a warning box indicating that the workbook is protected.

7. Click OK to close the message box.
   At this point you are prevented from modifying the workbook structure. You can still work normally within the worksheets, however.

8. Choose Tools→Protection→Unprotect Workbook from the menu bar.

9. Double-click the Master worksheet tab and notice that you can change the name if desired.

10. Click anywhere in the worksheet to cancel the action.

Protect a Worksheet

11. Choose Tools→Protection→Protect Sheet from the menu bar.

12. Take a moment to browse the Protection options then click OK.

13. Click any cell in the worksheet and try entering new text or numbers.
Excel will display a message box indicating that the cell cannot be changed.

14. Click OK to close the message box.

Unprotect the Sheet

15. Choose Tools→Protection→Unprotect Sheet from the menu bar.

16. Click any empty cell in the worksheet and enter any number or text.

17. Click the Undo button to reverse the editing change.

18. Use the Tools→Protection→Protect Sheet command to protect the sheet again.
At this point only the Master sheet is protected. You will protect the other sheets later.

19. Save the changes to your workbook and continue with the next topic.

Unlocking Cells in Protected Worksheets

Excel lets you unlock specific cells within a protected worksheet. Unlocked cells can be edited even though the overall worksheet is protected. This way, you can protect important cells and objects while allowing data entry in less important parts of the sheet. You must unlock the cells before protecting the worksheet.

QR

QUICK REFERENCE: UNLOCKING CELLS

Task	Procedure
Unlock cells	■ Select the cells you want to unlock.
	■ Choose Format→Cells and click the Protection tab.
	■ Remove the checkmark from the Locked box and click OK.
	■ Use the Tools→Protection→Protect Sheet command to protect the worksheet.

Hands-On 3.11 Unlock Cells in Worksheets

In this exercise, you will unlock several cells in the Postage and Salaries sheets. You will then protect the sheets to prevent the formulas and overall structure from being changed.

Unlock Cells in the Postage Sheet

1. Click the Postage sheet tab and select the range B4:B15.
    This range includes all cells in column B between the Amount Spent heading and cell B16.

2. Choose Format→Cells from the menu bar and click the Protection tab.

3. Remove the checkmark from the Locked box and click OK.
    This action will have no effect on your sheet until you protect it in the next step.

Protect the Sheet and Enter Data

4. Use the Tools→Protection→Protect Sheet command to protect the sheet.

5. Click cell B16 and try entering data in the cell.
    A message box will appear, indicating that the cell is protected.

6. Click OK to close the message box.

7. Click cell B8 and enter **800**.
    Excel lets you enter the number because you unlocked the cell prior to protecting the sheet.

Unlock Cells and Protect the Salaries Sheet

8. Click the Salaries sheet tab and select the range B4:F15.

9. Choose Format→Cells from the menu bar.

TIP! *Remember, you can display the Format→Cells dialog box by right-clicking on selected cells.*

10. Remove the checkmark from the Locked box and click OK.

11. Protect the worksheet.
    All cells in this sheet will now be protected, except for the data entry cells in the range B4:F15.

12. Save the changes and continue with the next topic.

Using 3-D Selecting and Formatting

You can use a variety of techniques to select and format several worksheets at the same time. These techniques are commonly known as 3-D techniques because worksheets have a 3-D (three-dimensional) arrangement within workbooks. 3-D selecting and formatting is most effective when all of the affected worksheets contain the same structure. For example, the Equipment, Instructional Materials, and Mileage worksheets all have the same structure. The critical step in using 3-D techniques is to select all of the desired worksheets before issuing a command. This way, all of the selected worksheets are affected when the command is issued.

You can select multiple worksheets by pressing the [Ctrl] key and clicking the desired sheet tabs. You can select a range of sheets by clicking the first sheet in the desired range, pressing the [Shift] key and clicking the last sheet in the range. All sheets between the first and last sheets are selected.

 ## Hands-On 3.12   Unlock Cells and Add Protection

In this exercise, you will select multiple sheets, unlock a cell range, and protect the sheets so data can only be entered in the unlocked cells.

1. Click the Equipment sheet tab.

2. Press and hold down the [Ctrl] key while you click the Instructional Materials sheet tab.
   Both the Equipment and Instructional Materials tabs will appear white in color.

3. Continue to hold down [Ctrl] while you click the Mileage sheet tab.
   Now all three tabs will be white, indicating that they are selected. Any commands that you issue in the Equipment sheet will be applied to the same range of cells in the other two sheets. You will learn more about working with multiple worksheets as a group in Microsoft Office Excel 2003: Quick Course 3.

4. Release the [Ctrl] key, and then select the range B4:B15 in the Equipment sheet.

5. Click the Instructional Materials sheet tab then click the Mileage sheet tab and notice that the range B4:B15 is selected in those sheets as well.

6. Use the Format→Cells command to unlock the cells.
   The three sheets should still be selected.

7. Choose Tools→Protection from the menu bar and the Protect Sheet option will not be available.
   The 3-D selection techniques let you issue commands that affect ranges of cells. However, some commands, such as Protect Sheet, are not available when multiple sheets are selected.

8. Click anywhere in the worksheet to close the menu.

9. Click the Postage sheet tab and the three sheets will no longer be selected.
   You can deselect multiple selected sheets by clicking a sheet tab not included in the selection.

10. Click the Equipment sheet tab and use the Tools→Protection→Protect Sheet command to protect just that sheet.

11. Protect the Instructional Materials sheet, and then protect the Mileage sheet.

Now you can only enter data in the B4:B15 cell ranges of the Equipment, Instructional Materials, and Mileage sheets. All other cells in the sheets are locked.

12. Save the changes to your workbook and close it.

Digital Signatures

A digital signature is used to guard against files containing viruses. You can authenticate that your workbook is virus free, that it originated from you, and that it has not been altered by adding a digital signature. Since one of its purposes is to verify that the worksheet has not been altered, if you modify the worksheet in any way then save the changes, you will receive a warning that the digital signature will be removed. If you save the file, you will need to reapply digital signature.

 NOTE! *Digital Signatures also work with macro security levels. You will learn about the macro security levels in* Microsoft Office Excel 2003: Quick Course 3.

You add a digital signature to a file by attaching a digital certificate. Digital certificates can be obtained from third-party vendors or you can create one of your own. Usually, if you will be sharing worksheets over an intranet or the Internet, your network administrator will provide you with an authentic digital certificate.

You can create your own digital certificate using the Selfcert.exe tool. A certificate you create using the Selfcert.ext tool is considered unauthenticated and will produce a warning if the security level is set to High in a document.

A digital signature can be removed at any time using Tools→Options→Security. Note, however, that the digital certificate is removed from Internet Explorer, not Excel.

 IMPORTANT! *Your network security administrator may provide the digital signatures for your company, so check with that person before creating your own.*

QUICK REFERENCE: CREATING A DIGITAL SIGNATURE	
Task	**Procedure**
Create a digital certificate	■ Click Start then click Run.
	■ Type `C:\Program Files\Microsoft\OFFICE11\selfcert.exe.`.
	■ Type a name for the certificate in the Create Digital Certificate dialog box and click OK.
Create a digital signature	■ Choose Tools→Options.
	■ Click the Security tab then click the Digital Security button.
	■ Click the Add button in the Digital Security dialog box.
	■ Click on the certificate name you created.
	■ Click OK to accept the name.
	■ Click OK to close the Digital Security box then click OK again to close the Options box.

Hands-On 3.13   Create a Digital Signature

In this exercise, you will create a digital certificate using the Selfcert.exe tool. You will then add a digital signature to the file using the digital certificate.

Create a Digital Certificate

1. Open the High Level Grant workbook.

2. Click the Start button then click Run.

3. In the Open box, type `c:\Program Files\Microsoft Office\OFFICE\ selfcert.exe`.

TIP! *You must use the correct path to the Selfcert.exe file. If your Office 2003 installation is in a different location, you must modify the path. If you don't know the correct path, use Windows' Search command to scan your C: drive (including hidden and system files) for selfcert.exe.*

4. Follow these steps to create a digital certificate:

A Click in the Your Certificate's Name box and type **Excel Test.**

B Click OK twice.

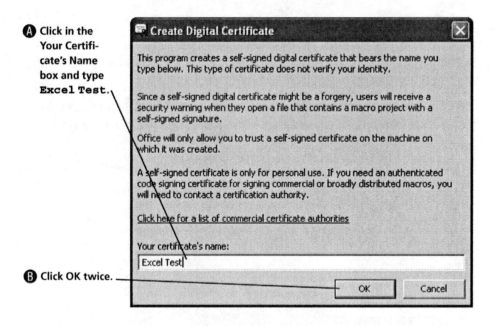

Now that you have made the digital certificate, you will create a digital signature using the Tools→Options dialog box.

Create a Digital Signature

5. Click Tools→Options.

6. Click the Security tab, and then click the Digital Signatures button.
   You may be asked to save the file first. If so, click Yes to save it. You will use the Digital Signature dialog box that displays to complete this procedure.

7. Follow these steps to create your digital signature for this workbook:

A Click the Add button. The Select Certificate dialog box opens and displays the digital certificate name you created (Excel Test).

B Click the Excel Test certification and click OK. The Select Certificate dialog box closes and you are returned to the Digital Signature dialog box.

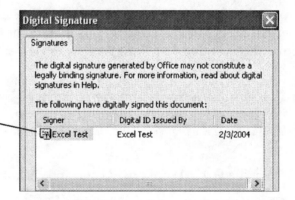

C The Digital Signature dialog box displays and indicates that the new digital signature, Excel Test, was generated and that it has signed the document. Click OK twice, first to close the Digital Signatures dialog box then to close the Options dialog box.

You now have a digital certificate that you can use for a digital signature on this and other files. You have also applied a digital signature to the High Level Grant workbook, which verifies that it originated from you and has not been altered.

8. Click the Save 🖫 button.
A message displays, warning that if you save this file you will remove the digital signature. This is because the digital signature ensures to the user that the file has not been altered.

9. Click No, and then close the file without saving.

Printing Multiple-Sheet Workbooks

Excel prints the current worksheet when you click the Print ![print] button. If you are working with a multiple-sheet workbook, you can use a variety of techniques to set up and print multiple sheets.

Applying Page Setup Options to Multiple Sheets

The Page Setup dialog box lets you adjust the margins, page orientation, headers and footers, and a variety of other settings that affect the printed worksheet. You can apply these settings to multiple worksheets by first selecting the desired sheets. You learned how to select multiple worksheets in an earlier topic.

Printing All Sheets

You can print all sheets in a workbook by selecting the sheets and clicking the Print button. You can also print all sheets by issuing the File→Print command and choosing the Entire Workbook option. You do not have to select the sheets if you use the File→Print technique.

Printing Selected Sheets

You can print just certain sheets by selecting the desired sheets and clicking the Print button. Selected sheets can also be printed by issuing the File→Print command and choosing the Active Sheets option. Use Print Preview to view selected sheets.

 Hands-On 3.14   Preview and Print Selected Sheets

In this exercise, you will preview the Master sheet alone then select multiple sheets and preview them all at once.

1. Open the Federal Grant workbook and click the Master sheet tab.

2. Click the Print Preview ![icon] button.
   Notice that the Next button is unavailable. Excel only displays the selected sheet(s) in Print Preview.

3. Close the Print Preview window.

4. Press the [Shift] key and click the Salaries sheet tab.
   All sheets should be selected. The [Shift] key technique is useful for selecting a continuous range of sheets.

5. Click the Print Preview ![icon] button.

6. Use the Next button to browse through the worksheets.
   Notice that all six sheets are available because you selected them prior to clicking Print Preview. These same sheets would have printed if you clicked the Print button instead of Print Preview.

7. Click the Print button on the Print Preview toolbar.
   Notice that the Active Sheet(s) option is chosen. All six sheets are active and would print if you were to click OK. Notice the Entire Workbook option. This option can be used to print the entire workbook without having to first select the sheets.

8. Click the Cancel button to exit from the Print dialog box.

9. Save and close the workbook.

Concepts Review

True/False Questions

1. Linking formulas are inserted in the source worksheet.	TRUE	FALSE
2. Linking formulas can be typed or created using point mode.	TRUE	FALSE
3. The Format Painter can be used to copy formats between worksheets.	TRUE	FALSE
4. The Select All ☐ button can be used to select an entire worksheet.	TRUE	FALSE
5. Spaces are allowed in cell names.	TRUE	FALSE
6. Cell names can only be used within the worksheet in which they were created.	TRUE	FALSE
7. You can move to a named cell by choosing the name from the Name list.	TRUE	FALSE
8. You must unlock cells after a worksheet has been protected to edit those cells.	TRUE	FALSE
9. You can change the default number of worksheets.	TRUE	FALSE
10. You can protect just one worksheet in a multiple-worksheet workbook.	TRUE	FALSE

Multiple Choice Questions

1. Which of the following procedures is used to create a cell name?
   a. Click the desired cell, click in the Name box, type the desired name, and tap Enter.
   b. Click the desired cell and type the desired name.
   c. Click the desired cell, click in the Name box, type the desired name, and click the Enter button on the Formula bar.
   d. None of the above

2. Which command is used to change or delete a cell name?
   a. Insert→Name→Create
   b. Tools→Name→Create
   c. Insert→Name→Define
   d. None of the above

3. Which command is used to create cell names from existing column or row titles?
   a. Insert→Name→Create
   b. Tools→Name→Create
   c. Insert→Name→Define
   d. None of the above

4. Which key is used to select multiple worksheets?
   a. Shift
   b. Ctrl
   c. Alt
   d. Both a and b

Skill Builders

Skill Builder 3.1   Copy and Format Worksheets

In this exercise, you will copy a worksheet twice to create three identical worksheets. You will then use the Format Painter to ensure consistent formatting between the sheets. Finally, you will create a named range and use it in a formula.

Copy a Worksheet

1. Open the Testing workbook and click cell B10.

2. Click the drop-down button on the AutoSum Σ button and choose Average from the function list.
   Excel will propose the formula =Average(B6:B9).

located on formula bar next to fx

3. Click the Enter ✔ button on the Formula bar to accept the proposed formula.
   The formula result should equal 18.5.

4. Copy the formula to cells C10 and D10.

5. Click the Select All ▢ button, and then click the Copy 🗐 button.

6. Click the Sheet2 tab and Paste 📋 the sheet.

7. Paste the sheet into Sheet3.

8. Rename the sheets **Test1**, **Test2**, and **Test3**.

9. Change the headings in row 3 of the Test2 and Test3 sheets to **Test 2** and **Test 3**.

10. Change a few of the numbers in the Test2 and Test3 sheets so the sheets contain different data.

Format the Test1 Sheet and Copy the Formats

11. Click the Test1 tab, and then click cell A1.

12. Increase the font size to 14 and apply a color to the text.

13. Click cell A3, increase the size to 12, and apply the same color you used in the previous step.

14. Format the Average row in any way you desire.

15. Click the Select All ▢ button to select the entire sheet.

16. Double-click the Format Painter 🖌 button.

17. Click the Test2 sheet tab.

18. Click the Select All ▢ button to copy the formats to that sheet.
    You were able to copy the formats in this manner because the sheets are identical.

19. Click the Test3 sheet tab, and then click the Select All ▢ button to copy the formats to that sheet.

20. Click the Format Painter 🖌 button to turn it off.

Experiment with Range Names

21. Click the Test1 sheet tab.

22. Select cells B10:D10 and tap [Delete] to delete the average formulas.

23. Select the Ozone data in cells B6:B9.

24. Click in the Name box, type **Ozone**, and tap [Enter].

25. Click cell B10, type the formula **=AVERAGE(Ozone)**, and tap [Enter].
The correct average, 18.5, should be displayed. You can assign names to any range and use the names in formulas.

26. Assign the name **Carbon_Monoxide** to the range C6:C9.

27. Enter an average formula in cell C10 that references the range name.

28. Assign the name **Particulate_Matter** to the range D6:D9.

29. Enter an average formula in cell D10 that references the range name.

30. Save the changes to the workbook then close it.

Skill Builder 3.2   Copy and Insert Worksheets

In this exercise, you will set up a master worksheet then copy the entire sheet to create three detail sheets. You will edit the titles on each detail sheet and rename the sheet tabs. Don't worry about formatting your worksheet yet. You'll take care of that in Skill Builder 3.4

Create the Master Sheet

1. Start a new workbook and set up the following worksheet. You will need to widen columns A–E to 15. You can widen the columns by selecting them and using the Format→ Column→Width command.

	A	B	C	D	E
1	2003 Sales - Consolidated Systems, Inc.				
2					
3		Q1	Q2	Q3	Q4
4	Eastern Region				
5	Central Region				
6	Western Region				
7	Total Sales				

2. Change the name of the sheet to **National**.

Set Up the First Source Sheet

3. Change the name of Sheet2 to **Eastern Region** and create the following worksheet. Type the numbers shown in rows 4–7 and use AutoSum to calculate the Total Sales in row 8. Make sure to format the cells as shown, widening the columns to 15.

	A	B	C	D	E
1	2003 Eastern Region Sales				
2					
3		Q1	Q2	Q3	Q4
4	Boston	500,000	350,000	340,000	300,000
5	New York	560,000	450,000	280,000	700,000
6	Atlanta	700,000	325,000	450,000	650,000
7	Miami	650,000	600,000	200,000	230,000
8	Total Sales	$ 2,410,000	$ 1,725,000	$ 1,270,000	$ 1,880,000

4. Save the workbook as **2003 Sales**.

Copy the Eastern Region Sheet to Sheet3 and Sheet4

5. Click the Sheet3 tab and choose Insert→Worksheet from the menu bar.
   A new worksheet named Sheet4 will appear.

6. Click the Eastern Region sheet tab.

7. Click the Select All ⬜ button and click the Copy 🖹 button.

8. Click the Sheet4 tab and Paste 🖹 the copied sheet.

9. Click the Sheet3 tab and Paste 🖹 the sheet again.

10. Rename Sheet4 **Central Region** and rename Sheet3 **Western Region**.

Edit the New Sheets

11. Click the Central Region sheet tab.

12. Change the title to **2003 Central Region Sales**.

13. Change the city names to **Chicago, Dallas, St. Louis**, and **Denver**.

14. Change all the numbers in row 4 to 500,000 by clicking cell B4 and dragging the fill handle three cells to the right.
    This will make the numbers slightly different from those in the Eastern Region sheet.

15. Click the Western Region sheet tab.

16. Change the title to **2003 Western Region Sales** and change the city names to **Los Angeles, San Francisco, Phoenix**, and **Seattle**.

17. Enter the number **800,000** in cell B4 and use the fill handle to copy the number to the next three cells to the right.

18. Save the changes and continue with the next exercise.

Skill Builder 3.3   Name Ranges and Link with Formulas

In this exercise, you will create names for each quarter in the Eastern, Central, and Western sheets. You will also create linking formulas to link the region sheets with the Master sheet. Finally, you will create two charts based on the data in the Master sheet.

Name the Cells in the Detail Sheets

1. Click the Eastern Region sheet tab then click cell B8.

2. Click in the Name box on the left end of the Formula bar.

3. Type the name **Eastern_Q1** and tap ⎡Enter⎤.

4. Assign names to the Total Sales cells for the second, third, and fourth quarters in the Eastern sheet. Use the same naming convention you used in step 3. For example, in cell C8, use **Eastern_Q2**.

5. Assign names to the Total Sales cells for all four quarters in the Central and Western sheets using the same naming convention you used in steps 3 and 4. For example, use the names **Western_Q1** for cell B8 in the Western sheet, **Central_Q1** for cell B8 in the Central sheet, and so forth.

Create Linking Formulas in the National Sheet

6. Click the National sheet tab, and then click cell B4.

7. Enter the linking formula **=Eastern_Q1**.
   The number 2410000 should appear in cell B4.

8. Create links in rows 4, 5, and 6 to the three detail sheets. You may want to copy the formula in cell B4 across the row, and then edit the formula in each cell by simply changing the Q1 to Q2, etc. You may also want to enter the formulas using point mode. Point mode is much faster in some situations.

9. Use AutoSum ⎡Σ ▾⎤ to calculate the Total Sales in row 7 of the National sheet.

10. Format the numbers in rows 4–6 as Comma Style with 0 decimals and format the totals in row 7 as Currency Style with 0 decimals. You may want to use the Format Painter to copy the formats from one of the detail sheets.

11. Create the column chart and pie chart shown in the following illustration.
    Notice that the column chart compares each region's numbers in the various quarters. The pie chart compares the contributions of each region to the total sales for the year. To create the pie chart, you will need to add column F, as shown in the illustration.

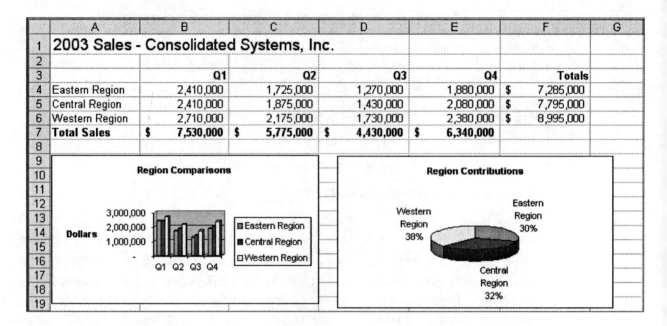

	A	B	C	D	E	F	G
1	2003 Sales - Consolidated Systems, Inc.						
2							
3		Q1	Q2	Q3	Q4	Totals	
4	Eastern Region	2,410,000	1,725,000	1,270,000	1,880,000	$ 7,285,000	
5	Central Region	2,410,000	1,875,000	1,430,000	2,080,000	$ 7,795,000	
6	Western Region	2,710,000	2,175,000	1,730,000	2,380,000	$ 8,995,000	
7	Total Sales	$ 7,530,000	$ 5,775,000	$ 4,430,000	$ 6,340,000		
8							

Region Comparisons

Dollars
3,000,000
2,000,000
1,000,000
-
Q1 Q2 Q3 Q4

■ Eastern Region
■ Central Region
□ Western Region

Region Contributions

Western Region 38%
Eastern Region 30%
Central Region 32%

Edit the Eastern Region Numbers

Notice that the Eastern Region percentage in the pie chart is currently 30%. This number will change when you change numbers in the Eastern detail sheet in the next few steps.

12. Click the Eastern Region sheet tab and click cell B4.

13. Enter the number **1,000,000** and copy it across the row.
    This will make the Eastern numbers substantially larger.

14. Click the National sheet tab and notice that the Eastern Region pie chart percentage is now 37%.

15. Save the changes to the workbook and continue with the next exercise.

Skill Builder 3.4　Format Multiple Sheets

In this exercise, you will format the sheets then use Page→Setup to prepare the sheets for printing.

1. Format the title in row 1, the headings in row 3, and the total sales in row 7 of the National sheet. Use whichever font sizes and colors you desire.

2. Select rows 1–3 of the Master sheet by dragging the mouse pointer down the row headings.

3. Double-click the Format Painter ![button] button.

4. Click the Eastern Region sheet tab, and then select rows 1–3 by dragging the mouse pointer down the row headings.
   The formats from the National sheet should be copied to rows 1–3. Notice that you were able to copy the formats because rows 1–3 have the same structure in both sheets.

5. Click the Central Region sheet tab and paint the formats to rows 1–3 of that sheet.

6. Paint the formats to rows 1–3 of the Western Region sheet.

7. Use the Format Painter 🖌 button to paint the formats from row 7 of the National sheet to row 8 of the Detail sheets.

Add a Header to All Sheets

In the next few steps, you will create a header on all four sheets. You will display the Page Setup dialog box directly from the worksheet with the File→Page Setup command. You must display the Page Setup dialog box from the worksheet if you want the Page Setup options to take effect on all of the selected sheets. The Page Setup options will not affect all selected sheets if you display the dialog box from Print Preview.

8. Press and hold down the Ctrl key while you click all four sheet tabs.

9. Choose File→Page Setup from the menu bar.

10. Click the Header/Footer tab, and then click the Custom Header button.

11. Type the text **Folsom Technical College** in the Left Section box.

12. Click in the Center Section box, and then click the Sheet Name 🗐 button.
    The &[Tab] code will appear. This code places the sheet name in the header.

13. Click in the Right Section box, and then click the Date 📆 button.
    The &[Date] code will appear. This code places the date in the header.

14. Click OK to complete the header, and then click the Print Preview button on the dialog box.

15. Use the Next button to browse through the pages.
    Notice that the National sheet is split by a page break. You will correct this soon. Also notice that the header appears on all pages.

16. Close the Print Preview window.

Change to Landscape Orientation on National Sheet

17. Click the National sheet tab.
    The other sheet tabs will be deselected.

18. Choose File→Page Setup from the menu bar.

19. Click the Page tab.

20. Set the orientation to Landscape and click OK.

21. Select all four sheet tabs and click the Print Preview 🔍 button.

22. Use the Next button to browse through the pages.
    The National sheet should be the only sheet with landscape orientation. This is because it was the only sheet tab selected when you set the orientation.

23. Close the Print Preview window.

24. Feel free to modify the worksheet in any way you desire. Try experimenting with the print options in the Page Setup dialog box.

25. Save the changes when you have finished, and then continue with the next exercise.

Skill Builder 3.5   Create a Digital Signature

In this exercise, you will create a digital certificate and apply a digital signature to the 2003 Sales workbook.

1. Click ![start], and then click Run.

2. In the Open box, type `c:\Program Files\Microsoft Office\OFFICE\ selfcert.exe` (or whatever your path is on your computer to the Selfcert.exe file).

3. Create a digital certificate named **2003 Sales** and click OK.

4. Display the Digital Signatures dialog box in the Tools→Options→Security dialog box.

5. Add a digital signature using the 2003 Sales digital certificate.

6. Click File→Save and choose No since saving the file will automatically remove the digital signature.

7. Close the workbook without saving.

Remove the Digital Signatures

In this section of the exercise, you will remove the digital signatures you created for the Testing and 2003 Sales workbooks.

8. Open the Testing workbook.

9. Click Tools→Options, and then click the Security tab.

10. Click the Digital Signatures button, select Excel Test, and click the Remove button.

11. Click OK twice, and then save and close the workbook.

12. Open the 2003 Sales workbook, remove the digital signature, and save the changes.
    Leave the workbook open.

Remove the Digital Certificate

In this section of the exercise, you will open Internet Explorer and use the Internet Options command under the Tools menu to remove both digital certificates you created in this lesson.

13. Click Start→(All) Programs→Internet→Internet Explorer.

14. Click Tools→Internet Options.

15. Click the Certificates button, select Excel Test, and click Remove.

16. Remove the 2003 Sales digital certificate.

17. Close any open dialog boxes, and then close Internet Explorer.

18. Close the 2003 Sales workbook.

Assessments

Assessment 3.1   Create a Linked Workbook

In this exercise, you will create a new workbook that contains three worksheets. You will also create cell names, and then use those names in linking formulas.

1. Follow these guidelines to create a new workbook with the three worksheets shown in the following illustrations:

   ■ Enter the numbers and text shown into three separate sheets.

   ■ Use AutoSum to calculate the totals in all three sheets. The SUM functions in the Totals row of the master sheet should sum the cells in rows 6 and 7 even though the cells are currently empty.

   ■ Name the master sheet **Both Stores** and name the detail sheets **Eastside Store** and **Westside Store**.

   ■ Create cell names for each total in row 11 of the detail sheets. Name the totals in the Eastside sheet **Eastside_January**, **Eastside_February**, and **Eastside_March**. Use a similar naming convention for the Westside sheet.

   ■ Use linking formulas to create links in rows 6 and 7 of the master sheet to the totals in the detail sheets.

   ■ Format the titles, headings, and numbers as shown. Use the Currency Style format with 0 decimals for the totals in all Totals rows. Make sure to use consistent formatting across the worksheets by using Format Painter. Use whichever font color you desire.

	A	B	C	D	E
1	**Jane's Collectibles**				
2					
3	**January - March Sales**				
4					
5		January	February	March	
6	Eastside Store				
7	Westside Store				
8	**Totals**				

	A	B	C	D	E
1	**Jane's Collectibles - Eastside Store**				
2					
3	**January - March Sales**				
4					
5		January	February	March	
6	Dolls	5,000	3,450	4,500	
7	Spoons	1,500	3,400	3,700	
8	Figurines	2,750	2,000	2,300	
9	Antiques	5,600	4,500	3,400	
10	Crystal	3,400	2,700	2,900	
11	**Totals**				

	A	B	C	D	E
1	**Jane's Collectibles - Westside Store**				
2					
3	**January - March Sales**				
4					
5		January	February	March	
6	Dolls	7,500	4,000	6,000	
7	Spoons	2,000	4,000	5,000	
8	Figurines	2,950	3,000	3,700	
9	Antiques	6,000	5,000	4,000	
10	Crystal	5,000	3,000	3,200	
11	**Totals**				

2. Save the completed workbook as **Jane Jan Mar Sales** then close it.

Assessment 3.2   Set Up Linked Worksheets

In this exercise, you will create a new workbook and insert a new worksheet. You will also create names for all the sheets then use those names to create linking formulas.

1. Follow these guidelines to create a new workbook with the four worksheets shown in the following illustrations:

   - Enter the numbers and data shown into four separate sheets. You will need to insert one new worksheet.

   - Use AutoSum to calculate the totals in all four sheets.

   - Name the master sheet **Transaction Summary** and name the detail sheets **January, February,** and **March.**

   - Create cell names for each total in cell C10 of the detail sheets. Name the total in cell C10 of the January sheet **January_Total**. Likewise, name the totals in the February and March sheets **February_Total** and **March_Total**.

   - Create links in column D of the Transaction Summary sheet to the totals in the detail sheets. Use the cell names from the detail sheets in the linking formulas.

   - Format the titles, headings, and numbers as shown. Use the Currency Style format with 2 decimals for all totals. Make sure to use consistent formatting across the detail worksheets with the Format Painter. Use whichever font color you desire.

	A	B	C	D
1	2004 Visa Card Transaction Summary			
2				
3	Month	Finance charge	Payment	Transactions
4	January	120	900	
5	February	85	100	
6	March	90	100	
7	April			
8	May			
9	June			
10	July			
11	August			
12	September			
13	October			
14	November			
15	December			
16	Total			

	A	B	C
1	January Transactions		
2			
3	Date	Description	Amount
4	1/2/2004	BayView Health Club	35.00
5	1/7/2004	Bob's Pizza	14.90
6	1/9/2004	Century Cinemas	34.90
7	1/14/2004	William's AutoCare	230.75
8			
9			
10	Total		

	A	B	C
1	February Transactions		
2			
3	Date	Description	Amount
4	2/2/2004	BayView Health Club	35.00
5	2/4/2004	Southeast Airlines	230.00
6	2/8/2004	Western Dental	120.50
7	2/16/2004	Mel's Diner	45.80
8			
9			
10	Total		

	A	B	C
1	March Transactions		
2			
3	Date	Description	Amount
4	3/2/2004	BayView Health Club	35.00
5	3/6/2004	Home Depot	40.90
6	3/23/2004	Aetna Insurance	200.00
7			
8			
9			
10	Total		

2. Save the workbook as **2004 Visa Summary** then close it.

Critical Thinking

Critical Thinking 3.1   On Your Own

Set up a revenue and expense workbook for Berkeley Bicycles—a retailer of racing and mountain bicycles. Include four sheets in the workbook. The first sheet should be a summary sheet and sheets 2–4 should contain revenue and expense data for Store 1, Store 2, and Store 3. Include revenue and expense data for four quarters (Q1, Q2, Q3, and Q4). The expenses should include employee costs, lease costs, inventory, and overhead. Use whatever revenue and expense numbers you think would be appropriate for a small bicycle retailer. Calculate the profit or loss of each store for each quarter by subtracting the expenses from the revenue.

Use linking formulas in the summary sheet to calculate the revenue and expenses for the combined stores for each quarter. This should be easy to do if the structure of your summary sheet is identical to the three source sheets.

Format the numbers with either the Currency Style or Comma Style format. Use AutoFormat to format all of the worksheets to be visually attractive. Create a digital certificate named **Revenue Expense** and use it to apply a digital signature to this file. Save the workbook as **Bike Rev Exp** then close it.

Critical Thinking 3.2   Web Research

Open the College Costs workbook. David's parents want to compare the costs of attending Yale and Princeton to the cost of attending Harvard. Copy the data and formatting from the Harvard sheet to the other two sheets in the workbook. Name the sheets **Harvard**, **Yale**, and **Princeton**. Use Internet Explorer and a search engine of your choice to locate the Websites of Princeton University and Yale University. Determine the approximate tuition, fees, room, board, and personal expenses for a full-time, undergraduate student. Enter the expense numbers into the cells in column B of both the Princeton and Yale sheets. The estimated expenses for the remaining years will be automatically calculated by the formulas that were set up in the original Harvard sheet. Save the changes to the workbook and close it.

Critical Thinking 3.3   On Your Own

Stefanie Martin is the owner of Stefanie's Used Computer Stores, which has three locations in various parts of the city. She instructs each of her store managers to prepare an Excel worksheet that lists the number of computers, monitors, printers, scanners, and keyboards purchased by the stores in the past month. In addition, Stefanie wants the items categorized as Poor Condition, Good Condition, or Excellent Condition. Stefanie emails each store manager an Excel worksheet to use as the basis for the worksheets they submit. This way, each worksheet will have an identical format and Stefanie can easily summarize the data from the three stores.

Set up a workbook using the criteria discussed above. Create four worksheets: one sheet will contain data for Store 1, the second sheet will be for Store 2, the third for Store 3, and the fourth for a summary sheet. You should set up the structure of the worksheet, including the headings.

Use linking formulas to summarize the data from the various sheets on your summary sheet. Use AutoFormat to make all sheets visually attractive. Save the completed workbook as **Store Inventory**.

LESSON 4

Using Financial Functions and Data Analysis

Excel's built-in financial functions can be used for various types of financial analyses. In this lesson, you will use the PMT (Payment) function to determine the monthly payment for a new automobile. In addition, you will use the FV (Future Value) function to determine the future value of investments. Excel also provides tools to help you find solutions to financial questions and other data analyses. In this lesson, you will use Goal Seek, Solver, and the Analysis ToolPak to answer a variety of questions.

Microsoft Office Excel 2003 and Microsoft Office Excel 2003 Expert objectives covered in this lesson

Objective Number	Skill Sets and Skills	Concept Page References	Exercise Page References
XL03S-2-4	Use statistical, date and time, financial, and logical functions	104	105–107
XL03E-1-7	Perform data analysis using automated tools	108, 110, 112	108–113

Case Study

Ashley Diehl has often dreamed of owning a shiny, new Chevrolet Corvette. Recently, she was promoted in her job and received a significant pay raise. She has also profited handsomely from some wise investments. Ashley decides it is time to explore the idea of making her dream come true by purchasing a new Corvette. Ashley sets up an Excel worksheet that calculates the monthly payment on a car loan using a variety of input variables. She uses the PMT (Payment) function to calculate the monthly payment and Excel's Goal Seek and Solver tools to explore various financing scenarios. Ashley is also considering buying a house in five years. Realizing that she cannot possibly save enough on her own for a house, Ashley decides to move back in with her parents. She figures she'll be able to save $225 per month this way and wants to see, given her current interest rate, how much money she will have at the end of five years. She will use the FV (Future Value) function to calculate the total.

	A	B	C	D	E
1	Car Loan Analysis for Ashley Diehl				
2					
3	Make and Model	2004 Corvette Coupe			
4	Purchase Price	$37,000			
5	Down Payment	10,000			
6	Loan Amount	$27,000			
7	Interest Rate	6%			
8	Number of Months	60			
9	Monthly Payment	$521.99			
10	Total Interest	$4,319.14			
11	Total Vehicle Cost	$41,319.14			
12					

Interest vs. Purchase Price

Purchase Price 90%

Total Interest 10%

Using Financial Functions

Excel provides more than 50 financial functions that calculate important financial numbers. For example, Excel has basic financial functions for determining monthly payments on loans, the total interest paid on loans, the future value of investments, and other such questions. Excel also has advanced financial functions for calculating depreciation of assets, internal rates of return, and other more advanced topics.

Introducing the PMT and FV Functions

In this lesson, you will use the PMT (Payment) and FV (Future Value) functions. These are the most useful financial functions for the average Excel user. The PMT function calculates the required payment for a loan when you specify the loan amount, interest rate, and number of payments you will make. The FV function calculates the total amount you will have when you specify the interest rate and the amount and number of deposits you make.

You can use actual values or cell references in the formulas. Keep in mind that using the cell reference offers more flexibility. For example, you can easily see the total amount saved change if you change the number of deposits in an FV function.

Financial Functions Syntax

You can enter financial functions using the Insert Function dialog box or by entering them with the keyboard. Like all functions, financial functions have a specific syntax you must follow. The generic syntax of the PMT and FV functions is shown in the following table.

Function	Syntax
PMT (Payment)	PMT(rate, periods, loan amount)
FV (Future Value)	FV(rate, periods, payment)

Most car loans and fixed-rate mortgages have payment amounts that remain constant throughout the term of the loan. The PMT and FV functions can be used when the payment amount remains constant. The various arguments in the PMT and FV functions are outlined in the following Quick Reference table.

QUICK REFERENCE: USING FINANCIAL FUNCTION ARGUMENTS

Argument	Description
Periods	This is the number of payments you will make. Most loans have a monthly payment period, so you should specify the number of months instead of the number of years. For example, you should use 60 as the number of periods for a 5-year auto loan (5 years*12 months per year).
Rate	This is the interest rate for each period. Most loans have a monthly period, though they are quoted as annual rates. Therefore, you will need to divide the interest rate by 12 in the formula.
Payment	This is the payment amount for each period. The payment must be the same for each period.
Loan amount	This is the opening balance or amount borrowed for a loan.

Hands-On 4.1   Use the PMT and FV Functions

In this exercise, you will set up a loan worksheet that will calculate the monthly payment on a car loan using the PMT function and insert a pie chart to visually compare the Total Interest to the Purchase Price. You will also calculate the monthly deposit required to save the $10,000 down payment.

Create a PMT Function

1. Start a new workbook.

2. Enter the following data. Format the numbers and widen columns A and B as shown.

	A	B
1	Car Loan Analysis for Ashley Diehl	
2		
3	Make and Model	2004 Corvette Coupe
4	Purchase Price	$37,000
5	Down Payment	10,000
6	Loan Amount	
7	Interest Rate	
8	Number of Months	
9	Monthly Payment	
10	Total Interest	
11	Total Vehicle Cost	

3. Click cell B6 and enter the formula **=B4-B5**.
   The loan amount is the purchase price minus the down payment. The PMT function will use the loan amount as one of its arguments. The result should equal 27,000.

4. Click cell B7 and enter the interest rate **6%**.

5. Click cell B8 and enter **60** as the number of months.

6. Click cell B9 and enter the formula **=PMT(B7,B8,B6)**.
   The result should equal ($1,670.64). The generic PMT function syntax is =PMT(rate, periods, loan amount). Notice that the B7, B8, and B6 references in the function refer to the interest rate, number of months, and loan amount in the worksheet.

   Notice that Excel formats the payment with the Currency Style format and that the payment is red and in parentheses. The red color and parentheses indicate that this is a negative number. Excel treats payments as debits (money you are paying) so they are assigned a negative number. This is a convention that bankers and other financial professionals use. You will convert this number to a positive number in the following steps.

   Finally, notice that $1,670.64 is a very large payment. This is because the interest rate in cell B7 is an annual rate of 6%. These financial functions have monthly periods so you are paying 6% interest per month! The interest rate must be divided by 12 (the number of months in a year) to use a monthly interest rate in the function. You will do this in the following steps.

7. Make sure the highlight is in cell B9.

8. Click in the Formula bar and edit the formula as follows:

- Insert a minus (−) sign between the comma and B6 in the formula.
- Divide the B7 reference by 12. The completed formula is =PMT(B7/12,B8,-B6).

9. Complete the entry. The new payment should equal $521.99.
This payment will certainly be more affordable. The minus sign converts the number to a positive and the B7/12 argument establishes a 0.5% per month rate.

10. Click cell B10 and enter the formula **=B9*B8-B6**.
This formula calculates the total interest, which first multiplies the monthly payment by the number of months to determine the total payments. The loan amount in cell B6 can then be subtracted from the total payments to determine the total interest in cell B10, which should equal $4,319.14.

11. Click cell B11 and enter the formula **=B9*B8+B5**.
This formula calculates the total vehicle cost, which is simply the total payments plus the down payment. The result should equal $41,319.14. As you can see, the purchase price of $37,000 plus the total interest of $4,319.14 equal $41,319.14.

12. The completed worksheet is shown in the following illustration:

	A	B
1	Car Loan Analysis for Ashley Diehl	
2		
3	Make and Model	2004 Corvette Coupe
4	Purchase Price	$37,000
5	Down Payment	10,000
6	Loan Amount	$27,000
7	Interest Rate	6%
8	Number of Months	60
9	Monthly Payment	$521.99
10	Total Interest	$4,319.14
11	Total Vehicle Cost	$41,319.14

This example also shows selected data that will be used to create a chart in the next few steps.

Create a Pie Chart

13. Select cells A4:B4 and A10:B10 as shown in the preceding illustration (you must use the [Ctrl] key).
This selection will allow the pie chart to compare the total interest to the purchase price.

14. Click the Chart Wizard button.

15. Use the Chart Wizard to create the embedded pie chart shown to the right.

16. Rename Sheet1 **Car Loan**.

17. Save the workbook as **Car Loan**.

Interest vs. Purchase Price

Purchase Price 90%

Total Interest 10%

Create the FV Function

18. Click the Sheet2 tab, enter the following data, and then click cell B7.

	A	B
1	Saving for down payment	
2		
3		
4	Amt Saved Each Month	$225
5	Interest Rate	2.5%
6	Number of Months	60
7	Total Saved in 5 Years	

19. Click the Insert Function *fx* button.

20. Follow these steps to choose the FV function:

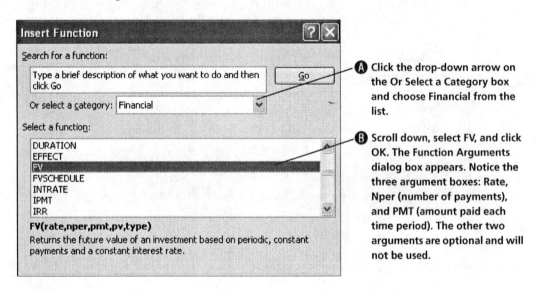

A Click the drop-down arrow on the Or Select a Category box and choose Financial from the list.

B Scroll down, select FV, and click OK. The Function Arguments dialog box appears. Notice the three argument boxes: Rate, Nper (number of payments), and PMT (amount paid each time period). The other two arguments are optional and will not be used.

21. Follow these steps to specify the function arguments:

A Click the Rate box then click cell B5 and type **/12**. If the Function Arguments dialog box is covering cell B5, move it over by dragging the title bar. Interest rates are typically quoted as annual figures, so you are dividing the rate by 12.

B Click the Nper box then click cell B6. The B6 cell reference appears in the Nper box and the value (60) appears on the right side of the box.

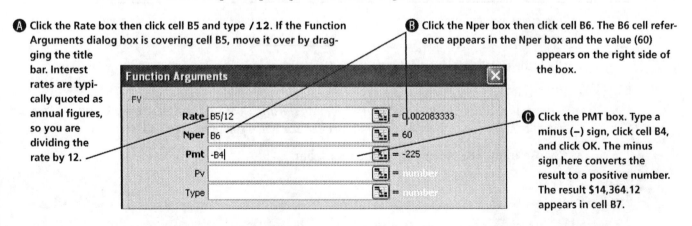

C Click the PMT box. Type a minus (–) sign, click cell B4, and click OK. The minus sign here converts the result to a positive number. The result $14,364.12 appears in cell B7.

22. Rename Sheet2 **Savings**, save the changes, and continue with the next topic.

Introducing Data Analysis Tools

Excel provides several tools, including Goal Seek and the Solver, to let you perform advanced what-if analyses. Other data analyses, such as the Rank and Percentile tool, use the Data Analysis ToolPak. Goal Seek lets you see how changing the values in cells affects the outcome of formulas. The Solver determines a value of one cell by changing other cells. You can also restrict the values Solver uses in calculations. The Data Analysis ToolPak performs functions determined by the data and parameters you provide.

Using Goal Seek

In this topic, you will use the Goal Seek tool. Goal Seek lets you set a goal for a cell that contains a formula. For example, you will set a goal of $550 for the Monthly Payment in cell B9 of the Car Loan worksheet. You can instruct Goal Seek to choose another cell whose contents it will change. The cell with the formula must be dependent on the second cell. For example, you will let Goal Seek adjust the down payment to achieve the $550 monthly payment.

QUICK REFERENCE: USING GOAL SEEK

Task	Procedure
Use Goal Seek	▪ Develop and test the worksheet to make sure it is functioning properly.
	▪ Click the cell for which you want to set a goal. The cell must contain a formula.
	▪ Choose Tools→Goal Seek from the menu bar.
	▪ Type the desired goal (number) in the To Value box.
	▪ Click the By Changing Cell box and specify the cell whose value you want Goal Seek to adjust.
	▪ Click OK then click OK again to confirm the change.

 Hands-On 4.2   Use Goal Seek

In this exercise, you will use Goal Seek to adjust the down payment based on a monthly payment that you determine.

1. Click the Car Loan sheet tab.

2. Click cell B9.
   Clicking the cell you want to set a goal for prior to starting Goal Seek will ensure you set the goal for the correct cell. The cell will already be in the Set Cell box when you open Goal Seek.

3. Choose Tools→Goal Seek from the menu bar.

4. Follow these steps to set the Goal Seek parameters:

A The Set Cell option should already be set to B9. This is the cell for which you are setting a goal.

B Click in the To Value box and type **550**. This is the monthly payment goal for cell B9.

C Click in the By Changing Cell box then click cell B5 in the worksheet. Excel will insert the absolute reference B5 in the By Changing Cell box. Notice that you can type entries in the Goal Seek or use point mode (as you just did).

Goal Seek	☒
Set cell:	B9
To value:	550
By changing cell:	B5
OK	Cancel

Click in CELL B5 or enter B5

5. Click OK and Goal Seek will indicate that it has found a solution to the goal.
   The down payment in the worksheet has been adjusted to 8,551.

6. Click OK on the Goal Seek Status box to confirm the change to the down payment.
   As you can see, a smaller down payment is required to achieve a $550 monthly payment.

Use Goal Seek to Adjust the Interest Rate

7. Click the Undo ↺ button to reverse the change to the down payment.

8. Click cell B9 and choose Tools→Goal Seek from the menu bar.

9. Type **550** in the To Value box.

10. Click in the By Changing Cell box, and then click cell B7 in the worksheet (the Interest Rate cell).

11. Click OK and the interest rate will be set to 8%.

12. Click OK again to confirm the change to the interest rate.
    Notice the impact this change has on the chart. The total interest (in the chart) has decreased to 14%.

Create a What-If Analysis

You can also experiment with what-if analyses by changing the interest rate, down payment, purchase price, and other values.

13. Click cell B4 and change the purchase price to **$20,000**.
    What impact does this change have on the other variables and the chart?

14. Feel free to experiment with Goal Seek.

15. Save the changes when you have finished, and then continue with the next topic.

Using Solver

Goal Seek is easy to use but it is somewhat limited. It can only adjust one variable at a time. Excel's Solver tool can solve problems when more than one variable requires adjustment. You display the Solver dialog box with the Tools→Solver command.

Solver also gives you additional options for specifying the value of the target cell. You can specify a precise value, as with Goal Seek, or you can specify a MIN or MAX value. For example, you can create a Solver scenario and specify a maximum monthly payment of $650. In addition, Solver lets you specify one or more constraints. Constraints give you extra control over the scenario by allowing you to specify a range of values that a particular cell has.

The Equal To options are used to specify the target cell value. You can specify an exact value or a MIN or MAX value.

Multiple variable cells are entered here. Solver will adjust all variables to find a solution.

You can specify one or more constraints. Constraints are added by clicking the Add button and filling in the options in the Subject to the Constraints box.

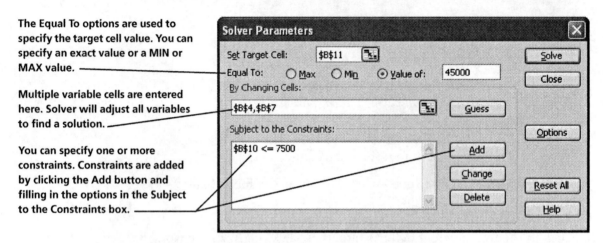

Installing Solver

Solver is not part of the typical Office 2003 installation. It is an add-in program that only appears on the Tools menu if a full installation of Excel was performed. If Solver does not appear on the Tools menu, you can choose Tools→Add Ins, and then choose Solver Add-In from the Add-Ins box.

 Hands-On 4.3   Use Solver

In this exercise, you will use Solver to determine the purchase price and interest rate required to achieve the total vehicle purchase price you specify.

NOTE! *To complete this exercise Solver must be installed using the procedure discussed in the preceding topic.*

1. Click cell B11 and choose Tools→Solver from the menu bar.

2. Follow these steps to set the target cell value and specify the variable cells:

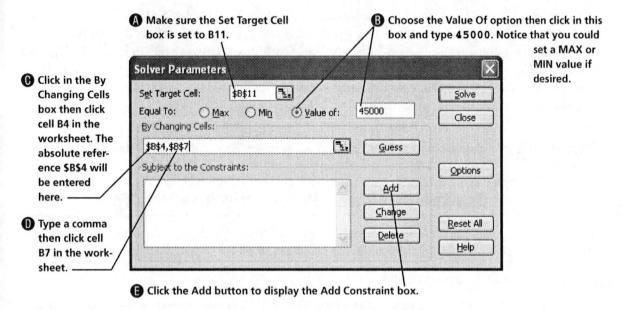

A Make sure the Set Target Cell box is set to B11.

B Choose the Value Of option then click in this box and type **45000**. Notice that you could set a MAX or MIN value if desired.

C Click in the By Changing Cells box then click cell B4 in the worksheet. The absolute reference B4 will be entered here.

D Type a comma then click cell B7 in the worksheet.

E Click the Add button to display the Add Constraint box.

3. Follow these steps to specify a constraint:

A Click cell B10 in the worksheet to enter that reference in this box.

B Make sure the Constraint option is set to <= (less than or equal to).

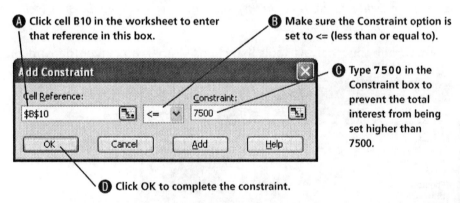

C Type **7500** in the Constraint box to prevent the total interest from being set higher than 7500.

D Click OK to complete the constraint.

The constraint will appear in the Subject to the Constraints box of the Solver Parameters box.

4. Take a moment to review the parameters you have set prior to initiating Solver.

5. Click the Solve button and the Solver will go to work.
When the Solver has completed its work, the Solver Results box should report that a solution has been found.

6. Be sure the Keep Solver Solution option is chosen and click OK.
The completed solution should match the example shown to the right.

7. Take a few minutes to experiment with Solver.

8. When you have finished, save the changes and close the workbook.

	A	B
1	Car Loan Analysis for Ashley Diehl	
2		
3	Make and Model	2004 Corvette Coupe
4	Purchase Price	$37,500
5	Down Payment	10,000
6	Loan Amount	$27,500
7	Interest Rate	10%
8	Number of Months	60
9	Monthly Payment	$583.33
10	Total Interest	$7,500.00
11	Total Vehicle Cost	$45,000.00

Using the Analysis ToolPak

The Analysis ToolPak contains a set of data analysis tools. You display a dialog box that contains all the tools using Tools→Data Analysis. If Data Analysis is not on the menu, you must add it by choosing Tools→Add Ins, checking Analysis ToolPak, and clicking OK. The tool you choose to use actually performs the appropriate statistical or engineering macro function then displays the results either on the same sheet as the data or on a separate worksheet. You will use the Rank and Percentile analysis tool in this course.

 WARNING! *Depending on your installation, you may need to check both Analysis ToolPak and Analysis ToolPak VBA.*

 Hands-On 4.4   Use the Rank and Percentile Analysis Tool

In this exercise, you will use the Rank and Percentile Analysis Tool to produce a table in the same worksheet as the data, and that contains the rank and percentile of each score.

1. Open the Evaluations workbook.

2. In cell A16, type **First Test Ranking** and in cell F16, type **Second Test Ranking**.

3. Choose Tools→Data Analysis from the menu bar.
   Remember, if Data Analysis is not in the menu you must add it by choosing Tools→Add Ins, checking Analysis ToolPak, and clicking OK.

4. Scroll through the Analysis Tools list, choose Rank and Percentile, and click OK.

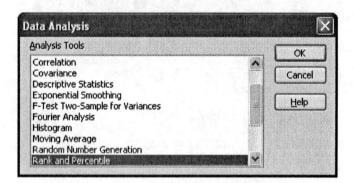

The Rank and Percentile dialog box appears. You must specify the cell range to be analyzed in the Input Range box and where you would like to display the results in the Output Range box. Notice the Help button on the dialog box. You can use this to get a description of each tool in the list.

5. Follow these steps to specify the rank and percentile settings:

A Click the Input Range box then drag over cells C6:C11 in the worksheet.

B Click the Output Range option, and then type **A17** in the box.

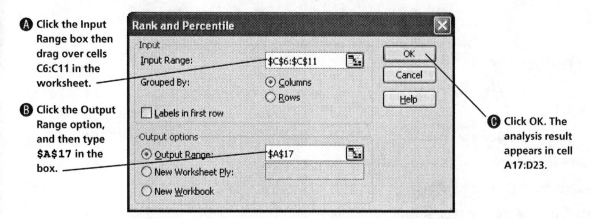

C Click OK. The analysis result appears in cell A17:D23.

Notice that the scores are now ranked from the highest to the lowest; that is, 78 is the highest score and is ranked number 1 (out of 6) and 100%, and 64 is the lowest score so it is ranked 6 and 0%.

6. Using same technique described in steps 4 and 6, analyze the Second Test Scores in column E. Display the results beginning in cell F17.
Take a few minutes to look at the data in the analysis tables and how they correlate to the data in cells C6:C11 and E6:E11.

7. When finished, save the changes and close the workbook.

Concepts Review

True/False Questions

1. The PMT function can only be used if the payment amount is the same for each payment period. TRUE FALSE

2. Most loans have a yearly payment period. TRUE FALSE

3. The cell for which you are seeking a goal must contain a formula. TRUE FALSE

4. Solver can adjust more than one variable. TRUE FALSE

5. Solver is installed as part of the typical Office 2003 installation. TRUE FALSE

6. The FV function is used to calculate the future value of investments. TRUE FALSE

7. You must insert a minus sign in the PMT argument to have the result display as a positive value. TRUE FALSE

8. The PMT and FV functions both require four arguments. TRUE FALSE

9. You should click the cell you want to set a goal for before you open Goal Seek. TRUE FALSE

10. You can analyze data in your worksheet using the Analysis ToolPak. TRUE FALSE

Multiple Choice Questions

1. Which command is used to initiate Goal Seek?
   a. Edit→Goal Seek
   b. Format→Goal Seek
   c. Tools→Goal Seek
   d. None of the above

2. Which of the following PMT functions has the arguments in the correct positions?
   a. =PMT(rate, periods, loan amount)
   b. =PMT(rate, loan amount, periods)
   c. =PMT(periods, rate, loan amount)
   d. None of the above

3. Which command is used to initiate Solver?
   a. Edit→Solver
   b. File→Solver
   c. Format→Solver
   d. None of the above

4. With which tool are constraints used?
   a. Solver
   b. Goal→Seek
   c. PMT function
   d. FV function

Skill Builders

Skill Builder 4.1   Use the PMT Function and Solver

In this exercise, you will use the PMT function to calculate mortgage payments on a 30-year fixed mortgage. You will multiply the 30 years by 12 within the PMT function to determine the total number of periods in the loan. The generic syntax of the PMT function is repeated below for your convenience. You will also use Solver to determine the purchase price and interest rate required for a specified total cost.

Payment Function Syntax =PMT(rate, periods, loan amount)

Create PMT Function

1. Start a new workbook and set up the worksheet shown to the right.
   Be sure you use a formula to calculate the loan amount in cell B5 as the Purchase Price – Down Payment.

	A	B
1	**30-Year Mortgage Worksheet**	
2		
3	Purchase Price	260,000
4	Down Payment	25,000
5	Loan Amount	235,000
6	Interest Rate	9%
7	Number of Years	30
8	Monthly Payment	
9	Total Interest	
10	Total Cost of Home	

2. Click cell B8 and enter the formula **=PMT(B6/12,B7*12,-B5)**.
   The result should equal $1,890.86. Notice that the formula has a minus sign between the comma and B5. Also, the first argument divides the interest rate in cell B6 by 12 because the argument requires the monthly rate. Likewise, the second argument multiplies the number of years in cell B7 by 12 because the argument requires the number of months. Excel formats the result with the Currency Style because you used the PMT function.

3. Click cell B9 and enter **=B8*B7*12-B5** to calculate the total interest.
   The result should equal $445,710.73. Take a few moments to study the formula and notice that it calculates the total payments over the term of the loan and subtracts the loan amount. Also notice that the number of months is determined by multiplying the number of years in cell B7 by 12.

4. Click cell B10 and enter **=B9+B3** to calculate the total cost of the home.

Create a Pie Chart

5. Select cells A3:B3 and A9:B9, as shown to the right.
   This selection will allow the pie chart to compare the Total Interest to the Purchase Price.

	A	B
1	**30-Year Mortgage Worksheet**	
2		
3	Purchase Price	260,000
4	Down Payment	25,000
5	Loan Amount	235,000
6	Interest Rate	9%
7	Number of Years	30
8	Monthly Payment	$1,890.86
9	Total Interest	$445,710.73
10	Total Cost of Home	$705,710.73

6. Click the Chart Wizard ⊞ button and create the embedded pie chart shown to the right.

Interest vs. Purchase Price

Use a What-If Analysis

7. Click cell B6.
Notice that the monthly payment in cell B8 is approximately $1,890.

Purchase Price
37%

Total Interest
63%

8. Change the Interest Rate to **8%** and notice the impact it has on the monthly payment.

9. Experiment with various interest rates. Also, try changing the down payment and note the impact it has on the monthly payment.

Use Solver

10. Click cell B10 and choose Tools→Solver.

11. Follow these guidelines to complete the options in the dialog box:

- Set the Value Of option to **600000**.
- Set the By Changing Cells by inserting the Purchase Price and Interest Rate cells separated by a comma.
- Add a constraint and set the total interest not to exceed **400000**.

The new interest rate should be 7%. The monthly payment is automatically recalculated since it uses the purchase price and interest rate in its formula. The monthly payment is now $1,597.22.

12. Save the workbook as **Home Mortgage** then close it.

Skill Builder 4.2   Use the FV Function

In this exercise, you will use the Future Value (FV) function to determine the future value of a college fund. This could be important if you are planning on saving for a college education, but the worksheet can also be used to determine the future value of nearly any investment that has consistent contributions. The generic syntax of the FV function is repeated below for your convenience.

Future Value Function Syntax =FV(rate, periods, payment)

1. Start a new workbook.

2. Use the Format→Column→Width command to set the width of column A to 19 and column B to 14.

3. Enter the data shown to the right.

4. Click cell B6 and enter the function =FV(B3/
   12,B4*12,B5).
   *The result should equal ($96,017.23). The FV function
   returns a negative number, as did the PMT function. Also,
   notice that the interest rate in cell B3 is divided by 12 to give*
   a monthly rate. The number of years in cell B4 is multiplied by 12 to give the total number of monthly
   payments.

	A	B
1	Ted's College Fund	
2		
3	Interest Rate	8%
4	Number of Years	18
5	Monthly Contribution	200
6	Future Value	

5. Click cell B6 then click in the Formula bar and insert a minus (-) sign between the comma
   and B5.

6. Complete the entry and the result should be positive.

7. Save the workbook as **Original College Fund**.
   You will continue to use this workbook in the next exercise.

Skill Builder 4.3   Use Goal Seek

*In this exercise, you will use Goal Seek to determine the interest rate required to have $200,000 saved by
contributing $300 monthly for 18 years.*

Use the Goal Seek

1. Click cell B5 and change the monthly contribution to **$300**.
   *Notice that this increases the future value of the investment to approximately $144,000. In the next few
   steps, you will use Goal Seek to determine the interest rate necessary to have a future value of $200,000
   with a monthly contribution of $300.*

2. Click cell B6 and choose Tools→Goal Seek from the menu bar.

3. Set the To Value option to **$200,000**.

4. Set the By Changing Cell option to **B3** (the Interest Rate cell).

5. Click OK and notice that an 11% interest rate is required.

6. Click Cancel on the Goal Seek Results box to cancel the change to the interest rate.

7. Use Goal Seek to determine the interest rate required to achieve a **$275,000** future value
   with a **$325** monthly contribution.

8. Save the workbook as **College Fund Goal** then close it.

 # Assessments

Assessment 4.1   Use FV Function

In this exercise, you will calculate the future value of a mutual fund.

1. Create the following worksheet, using the FV function to calculate the future value in cell B7:

	A	B
1	Investment Projections	
2		
3	Account	Utilities Mutual Fund
4	Projected Annual Rate of Return	11%
5	Number of Years	20
6	Monthly Contribution	$800
7	Future Value	

2. Format all cells as shown and adjust the width of columns A and B to 19.

3. Print the worksheet, save the workbook as **Invest Projection**, and close the workbook.

Assessment 4.2   Use PMT Function

In this exercise, you will calculate the monthly payment for a home equity loan.

1. Create the following worksheet using the PMT function to calculate the monthly payment in cell B7. Be sure the answer displays as a positive number.

	A	B
1	Home Equity Loan Analysis	
2		
3	Lender	Wells Fargo
4	Interest Rate	6.00%
5	Number of Years	10
6	Loan Amount	$15,000
7	Monthly Payment	

2. Format all cells as shown and adjust the width of column A to 24 and column B to 11.

3. Save the workbook as **Home Equity Loan**.
You will continue to use this workbook in the next exercise.

Assessment 4.3   Use Goal Seek

In this exercise, you will use Goal Seek to determine the amount you could borrow with a monthly payment of $200.

1. Display the Goal Seek dialog box.

2. Set the options in the dialog to determine what the loan amount would be if the monthly payment was $200.

3. Save the changes, print the worksheet, and close the workbook.

Critical Thinking

Critical Thinking 4.1   On Your Own

Ashley Sinclair is part of the new wave of independent investors who are taking control of their own investment portfolios. Ashley recently discovered a corporate bond fund in which she feels her principal will be quite safe. It pays an 8% annual return. Ashley makes every investment decision with retirement in mind. She is 38 years old and plans to retire when she is 58. Ashley wants to contribute $350 per month over the next 20 years. Set up a worksheet that uses the Future Value function to determine the future value of her bond fund investment. Save the workbook as **Ashley's Bond Fund**. Leave the workbook open because you will continue to use it.

Critical Thinking 4.2   On Your Own

After analyzing the future value of her potential bond fund investment, Ashley realizes that her investment just won't be large enough after 20 years to give her the income she will need at retirement. Ashley has other investments in stocks and real estate and she can count on social security; however, she expects a large part of her retirement income to come from the bond fund. Ashley decides to explore other bond funds and considers increasing her monthly contributions. Use Goal Seek and the worksheet you set up in Critical Thinking 4.1 to answer the following questions. Write your answers in the space provided.

■ If the annual rate of return is 11% and the number of years is 20, what must be the monthly contribution to have a future value of $1,000,000? _____

■ If the rate of return is 11% and the monthly contribution is $800, what must be the number of years to have a future value of $1,000,000? _____

■ If the number of years is 20 and the monthly contribution is $800, what must be the rate of return to have a future value of $1,000,000? _____

Leave the workbook open, as you will continue to use it.

Critical Thinking 4.3   On Your Own

Ashley purchased her home 15 years ago. Since that time, she has built up more than $100,000 of equity in the house. Recently, Ashley's financial advisor recommended that she consider taking out a home equity loan to pay off some bills and consolidate the rest of her debts. Set up another sheet in the Ashley's Bond Fund workbook that uses the PMT function to determine monthly payments on a home equity loan. Assume an annual interest rate of 8%, a 10-year term, and a loan amount of $15,000. Save the workbook and leave it open.

Critical Thinking 4.4   On Your Own

Use Goal Seek and the payment worksheet you set up in Critical Thinking 4.3 to answer the following questions. Write your answers in the space provided.

- If the interest rate is 9% and the number of years is 10, what must be the loan amount to have a monthly payment of $175? _____

- If the interest rate is 7% and the loan amount is $15,000, what must be the number of years to have a monthly payment of $175? _____

- If the number of years is 10 and the loan amount is $15,000, what must be the interest rate to have a monthly payment of $175? _____

Save and close the workbook.

Critical Thinking 4.5   Web Research

Carl Jenkins is considering the purchase of a new Volvo station wagon. Carl has $15,000 for a down payment and figures he can afford $500 for the monthly payment plus an additional $100 per month for insurance. Use Internet Explorer and a search engine of your choice to help Carl determine whether or not he can afford the vehicle. First, locate a site where you can determine the cost of the Volvo. You may need to make decisions on vehicle options to help Carl meet his budget. Record the information you find in an Excel workbook. Next, locate one or more sites that offer automobile loan information. If you are requested to enter personal and credit information, use Carl's information as listed below. Record all of the loan information in the workbook. Be sure to include the Website URL, interest rate, amount borrowed, term, and monthly payment.

Carl's Information	
Age:	37
Income:	$42,000 per year
Monthly Mortgage Payment:	$650
Other debts (including student loans and credit cards):	$0
Location:	Richmond, CA 94803
Driving record:	Perfect (before buying the Volvo)

Finally, locate several sites that offer automobile insurance quotations. Use Carl's information to obtain a rate quote. Choose a $500 deductible, full coverage, and $100,000/$300,000 liability limits. You may find that the rates vary considerably from one company to the next. Record your findings in the workbook and determine if Carl can afford the vehicle. Keep in mind that you have a $600 per month budget to work with. Carl doesn't mind if the payment is a little more than $500 or if the insurance is less than $100—as long as the total monthly expenditure is $600 or less. Save your completed workbook as **2004 Volvo**.

LESSON 5

Introducing Databases

Excel is often used to store lists of information and databases. Excel worksheets provide the perfect structure for organizing such data and have several tools to help you enter, view, and analyze information stored in a database structure. In this lesson, you will set up a database and use Excel's Data Form tool to enter data into it. In addition, you will use subtotals to analyze data and filters to view data in various ways.

Microsoft Office Excel 2003 Expert objectives covered in this lesson

Objective Number	Skill Sets and Skills	Concept Page References	Exercise Page References
XL03E-1-1	Use subtotals	129–130	131–132
XL03E-1-2	Define and apply advanced filters	132–133	133–134
XL03E-1-10	Use Database functions	135–136	137

Additional learning resources are available at labpub.com/learn/excel03/

Case Study

National Computing Solutions is a nationwide provider of customized hardware and software solutions for businesses. Donna Boyer, the National Sales Manager, wants to track and analyze the performance of her sales representatives. Donna wants the sales data separated by hardware and software sales. In addition, she wants to organize the sales representatives by region and position. You will develop a database that lets Donna organize the data and analyze it using subtotals and filters. The completed database you will create is shown below.

	A	B	C	D	E	F	G	H
1	National Computing Solutions							
2	2004 Sales Database							
3								
4	Last Name	First Name	Years Employed	Position	Region	State	SW Sales	HW Sales
5	Zain	Beth	7	Senior Sales Rep	Western	CA	340,000	800,000
6	Alvizo	Alex	7	Senior Sales Rep	Western	CA	450,000	340,000
7	Brown	Bill	3	Telemarketer	Western	CA	546,000	120,000
8	Smith	Bob	3	Sales Rep	Western	CA	200,000	180,000
9	Williams	Michael	3	Sales Rep	Eastern	FL	120,000	340,000
10	Martinez	Carlos	4	Senior Sales Rep	Eastern	FL	450,000	450,000
11	Hubbs	Daniel	4	Telemarketer	Eastern	FL	340,000	230,000
12	Wilson	Bernie	1	Sales Rep	Central	IL	120,000	170,000
13	Thomas	Will	2	Sales Rep	Central	IL	230,000	120,000
14	Cain	Mary	5	Senior Sales Rep	Central	IL	234,000	560,000
15	Watson	Tom	8	Sales Rep	Eastern	MA	230,000	340,000
16	Smith	Michael	5	Telemarketer	Eastern	MA	123,000	230,000
17	Richards	Paul	4	Telemarketer	Western	WA	234,000	546,000
18	Cray	Zip	6	Telemarketer	Western	WA	900,000	780,000

Creating Excel Databases

Databases let you store and manage sets of related data. For example, in this lesson you will create a database that holds sales data for sales representatives. The database will store all of the information for the sales representatives. It will also let you analyze the sales data with automatic subtotaling and filters.

Records

In Excel, each row in a database is called a record, and each record is a collection of facts about a certain person, event, or other item. For example, your sales representative database will have one record per sales representative.

Fields

In Excel, each column in a database is called a field. Each record in a database is divided into fields, and records can have many fields. For example, your sales representative database will have fields for each sales representative's name, position, length of employment, and sales results.

Database Tools

Excel provides a number of features designed specifically to work with databases. For example, Excel can display a data entry form to make entering records into a database easy. You can sort databases (in ascending or descending order), find records, create subtotals, and analyze data with very little effort.

Setting Up a New Database

You create a database as you would create any other worksheet. However, there are three rules you should follow when setting up a new database. These rules are described in the following illustration.

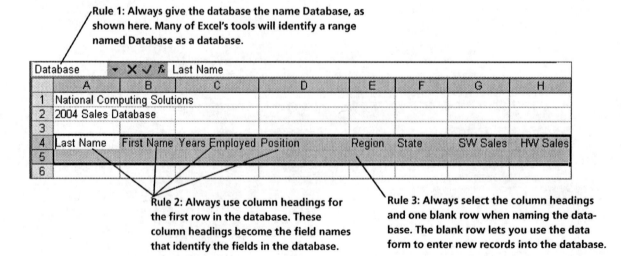

Rule 1: Always give the database the name Database, as shown here. Many of Excel's tools will identify a range named Database as a database.

Rule 2: Always use column headings for the first row in the database. These column headings become the field names that identify the fields in the database.

Rule 3: Always select the column headings and one blank row when naming the database. The blank row lets you use the data form to enter new records into the database.

Hands-On 5.1   **Set Up the Database**

In this exercise, you will create a database for National Computing Solutions' sales force. You will expand on and work with this database throughout the lesson.

Adjust Column Widths and Enter Data

1. Start Excel to display a new workbook.

2. Make sure the highlight is somewhere in column A and choose Format→Column→Width from the menu bar.

3. Set the width to **11** and click OK.

4. Adjust the other column widths as shown in the following table:

Column	Use This Width
B	9
C	14
D	15
E	AutoFit
F	Leave as is
G and H	10

5. Enter the following data:

	A	B	C	D	E	F	G	H
1	National Computing Solutions							
2	2004 Sales Database							
3								
4	Last Name	First Name	Years Employed	Position	Region	State	SW Sales	HW Sales

Name the Database

6. Follow these steps to name the database:

A Select the range A4:H5. Be sure to select the empty cells in row 5 as shown. Also, select only the cells shown (not the entire rows).

Database	▾ ✕ ✓ *fx*	Last Name						
	A	B	C	D	E	F	G	H
1	National Computing Solutions							
2	2004 Sales Database							
3								
4	Last Name	First Name	Years Employed	Position	Region	State	SW Sales	HW Sales
5								
6								

B Click in the Name box, type **Database**, and tap ⌷Enter⌷.

You should always name a database using this technique. Including the blank cells in the selection allows Excel's Data Form tool to identify the location where new rows are to be added. It is also important to use the name Database. The Data Form tool easily identifies this name, as do many of Excel's other database tools.

Format the Cells and Numbers

7. Follow these steps to format several cells:

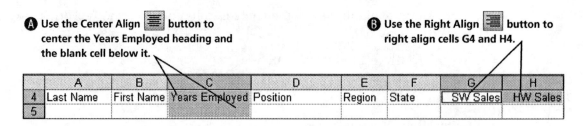

8. Follow these steps to format two blank cells:

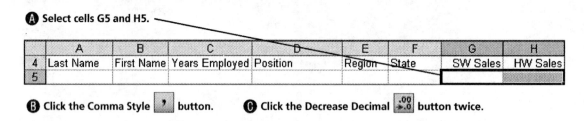

You won't be able to see the Comma Style in cells G5 and H5 until you enter numbers in those cells. All the formats you just set will be carried to each new record you add to the database.

9. Save the workbook as **2004 Sales Database**.

Working with Data Forms

The Data→Form command displays the Data Form dialog box. Data forms make entering, editing, and locating records in a database easy. When you issue the Data→Form command, Excel automatically identifies a database that has been given the name Database and displays a record in the data form.

 Hands-On 5.2   Use the Data Form to Enter Records

In this exercise, you will use the Data→Form command and enter several new records into the database.

1. Choose Data→Form from the menu bar.
Excel will identify your database (because you named it Database) and display the data form.

2. Follow these steps to enter the first record:

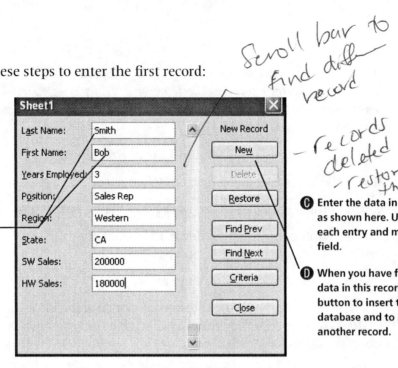

(handwritten note, top right) Scroll bar to find diff record

(handwritten note) - records can be deleted permanently
- restore only restores the last action 7 to 9

A Notice that Excel uses the field names from your database as labels for the boxes in the data form.

B Type **Smith** in the Last Name box, tap Tab to move to the First Name box, and then type **Bob**.

C Enter the data in the rest of the form as shown here. Use Tab to complete each entry and move to the next field.

D When you have finished entering the data in this record, click the New button to insert the record in the database and to prepare to enter another record.

3. If necessary, drag the Data Form dialog box slightly until you can see your database. *Notice that the record has been inserted below the heading row. The data form was able to insert the record in this location because you included a blank row in the selection when you named the database in Hands-On 5.1. Also, notice that the numbers in cells F5 and G5 have the Comma Style you set.*

4. Enter the following 13 records into the database:
You will need to click the New button after typing the data for each record. Be sure to enter all the records because you will need the data throughout this lesson. Also, there is no need to type the comma in the SW Sales and HW Sales numbers. Excel will format the numbers with the Comma Style format as they are entered in the database.

FROM THE KEYBOARD
Enter after the last field to insert the record

Name	Years Employed	Position	Region	State	SW Sales	HW Sales
Hubbs, Daniel	4	Telemarketer	Eastern	FL	340,000	230,000
Smith, Michael	5	Telemarketer	Eastern	MA	123,000	230,000
Watson, Tom	8	Sales Rep	Eastern	MA	230,000	340,000
Williams, Michael	3	Sales Rep	Eastern	FL	120,000	340,000
Martinez, Carlos	4	Senior Sales Rep	Eastern	FL	450,000	450,000
Wilson, Bernie	1	Sales Rep	Central	IL	120,000	170,000
Thomas, Will	2	Sales Rep	Central	IL	230,000	120,000
Cain, Mary	5	Senior Sales Rep	Central	IL	234,000	560,000
Zain, Beth	7	Senior Sales Rep	Western	CA	340,000	800,000
Alvizo, Alex	9	Senior Sales Rep	Western	CA	450,000	340,000
Brown, Bill	3	Telemarketer	Western	CA	546,000	120,000
Richards, Paul	4	Telemarketer	Western	WA	234,000	546,000
Cray, Zip	6	Telemarketer	Western	WA	900,000	780,000

5. Click the New button after entering the last record.
This button inserts the record into the database. This step is necessary because you will use the form to browse through and edit the records in the next few steps. You would lose the last record if you browsed prior to using the New button.

6. Click the Find Previous button until the Alvizo, Alex record is displayed.

7. Click in the Years Employed field and change the 9 to a **7**.

8. Use the vertical scroll bar in the Data Form dialog box to scroll through the records.

9. Drag the scroll box up and down and notice that the record number is displayed at the top-right corner of the Data Form box.

10. Move to record 4, and then move to record 10.

11. Notice the Delete and Restore buttons on the data form.
The Delete button permanently deletes a record while the Restore button lets you reverse your last action, such as an editing change. However, Restore will not let you recover a deleted record.

12. Click the Close button to return to the database.

13. Save the changes to your workbook and continue with the next topic.

Using Criteria to Find Records in a Data Form

The Data Form has a Criteria button that lets you locate records by specifying logical search criteria. For example, you may want to find a record where Last Name = Smith or you may want to find the next record where SW Sales is >700000. You can also use the asterisk (*) wildcard character with search criteria. This character is convenient if you know only the first part of the name or word for which you are searching. For example, if you enter Wood* in the Name field, Excel will locate the record containing Wood as the last name and the record containing Woodson as the last name. Search criteria are most useful in large databases with many records.

Hands-On 5.3   Use Criteria to Locate Records

In this exercise, you will search for existing records with various criteria using the Data→Form command.

1. Choose Data→Form to display the data form.

2. Click the Criteria button and notice that all of the field boxes appear empty.

TIP! *Criteria are not case sensitive.*

3. Click in the Last Name box and type **brown**.

4. Click the Find Next button or tap Enter and notice that the Bill Brown record appears.

5. Scroll to the top of the list. Then click the Criteria button, type **w***, and tap Enter. Notice that the Tom Watson record appears.

6. Click the Find Next button and notice that the Michael Williams record appears.

7. Take five minutes to practice locating records using various criteria. Try entering criteria in other boxes but make sure to click the Criteria button before entering each search criteria. *Excel may "beep" when you try to locate a record. If this happens, you will need to search in the opposite direction. For example, if you use the Find Next button and Excel beeps, try using the Find Prev button.*

8. Close the data form when you have finished.

Displaying Automatic Subtotals

You can use Excel's Subtotal tool to display subtotals and grand totals for numeric fields in a list. You can rapidly display subtotals to analyze your data and remove them just as easily. The following illustration shows the 2004 Sales Database with subtotals displayed.

Excel displays an Outline bar to let you increase or decrease the amount of information displayed in the subtotaled list.

In this example, the database is sorted on the State field and the SW Sales and HW Sales subtotals are inserted each time the State field changes. Excel automatically inserts the subtotals and grand total, and formats the worksheet as shown.

	A	B	C	D	E	F	G	H
1	National Computing Solutions							
2	2004 Sales Database							
3								
4	Last Name	First Name	Years Employed	Position	Region	State	SW Sales	HW Sales
5	Zain	Beth	7	Senior Sales Rep	Western	CA	340,000	800,000
6	Alvizo	Alex	7	Senior Sales Rep	Western	CA	450,000	340,000
7	Brown	Bill	3	Telemarketer	Western	CA	546,000	120,000
8	Smith	Bob	3	Sales Rep	Western	CA	200,000	180,000
9						CA Total	1,536,000	1,440,000
10	Williams	Michael	3	Sales Rep	Eastern	FL	120,000	340,000
11	Martinez	Carlos	4	Senior Sales Rep	Eastern	FL	450,000	450,000
12	Hubbs	Daniel	4	Telemarketer	Eastern	FL	340,000	230,000
13						FL Total	910,000	1,020,000
14	Wilson	Bernie	1	Sales Rep	Central	IL	120,000	170,000
15	Thomas	Will	2	Sales Rep	Central	IL	230,000	120,000
16	Cain	Mary	5	Senior Sales Rep	Central	IL	234,000	560,000
17						IL Total	584,000	850,000
18	Watson	Tom	8	Sales Rep	Eastern	MA	230,000	340,000
19	Smith	Michael	5	Telemarketer	Eastern	MA	123,000	230,000
20						MA Total	353,000	570,000
21	Richards	Paul	4	Telemarketer	Western	WA	234,000	546,000
22	Cray	Zip	6	Telemarketer	Western	WA	900,000	780,000
23						WA Total	1,134,000	1,326,000
24						Grand Tot	4,517,000	5,206,000

Sorting the List

The most important step in the subtotaling process is to first sort the list. You must sort the list on the field you want to base the subtotals. For example, sort on the State field if you want subtotals to appear each time the state field changes. When you issue the Subtotal command Excel will group all rows with the same state and calculate subtotals for the group.

The Subtotal Dialog Box

The Data→Subtotals command displays the Subtotal dialog box. The Subtotal dialog box lets you determine the fields for which subtotals are calculated and the function used in the calculations. The following illustration describes the options in the Subtotal dialog box.

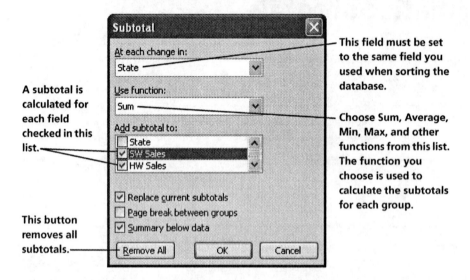

A subtotal is calculated for each field checked in this list.

This field must be set to the same field you used when sorting the database.

Choose Sum, Average, Min, Max, and other functions from this list. The function you choose is used to calculate the subtotals for each group.

This button removes all subtotals.

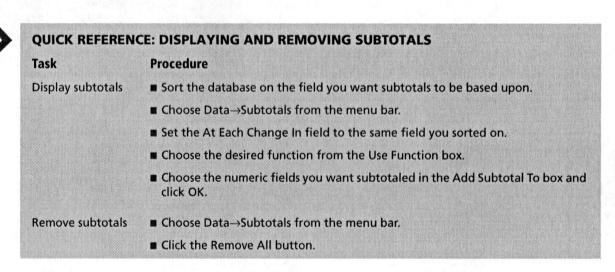

QUICK REFERENCE: DISPLAYING AND REMOVING SUBTOTALS

Task	Procedure
Display subtotals	■ Sort the database on the field you want subtotals to be based upon.
	■ Choose Data→Subtotals from the menu bar.
	■ Set the At Each Change In field to the same field you sorted on.
	■ Choose the desired function from the Use Function box.
	■ Choose the numeric fields you want subtotaled in the Add Subtotal To box and click OK.
Remove subtotals	■ Choose Data→Subtotals from the menu bar.
	■ Click the Remove All button.

In this exercise, you will sort the database list and display subtotals for each state. You will also use the Outline Bar to control the amount of detail displayed in the worksheet.

Sort the Database

1. Click cell F5.

2. Click the Sort Ascending ▲↓ button to sort the database based on the state field in column F.

All CA records will appear first, followed by FL, etc. When you issue the Subtotals command, Excel will create subtotals for the CA group, the FL group, etc.

Display Subtotals

3. Choose Data→Subtotals from the menu bar.

4. Follow these steps to set the subtotal options:

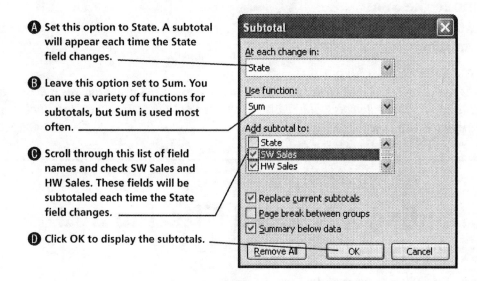

Ⓐ **Set this option to State.** A subtotal will appear each time the State field changes.

Ⓑ **Leave this option set to Sum.** You can use a variety of functions for subtotals, but Sum is used most often.

Ⓒ **Scroll through this list of field names and check SW Sales and HW Sales.** These fields will be subtotaled each time the State field changes.

Ⓓ **Click OK to display the subtotals.**

Take a few moments to review the subtotals before continuing.

Use the Outline Bar

5. Follow these steps to experiment with the Outline Bar on the left side of the worksheet:

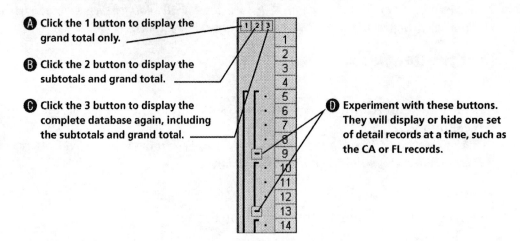

A Click the 1 button to display the grand total only.

B Click the 2 button to display the subtotals and grand total.

C Click the 3 button to display the complete database again, including the subtotals and grand total.

D Experiment with these buttons. They will display or hide one set of detail records at a time, such as the CA or FL records.

Remove the Subtotals

6. Make sure the highlight is somewhere in the database, and choose Data→Subtotals from the menu bar.

7. Click the Remove All button.

As you can see, subtotals are easy to display and remove. The key to subtotals is to sort the database on the field that the subtotals will be based. In this example, the control field was State, so subtotals were displayed each time the State field changed.

Understanding Advanced Filtering and Data Extraction

Excel's AutoFilter command lets you filter (temporarily hide rows) databases by choosing values from drop-down lists. AutoFilter will be covered in detail in *Microsoft Office Excel 2003: Quick Course 3*. The AutoFilter command is quite useful, though you will find that some situations require more advanced filtering techniques. The Data→Filter→Advanced Filter command displays the Advanced Filter dialog box. You can use advanced filtering to filter data in ways not available with AutoFilter. The most common uses of advanced filters are to specify an OR condition between two columns and to extract filtered data to another worksheet location. To set up an advanced filter, you must specify a criteria range above the list where filtering criteria are entered. The criteria range must include one or more column headings from the list and one or more filtering criteria. The following illustration discusses these concepts.

Rows have been inserted above the list and the criteria are entered in this criteria range.

The SW Sales and HW Sales headings used for columns G and H are also used in the criteria range.

	A	B	C	D	E	F	G	H
1	National Computing Solutions							
2	2004 Sales Database							
3								
4	SW Sales	HW Sales						
5	>300,000							
6		>300,000						
7								
8	Last Name	First Name	Years Employed	Position	Region	State	SW Sales	HW Sales
9	Zain	Beth	7	Senior Sales Rep	Western	CA	340,000	800,000
10	Alvizo	Alex	7	Senior Sales Rep	Western	CA	450,000	340,000
11	Brown	Bill	3	Telemarketer	Western	CA	546,000	120,000
12	Smith	Bob	3	Sales Rep	Western	CA	200,000	180,000
13	Williams	Michael	3	Sales Rep	Eastern	FL	120,000	340,000
14	Martinez	Carlos	4	Senior Sales Rep	Eastern	FL	450,000	450,000
15	Hubbs	Daniel	4	Telemarketer	Eastern	FL	340,000	230,000
16	Wilson	Bernie	1	Sales Rep	Central	IL	120,000	170,000
17	Thomas	Will	2	Sales Rep	Central	IL	230,000	120,000
18	Cain	Mary	5	Senior Sales Rep	Central	IL	234,000	560,000
19	Watson	Tom	8	Sales Rep	Eastern	MA	230,000	340,000
20	Smith	Michael	5	Telemarketer	Eastern	MA	123,000	230,000
21	Richards	Paul	4	Telemarketer	Western	WA	234,000	546,000
22	Cray	Zip	6	Telemarketer	Western	WA	900,000	780,000

The two >300,000 criteria are entered on separate rows. This creates a logical OR condition. If they were both entered on row 5, then a logical AND condition would be created.

Only records where the SW Sales are >300,000 OR the HW Sales are >300,000 are chosen.

Hands-On 5.5 Use Advanced Filtering and Data Extraction

In this exercise, you will insert blank rows above row 4 and enter criteria for the SW Sales and HW Sales fields. You will use the Advanced Filter command to filter data according to the set criteria and paste it below the existing data.

Filter and Extract the Data

1. Position the mouse pointer on the row 4 heading and drag down to select rows 4–7.

2. Choose Insert→Rows to insert four blank rows.

3. Enter the criteria shown in the preceding illustration into the range A4:B6. Be sure to enter the SW Sales and HW Sales headings exactly as shown.

4. Choose Data→Filter→Advanced Filter from the menu bar.
   Excel should automatically identify the list because you named it Database. The flashing marquee will surround the list.

5. Follow these steps to filter the list:

A Click the Copy to Another Location button. In a moment, you will use this option to extract the filtered data.

B Click in the Criteria Range box then select the criteria range A4:B6 in the worksheet. The range reference will be entered in the box.

C Click in the Copy To box then click cell A27 in the worksheet.

D Click OK and the filtered data will be extracted (copied) to the range beginning at cell A27.

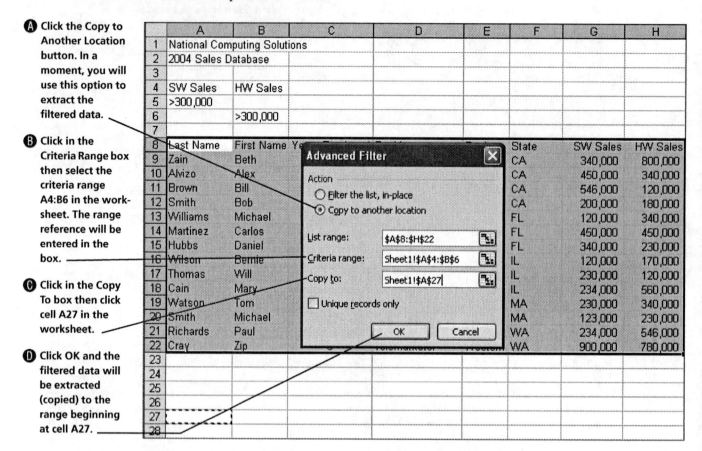

Notice that Excel copied the filtered data to the range beginning in cell A27. This is known as extracting the data. Extracting can be useful in large databases in which you want to copy just certain records. You can also extract to another worksheet in the workbook by simply clicking the desired worksheet tab in the workbook when entering the Copy To range in the Advanced Filter dialog box.

6. Feel free to experiment with advanced filtering.

7. When you have finished, save the changes to the workbook.

Using Database Functions

Excel provides database functions such as DSUM and DAVERAGE to summarize data in a list. In *Microsoft Office Excel 2003: Quick Course 1*, and Lesson 4, Using Financial Functions and Data Analysis, you learned about other types of functions including statistical, date and time, and financial. These functions use all the values in a range of cells to calculate the formula result. Database functions differ, however, in that you can define criteria to limit the cells the function uses for its result.

Syntax of Database Functions

You can enter database functions from the keyboard or by using the Insert Function f_x button on the Formula bar. Each database function uses three arguments: database, field, and criteria. These arguments refer to the ranges used by the function. See the following table for the generic syntax used in database functions.

Function	Syntax
DSUM	DSUM(database,field,criteria)
DAVERAGE	DAVERAGE(database,field,criteria)

The following illustration provides an example of arguments used in a DSUM function. You will use this function and its arguments later in your worksheet.

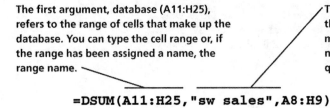

The first argument, database (A11:H25), refers to the range of cells that make up the database. You can type the cell range or, if the range has been assigned a name, the range name.

The second argument, field ("sw sales"), is the column that contains the numeric values to be calculated. You may click the column heading or type the heading name. If you type the name, it must be enclosed in quotation marks.

=DSUM(A11:H25,"sw sales",A8:H9)

The third argument, criteria (A8:H9), is the range that contains the specified conditions. Again, you can either select the range with the mouse or type it in yourself.

 TIP! *Selecting the ranges for a formula eliminates the chance of typing the cell range incorrectly; plus, you don't have to remember to type quotation marks around text fields.*

Criteria Ranges

The DSUM and DAVERAGE database functions require criteria ranges. You may need to insert additional blank rows in your worksheet to create a place to add the criteria rows. You must have at least one criteria label with at least one row below the label(s).

TIP! *The best place for your criteria range is above or to the side of the data list.*

	A	B	C	D	E	F	G	H
1	National Computing Solutions							
2	2004 Sales Database							
3								
4	SW Sales	HW Sales						
5	>300,000							
6		>300,000						
7								
8	Last Name	First Name	Years Employed	Position	Region	State	SW Sales	HW Sales
9					central		>200000	
10								
11	Last Name	First Name	Years Employed	Position	Region	State	SW Sales	HW Sales
12	Zain	Beth	7	Senior Sales Rep	Western	CA	340,000	800,000
13	Alvizo	Alex	7	Senior Sales Rep	Western	CA	450,000	340,000
14	Brown	Bill	3	Telemarketer	Western	CA	546,000	120,000
15	Smith	Bob	3	Sales Rep	Western	CA	200,000	180,000
16	Williams	Michael	3	Sales Rep	Eastern	FL	120,000	340,000
17	Martinez	Carlos	4	Senior Sales Rep	Eastern	FL	450,000	450,000
18	Hubbs	Daniel	4	Telemarketer	Eastern	FL	340,000	230,000
19	Wilson	Bernie	1	Sales Rep	Central	IL	120,000	170,000
20	Thomas	Will	2	Sales Rep	Central	IL	230,000	120,000
21	Cain	Mary	5	Senior Sales Rep	Central	IL	234,000	560,000
22	Watson	Tom	8	Sales Rep	Eastern	MA	230,000	340,000
23	Smith	Michael	5	Telemarketer	Eastern	MA	123,000	230,000
24	Richards	Paul	4	Telemarketer	Western	WA	234,000	546,000
25	Cray	Zip	6	Telemarketer	Western	WA	900,000	780,000
26	Total SW Sales over $200,000 for Central Region						464000	
27	Average SW Sales over $200,000 for Central Region						232000	

Three rows (8–10) have been inserted above the list to make room for the criteria range.

The headings from cells A11:H11 have been copied to row 8 and become the first row of the criteria range.

The two criteria, Central and >200000, are entered in row 9 below the column headings. This creates a logical AND condition.

The DSUM function is entered in cell G26. Only records from the Central Region with SW Sales greater than $200,000 are calculated (summed).

Using DSUM

The DSUM function adds the values of a specified field that matches set criteria. For example, you can use DSUM to calculate the total sales over or under a specified dollar amount sold in a specified region. Once the formula is created, you can change the criteria and view the updated results.

Using DAVERAGE

The DAVERAGE function averages the values of a specified column that matches conditions you specify in a criteria range. For example, you can use DAVERAGE to calculate the average amount of sales by employees with fewer than five year's experience.

Hands-On 5.6   Create and Edit Database Functions

In this exercise, you will calculate the total SW Sales beyond $200,000 for the Central Region using the DSUM function and calculate the average of those sales using DAVERAGE. You will later change the criteria to calculate the same values for the Eastern Region.

Create a DSUM Function

1. Position the mouse pointer on the row 8 heading and drag down to select rows 8–10.

2. Choose Insert→Rows to insert three blank rows.

3. Select cells A11:H11.

4. Using the right-drag method, copy the selected cells to cells A8:H8.

5. In cell E9, type **central** and in cell G9, type **>200000**.
   This instructs the criteria to use only those sales that are more than $200,000 from the Central Region in the calculation.

6. Click cell A26 and type **Total Central Region SW Sales Over $200,000**.

7. Click cell G26 and enter the formula **=DSUM(A11:H25,"sw sales",A8:H9)**.
   The result should be 464,000.

Create a DAVERAGE Function

8. Click cell A27 and type **Average Central Region SW Sales Over $200,000**.

9. Click cell G27 and enter the formula **=DAVERAGE(A11:H25,"sw sales",A8:H9)**.
   The result should be 232,000. Notice that the only change in this formula was the name of the function, DAVERAGE.

Edit the Function

10. Click cell E9 and type **eastern**.
    Notice the change in both the DSUM and DAVERAGE results in cells G26 and G27.

11. Revise the contents of cells A26 and A27 to reflect the new region, Eastern.

12. Experiment with changing the criteria value of cell G9 to see how it affects the formula results.

13. Experiment further by creating DSUM and DAVERAGE functions in cells H26 and H27 for the HW Sales.
    If you would like to use different criteria for the HW Sales, simply insert additional rows above the list, copy the headings, and set the criteria as you did for the SW Sales.

14. When finished, save the changes and close the workbook.

Querying Databases

Microsoft Query is a tool that can be used to import data from external data sources into Excel. External data sources include database programs such as Microsoft Access and Microsoft SQL Server. You can also use Query to extract data from an Excel list or database. Query lets you choose the fields to include in the extracted data and specify criteria to select only those records you wish to include in the extracted data. You can save queries and run them at any time.

Setting Up Queries

Query is not installed as part of the typical Office 2003 installation, so Excel will prompt you to install Query if it is your first time using it. Once installed, use the Data→Import External Data→New Database Query command to set up a new query. The Choose Data Source box is displayed and lets you select the data source from which the query will extract data.

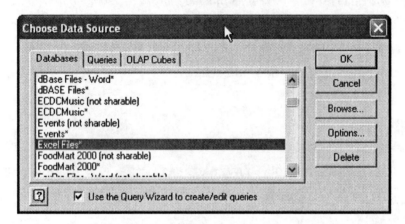

The Query Wizard

The Choose Data Source dialog box has a checkbox that initiates the Query Wizard. The Query Wizard guides you step-by-step through the process of setting up and running queries. It also lets you choose the fields (columns) to include in the query, specify criteria (filters), and sort the resulting worksheet data. The following sequence of screens shows a query being set up in 2004 Sales Database using the Query Wizard. The extracted worksheet data is also shown.

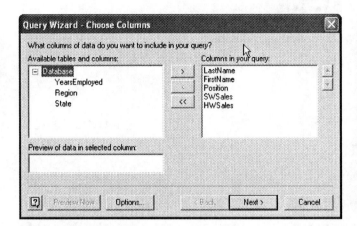

Query Wizard - Choose Columns

What columns of data do you want to include in your query?

Available tables and columns:

- Database
  - YearsEmployed
  - Region
  - State

Columns in your query:
- LastName
- FirstName
- Position
- SWSales
- HWSales

Preview of data in selected column:

Preview Now | Options... | < Back | Next > | Cancel

Query fields are specified

Query Wizard - Filter Data

Filter the data to specify which rows to include in your query.

If you don't want to filter the data, click Next.

Column to filter:
- LastName
- FirstName
- Position
- SWSales
- HWSales

Only include rows where:

SWSales

is greater than | 300000

○ And ● Or

○ And ○ Or

○ And ○ Or

< Back | Next > | Cancel

Criteria are set

For further information on Microsoft Query, use online Help. Since Query is an add-in that may not be installed on your computer system, there is no Hands-On exercise to accompany this topic.

	A	B	C	D
1	Name	Position	SW Sales	HW Sales
2	Alvizo, Alex	Senior Sales Rep	450,000	340,000
3	Brown, Bill	Telemarketer	546,000	120,000
4	Crag, Zip	Telemarketer	900,000	780,000
5	Hubbs, Daniel	Telemarketer	340,000	230,000
6	Martinez, Carlos	Senior Sales Rep	450,000	450,000
7	Zain, Beth	Senior Sales Rep	340,000	800,000

Extracted worksheet data

Concepts Review

True/False Questions

1. Database records are composed of fields.   TRUE   FALSE

2. You should always give the name Database to a database.   TRUE   FALSE

3. A data form can be used to locate data in a database.   TRUE   FALSE

4. You can use the =, <, and > operators in search criteria in a data form.   TRUE   FALSE

5. The first and most important step in the subtotaling process is to sort the list.   TRUE   FALSE

6. Databases can only be sorted in ascending order.   TRUE   FALSE

7. Filtered data can be extracted to a different location within the same worksheet.   TRUE   FALSE

8. Clicking OK on the Subtotal dialog box automatically sorts the database on the subtotal field.   TRUE   FALSE

9. You can display subtotals for only one field.   TRUE   FALSE

10. You can set criteria for database functions.   TRUE   FALSE

Multiple Choice Questions

1. Which command is used to display the Data Form dialog box?
   a. Format→Form
   b. Data→Form
   c. Tools→Form
   d. None of the above

2. Which button(s) can be used on the data form to locate records?
   a. Find Prev
   b. Find Next
   c. Criteria
   d. All of the above

3. Which command is used to display the Subtotals dialog box?
   a. Format→Subtotals
   b. Tools→Subtotals
   c. Tools→Database Subtotals
   d. None of the above

4. Which command is used to remove subtotals?
   a. Data→Subtotals→Remove Subtotals
   b. Tools→Subtotals→Remove Subtotals
   c. Format→Subtotals→Remove Subtotals
   d. None of the above

 # Skill Builders

Skill Builder 5.1   Use Subtotals

In this exercise, you will experiment with subtotals and totals in the Sales Database file.

1. Open Sales Database.

2. Click cell D12 then click the Sort Ascending  button.
   Remember, you must always sort on the field you want to base the subtotals.

3. Choose Data→Subtotals from the menu bar.

4. Set the At Each Change In field to Position.

5. Make sure both SW Sales and HW Sales are checked in the Add Subtotal To list.

6. Click OK to complete the subtotals.
   You should have a subtotal for each group of positions (Sales Rep, Senior Sales Rep, and Telemarketer).

7. Now, remove all subtotals from the database.

8. Save and close the workbook.

Skill Builder 5.2   Set Up a Database

In this exercise, you will set up a new database that tracks supporter information for a political campaign. You will enter data using a data form.

1. Start a new workbook and set up the following database structure. Select the range A4:F5 as shown and assign the name **Database** to it.

	A	B	C	D	E	F
1	Jake Reynolds for City Council					
2	Supporters Database					
3						
4	Name	Contact Type	Organization	Contribution 1	Contribution 2	Last Election Contribution
5						

2. Format the blank cells D5:F5 as Comma Style with 0 decimals.

3. Use the Data→Form command to display the data form.

4. Use the data form to enter the data shown in the following completed database:

	A	B	C	D	E	F
1	Jake Reynolds for City Council					
2	Supporters Database					
3						
4	Name	Contact Type	Organization	Contribution 1	Contribution 2	Last Election Contribution
5	Alex Gardner	Business Owner	Symtron	1,000	230	-
6	Betty Post	Business Owner	Café Ritz	300	350	100
7	Bill Evans	Union Member	Teamsters	1,000	1,250	2,000
8	Bill Jones	Private Individual	Homeowner	25	-	25
9	Dawn Newell	Union Member	UAW	750	250	1,000
10	Ed Watkins	Business Owner	Ron's Deli	450	450	200
11	Jason Lopez	Business Owner	PC Solutions	1,300	500	1,500
12	Jimmy Peters	Business Owner	Cablespace	250	200	250
13	Martha Adams	Private Individual	Homeowner	250	100	100
14	Sam Bond	Private Individual	Homeowner	85	100	100
15	Steven Rogers	Business Owner	Steve's Auto Care	350	250	500
16	Sylvia Porter	Union Member	AFLCIO	1,500	900	1,200
17	Ted Thomas	Union Member	UAW	800	1,000	1,000
18	Tom Carter	Private Individual	Homeowner	75	25	100
19	Wanda Wilson	Union Member	Teamsters	750	450	1,000

5. Save the database as **Jake Reynolds Supporters**.

   You will continue to use the database in the next two exercises so leave it open.

Skill Builder 5.3   Use Subtotals

In this exercise, you will create subtotals for the contribution amounts by each type of contact.

1. Use Excel's Subtotal tool to subtotal the database as shown in the following example. Be sure to sort the database on the Contact Type field before subtotaling.

	A	B	C	D	E	F
1	Jake Reynolds for City Council					
2	Supporters Database					
3						
4	Name	Contact Type	Organization	Contribution 1	Contribution 2	Last Election Contribution
5	Alex Gardner	Business Owner	Symtron	1,000	230	-
6	Betty Post	Business Owner	Café Ritz	300	350	100
7	Ed Watkins	Business Owner	Ron's Deli	450	450	200
8	Jason Lopez	Business Owner	PC Solutions	1,300	500	1,500
9	Jimmy Peters	Business Owner	Cablespace	250	200	250
10	Steven Rogers	Business Owner	Steve's Auto Care	350	250	500
11		**Business Owner Total**		3,650	1,980	2,550
12	Bill Jones	Private Individual	Homeowner	25	-	25
13	Martha Adams	Private Individual	Homeowner	250	100	100
14	Sam Bond	Private Individual	Homeowner	85	100	100
15	Tom Carter	Private Individual	Homeowner	75	25	100
16		**Private Individual Total**		435	225	325
17	Bill Evans	Union Member	Teamsters	1,000	1,250	2,000
18	Dawn Newell	Union Member	UAW	750	250	1,000
19	Sylvia Porter	Union Member	AFLCIO	1,500	900	1,200
20	Ted Thomas	Union Member	UAW	800	1,000	1,000
21	Wanda Wilson	Union Member	Teamsters	750	450	1,000
22		**Union Member Total**		4,800	3,850	6,200
23		**Grand Total**		8,885	6,055	9,075

2. Now subtotal the database as shown in the following example. The only difference between these subtotals and those in the previous step is that the Average function instead of the Sum function was chosen in the Subtotal dialog box.

	A	B	C	D	E	F
1	Jake Reynolds for City Council					
2	Supporters Database					
3						
4	Name	Contact Type	Organization	Contribution 1	Contribution 2	Last Election Contribution
5	Alex Gardner	Business Owner	Symtron	1,000	230	-
6	Betty Post	Business Owner	Café Ritz	300	350	100
7	Ed Watkins	Business Owner	Ron's Deli	450	450	200
8	Jason Lopez	Business Owner	PC Solutions	1,300	500	1,500
9	Jimmy Peters	Business Owner	Cablespace	250	200	250
10	Steven Rogers	Business Owner	Steve's Auto Care	350	250	500
11		**Business Owner Average**		608	330	425
12	Bill Jones	Private Individual	Homeowner	25	-	25
13	Martha Adams	Private Individual	Homeowner	250	100	100
14	Sam Bond	Private Individual	Homeowner	85	100	100
15	Tom Carter	Private Individual	Homeowner	75	25	100
16		**Private Individual Average**		109	56	81
17	Bill Evans	Union Member	Teamsters	1,000	1,250	2,000
18	Dawn Newell	Union Member	UAW	750	250	1,000
19	Sylvia Porter	Union Member	AFLCIO	1,500	900	1,200
20	Ted Thomas	Union Member	UAW	800	1,000	1,000
21	Wanda Wilson	Union Member	Teamsters	750	450	1,000
22		**Union Member Average**		960	770	1,240
23		**Grand Average**		592	404	605

3. Save the changes to your workbook and continue with the next exercise.

Assessments

Assessment 5.1   Set Up a Database

In this exercise, you will create a new workbook, set up a database, and assign the database range a name.

1. Follow these guidelines to create the database shown in the following illustration:
   - Enter the data in the same cells as shown.
   - Format the titles and column headings as shown. Use [Alt]+[Enter] to create the multi-line entries in cells C4 and D4.
   - Format the numbers in columns C and D with the Comma Style.
   - Assign the name **Database** to the range A4:D17.

2. Save the database as **Westside Employee Compensation**.

3. Leave the workbook open because you will continue to use it.

	A	B	C	D
1	Westside Electric Supplies			
2	*Employee Compensation Database*			
3				
4	Name	Category	2003 Compensation	2003 Retirement Plan Contributions
5	Jackson, Samuel	Salaried	45,000	4,700
6	Ellison, Linda	Salaried	32,000	2,500
7	Monroe, James	Hourly	34,000	4,250
8	Wilson, Larry	Salaried	89,000	21,890
9	Hughes, Ralph	Hourly	23,000	-
10	Peterson, Lisa	Hourly	31,000	2,300
11	Watson, Bill	Hourly	27,000	1,600
12	Templeton, James	Salaried	45,000	1,900
13	Barton, Lisa	Salaried	51,000	6,000
14	Erickson, Brian	Hourly	38,000	4,500
15	Thomas, Lynn	Salaried	34,000	2,700
16	Chin, Raymond	Salaried	56,000	3,450
17	Zurlow, Jack	Hourly	30,000	3,450

Assessment 5.2   Use Subtotals

In this exercise, you will copy the database on Sheet1 to a new sheet, rename both sheets, and calculate Average subtotals on the 2003 Compensation and 2003 Retirement Plan Contributions fields by category.

1. Copy the database in the Westside Employee Compensation worksheet to Sheet2.

2. Rename Sheet2 **Subtotals** and rename Sheet1 **Database**.

3. Follow these guidelines to subtotal the database in the Subtotals sheet:

   ■ Subtotal on the Category field. Subtotals should be calculated for each change in category.

   ■ Use the AVERAGE function to create subtotals for the 2003 Compensation and 2003 Retirement Plan Contributions fields.

4. Save the changes to the workbook.

Assessment 5.3   Use Database Functions

In this exercise, you will copy the database to a new sheet and rename it. You will also use the DSUM and DAVERAGE functions to perform calculations on the 2003 Compensation for salaries greater than $25,000 for the hourly employees.

1. Copy the list in the Database worksheet to Sheet3.

2. Rename Sheet3 **Functions**.

3. Use the DSUM function to calculate the total 2003 Compensation greater than $25,000 for the Hourly category.

4. Use the DAVERAGE function to calculate the average 2003 Compensation greater than $25,000 for the Hourly category.

5. Save the changes to the workbook, and then close it.

Critical Thinking

Critical Thinking 5.1   On Your Own

Linda Johnson is the owner of Linda's Home and Garden Supply. Linda's suppliers deliver products to her every Friday. She has asked you to set up an Excel worksheet that records the incoming supplies from the various suppliers. Currently, Linda receives supplies from Bay Area Garden Supply, Bright Flowers Supplies, and Home and Garden Warehouse. Set up a worksheet that lists the supplier name, product name, category ID, wholesale price, and retail price of each product. Name the worksheet **Subtotals**. The retail price should be calculated as the wholesale price multiplied by three. Assign the name **Database** to the list. Use the data form tool to enter the following data into the database:

Supplier	Product	Category ID	Wholesale Price
Bay Area Garden Supply	Shovels	Garden	12.95
Bay Area Garden Supply	Rakes	Garden	11.95
Bright Flowers Supplies	Orchids	Home	1.95
Bright Flowers Supplies	Potting Soil	Home	3.95
Home and Garden Warehouse	Pots	Home	2.35
Bright Flowers Supplies	Fertilizer	Home	2.35
Bay Area Garden Supply	Seeds	Garden	0.25
Home and Garden Warehouse	Bricks	Home	0.75
Home and Garden Warehouse	Stones	Home	2.35
Bay Area Garden Supply	Stakes	Garden	0.15
Bright Flowers Supplies	Planters	Garden	7.95
Bright Flowers Supplies	Watering Buckets	Garden	2.10
Bay Area Garden Supply	RotoTiller	Garden	545.00
Home and Garden Warehouse	Hoses	Home	4.50
Bay Area Garden Supply	Spades	Home	1.25
Home and Garden Warehouse	Miracle Grow	Garden	2.65
Bright Flowers Supplies	Azaleas	Home	0.69
Bright Flowers Supplies	Ferns	Home	0.35
Bright Flowers Supplies	Fake Plants	Home	13.95
Home and Garden Warehouse	Books	Home	2.95

Save your workbook as **Suppliers** and leave it open for the next exercise.

Critical Thinking 5.2   On Your Own

Linda Johnson wants the incoming supplies database subtotaled and filtered in several ways. Copy the entire worksheet to the other two worksheets in the workbook. Name the first worksheet **Home** and the second worksheet **Garden**. Subtotal the list in the first worksheet on the Category ID field, adding subtotals to both the wholesale and retail price fields. Use AutoFilter to filter the list in the second worksheet so only products with a Home Category ID are displayed. Filter the list in the third worksheet so only products with a Garden Category ID are displayed. When you are finished, save the workbook as **Suppliers Filtered** and close it.

Critical Thinking 5.3   On Your Own

Ned Armstrong is the returns manager for Parker Book Publishers, Inc. Ned has asked you to set up an Excel database to track and analyze customer returns. The database should have fields for the return authorization code, customer name, return date, title, book category, quantity returned, unit price, and refund amount. The refund amount is calculated as the quantity returned multiplied by the purchase price. Set up the database and enter the following data:

Return Auth Code	Customer	Return Date	Title	Category	Quantity	Unit Price
1122	Nita Wilson	2/3/04	Take Charge of Your Life	Self Improvement	1	21.00
1122	Nita Wilson	3/5/04	Walking for Your Heart	Fitness	1	9.95
1123	Ray Barker	3/5/04	Swim for Your Life	Fitness	1	15.00
1124	Bill Simms	3/6/04	Meals for Working Moms	Cooking	2	21.50
1125	Julia Wilson	3/7/04	Attitude is Everything	Self Improvement	1	22.95
1125	Julia Wilson	3/7/04	Soil Conservation Guide	Gardening	1	13.45
1125	Julia Wilson	3/7/04	The Fish Book	Cooking	1	22.00
1126	Alex Evans	3/7/04	You're Number One	Self Improvement	1	12.50
1127	Alexia Wilson	3/8/04	Walking for Your Heart	Fitness	2	9.95
1128	Betty Bird	3/9/04	Beefing Up	Cooking	3	16.55
1128	Betty Bird	3/9/04	Perfect Orchids	Gardening	1	12.95

Return Auth Code	Customer	Return Date	Title	Category	Quantity	Unit Price
1129	Carl Biltmore	3/9/04	Weight Training Guide	Fitness	3	11.95
1130	Billy Baskins	3/10/04	Healthy Relationships	Self Improvement	2	12.95
1131	Bobby Johnson	3/11/04	Steak Well Done	Cooking	4	21.25
1132	Rita Lane	3/11/04	Eating Right	Fitness	1	23.45
1132	Rita Lane	3/11/04	Organic Gardening	Gardening	3	18.50
1132	Rita Lane	3/11/04	Tomatoes and Potatoes	Gardening	2	12.50
1133	Cynthia Vincent	3/12/04	Weight Training Guide	Fitness	1	11.95
1134	Bill Brown	3/12/04	Healthy Relationships	Self Improvement	1	12.95
1135	Sheryl Barnett	3/13/04	Soil Conservation Guide	Gardening	1	13.45

Be sure to add a **Refund Amount** column and calculate the refund amount as the Quantity multiplied by the Unit Price. Subtotal the database on the Category field using the Sum function on the Unit Price field. Save the database as **Customer Returns** when you have finished.

LESSON 6

Using PivotTables, Styles, and Outlines

Excel has many features to help you perform sophisticated data analyses. Some of the most powerful data analysis tools in Excel are the PivotTable and the Pivot-Chart. PivotTables let you summarize worksheet data dynamically to view them in various ways. With simple drag and drop commands, you can arrange your data and have Excel automatically create summary formulas in the rows and columns. PivotCharts offer the same power and flexibility for charting data. Trendlines are another aid to analysis—helping you perceive and forecast trends in chart data. Excel's Styles feature lets you give a name to cell formatting then apply it with ease. Styles can help you format your worksheets more efficiently and consistently. Outlines and grouping let you selectively hide detail data with a single mouse click so it doesn't clutter your view of summary data.

Microsoft Office Excel 2003 and Microsoft Office Excel 2003 Expert objectives covered in this lesson

Objective Number	Skill Sets and Skills	Concept Page References	Exercise Page References
XL03S-3-2	Apply and modify cell styles	172–174, 176–177	174–178
XL03E-1-3	Group and outline data	178–179, 181	180–182
XL03E-1-8	Create PivotTable and PivotChart reports	152–155, 157–159, 167–168	155–157, 159–162, 169

Case Study

Allen is the assistant to the national sales manager at Acme Net Works. As part of his monthly routine, Allen gathers and presents sales data to the sales manager. Allen is expected to create various views of data that help the sales manager perceive trends and track the efficiency of the sales staff.

Allen knew the basics of working with values and formulas when he started his job, but he's always looking for ways to make his work easier. When he began this job, Allen would create workbooks with several views of the sales data, but this rather static view didn't allow him to analyze the data very efficiently. Allen recently heard about Excel's PivotTable feature at a one-day seminar for administrative assistants. He learned that PivotTables let you look at data in a variety of ways without the tedium of sorting and laying out the data manually. The following is just one example of how a PivotTable can be designed.

	A	B	C	D	E	F
1						
2						
3	Sum of SW Sale		Position ▼			
4	Region ▼	Name ▼	Sales Rep	Senior Sales Rep	Telemarketer	Grand Total
5	Central	Cain, Mary		$234,000		
6		Thomas, Will	$230,000			
7		Wilson, Bernie	$120,000			
8	Central Total		$350,000	$234,000		
9	Eastern	Hubbs, Daniel			$340,000	
10		Martinez, Carlos		$450,000		
11		Smith, Michael			$123,000	
12		Watson, Tom	$230,000			
13		Williams, Michael	$120,000			
14	Eastern Total		$350,000	$450,000	$463,000	
15	Western	Alvizo, Alex		$450,000		
16		Brown, Bill			$546,000	
17		Cray, Zip			$900,000	
18		Richards, Paul			$234,000	
19		Smith, Bob	$200,000			
20		Zain, Beth		$340,000		
21	Western Total					
22	Grand Total					

Allen is also expected to post data for the sales force to review. Rather than sending them out with email messages, Allen posts worksheets to the Web. He formats and organizes the data to enhance its readability and usefulness. Excel's Styles and Grouping features are useful tools for this task.

Styles allow Allen to quickly apply consistent formatting to worksheets. (You will add the Style command button to your toolbar later.)

The Grouping and Outline features allow Allen to expand and collapse the view of detail data. In this example, Allen has collapsed the outline to display only regional data. He can display the state data by expanding the outline with these plus signs.

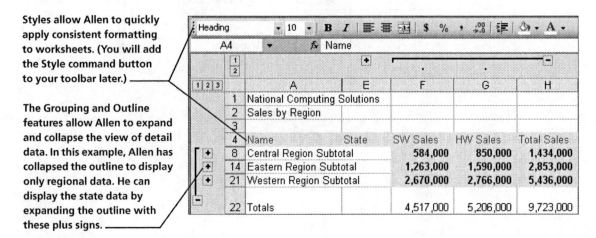

Working with PivotTables

PivotTables are powerful data analysis tools. They let you summarize data in various ways and instantly change the view you use. A PivotTable not only subtotals groups of related data but also goes a step further and compares one group to another. Compared to performing similar data analysis on a standard worksheet, PivotTables offer tremendous speed and flexibility. You create PivotTables from data on an Excel worksheet that is organized into a database. The following examples show two PivotTables based on the same worksheet data.

PivotTable Example 1

You have a worksheet that tracks product sales. Each row indicates the product name, region that made the sale, date sold, sale price, and quantity sold. Now, you could easily sort the worksheet by product and display subtotals to see which product sells the most; however, in this worksheet, you could not easily tell how one region compares to the others in sales for the same product. This is where the PivotTable comes into use. A PivotTable can summarize all data in any number of ways, and include grand totals for you. The following illustrations demonstrate the flexibility of PivotTables for displaying data in a variety of ways.

	A	B	C	D	E
1			2004 Stamp Sales		
2	**Product**	**Region**	**Date**	**Sales**	**Units**
3	Heritage	Bristol	01/01/2004	$ 20.00	2
4	Scenic	Bristol	02/01/2004	$ 40.00	4
5	Chesapeake Bay	Bristol	03/02/2004	$ 20.00	2
6	Children's Program - Hand	Richmond	03/02/2004	$ 100.00	10
7	Great Seal	Richmond	01/01/2004	$ 10.00	1
8	Disabled	Richmond	02/01/2004	$ 230.00	23
9	Scenic	Bristol	03/10/2004	$ 30.00	3
10	Great Seal	Bristol	01/01/2004	$ 20.00	2
11	Heritage	Staunton	02/01/2004	$ 50.00	5
12	Heritage	Staunton	02/01/2004	$ 440.00	44
13	Rescue Squad	Hampton	03/01/2004	$ 280.00	28
14	Children's Program - Hand	Hampton	03/01/2004	$ 50.00	5
15	Chesapeake Bay	Richmond	02/01/2004	$ 20.00	2
16	Heritage	Bristol	03/02/2004	$ 30.00	3
17	Scenic	Bristol	02/01/2004	$ 10.00	1
18	Great Seal	Richmond	01/02/2004	$ 60.00	6
19	Great Seal	Fairfax	02/01/2004	$ 110.00	11
20	Children's Program - Hand	Bristol	03/01/2004	$ 10.00	1
21	Rescue Squad	Fairfax	03/03/2004	$ 30.00	3
22	Scenic	Fairfax	03/01/2004	$ 70.00	7
23	Scenic	Richmond	01/01/2004	$ 10.00	1
24	Scenic	Fairfax	02/01/2004	$ 20.00	2
25	Rescue Squad	Hampton	02/01/2004	$ 30.00	3

This is the data list in the worksheet that will be used as the cell range for the PivotTable.

This Pivot-
Table shows
the complete
summary of
sales by
region for all
products sold.

	A	B	C	D	E	F	G
1	Sum of Sales	Region ▾					
2	Product ▾	Bristol	Fairfax	Hampton	Richmond	Staunton	Grand Total
3	Chesapeake Bay	20			20		40
4	Children's Program - Hand	10		50	100		160
5	Disabled				230		230
6	Great Seal	20	110		70		200
7	Heritage	50				490	540
8	Rescue Squad		30	310			340
9	Scenic	80	90		10		180
10	Grand Total	180	230	360	430	490	1690

PivotTables auto-
matically calcu-
late and include
a Grand Total of
the row data.

PivotTables also automatically calculate and include a
Grand Total of the column data.

Examine the PivotTable and notice that the Product field is being used for the row headings,
the Region field for the column headings, and the Sales field for the data area.

PivotTable Example 2

Using the same data as in the previous PivotTable, you can view the data differently: in this
case, summarized first by region, then by product. To create this type of view, the PivotTable
layout contains two fields for row headings, nothing for column headings, and one field in the
data area.

	A	B	C
3	Sum of Sales		
4	Region ▾	Product ▾	Total
5	Bristol	Chesapeake Bay	20
6		Children's Program - Hand	10
7		Great Seal	20
8		Heritage	50
9		Scenic	80
10	Bristol Total		180
11	Fairfax	Great Seal	110
12		Rescue Squad	30
13		Scenic	90
14	Fairfax Total		230
15	Hampton	Children's Program - Hand	50
16		Rescue Squad	310
17	Hampton Total		360
18	Richmond	Chesapeake Bay	20
19		Children's Program - Hand	100
20		Disabled	230
21		Great Seal	70
22		Scenic	10
23	Richmond Total		430
24	Staunton	Heritage	490
25	Staunton Total		490
26	Grand Total		1690

In this lesson, you will learn how to lay out both of these types of PivotTables and much more.

How PivotTables Work

PivotTables organize data into several different areas. Each area of the PivotTable plays a role in data organization. The areas of the PivotTable are explained in the following figure. You define a PivotTable by dragging and dropping various fields from the Excel database onto the PivotTable outline. Where you place fields into the outline determines how the PivotTable summarizes the data.

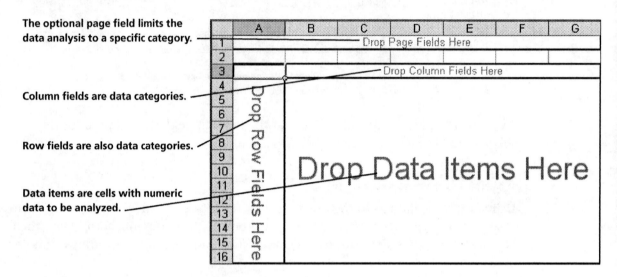

The optional page field limits the data analysis to a specific category.

Column fields are data categories.

Row fields are also data categories.

Data items are cells with numeric data to be analyzed.

After you drag and drop data fields into the PivotTable outline, Excel automatically summarizes the data for you. You can also drag fields out of the PivotTable and into new locations in the outline.

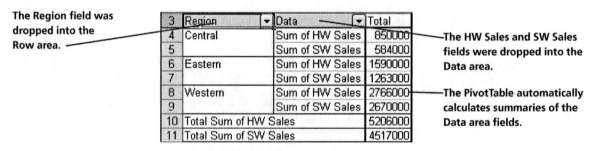

The Region field was dropped into the Row area.

The HW Sales and SW Sales fields were dropped into the Data area.

The PivotTable automatically calculates summaries of the Data area fields.

In this example, a PivotTable summarizes the breakdown of hardware and software sales by region.

Hands-On 6.1   Create a New PivotTable

The best way to understand the dynamic capabilities of a PivotTable is to create one. In this exercise, you will review the database and a worksheet-based method of analysis then create a new PivotTable from the database.

Review the Data

1. Open the 2004 Sales workbook.

2. Set the zoom level so all data on the worksheet is visible.
   The first worksheet contains the Excel database you will use to create a PivotTable. Look over the data fields in the column headings and the various records in the rows. Each record contains data for a specific salesperson.

   Notice that the numeric data is contained in the HW Sales and SW Sales columns. You will use these fields in the Data area of the PivotTable later in this exercise.

3. Display the Sales by Region worksheet. If necessary, set the zoom level so all data is visible.
   This layout summarizes the hardware and software sales by region. To create this summary, the database had to be sorted by region. Then, rows were added for the subtotal rows and total row.

4. Display the Sales by Position worksheet. If necessary, set the zoom level so all data is visible.
   This layout summarizes the hardware and software sales by the type of position each salesperson holds. To create this summary, the database had to be sorted by position and region. Then, rows were added for the subtotal rows and the total row. As you can imagine, it took quite some time and manual effort to create these two worksheets. A PivotTable can easily lay out the data for this type of analysis with much greater flexibility.

Create a PivotTable

Now you will create a PivotTable that summarizes HW and SW sales by region. This table will perform a function similar to the Sales by Region worksheet you viewed a moment ago.

5. Display the Sales Database worksheet and select cell A4.
   You should select a cell within the database before you create the PivotTable.

6. Choose Data→PivotTable and PivotChart Report from the menu bar.
   The PivotTable and PivotChart Wizard dialog box will appear to display Step 1 of 3.

7. Leave the default choices at Microsoft Office Excel List or Database and PivotTable in Step 1 of the wizard and click Next.
   A marquee (the "marching ants") surrounds the database, indicating the data to be used for the Pivot-Table. Since this is correct, there is no need to select another part of the worksheet.

8. Leave the default choice at Database in Step 2 of the wizard and click Next.

9. Leave the default choice at New Worksheet and click Finish.
   A new worksheet will appear with the PivotTable outline. The PivotTable toolbar and the PivotTable Field List are also displayed.

10. Rename Sheet 1 of the worksheet **PivotTable**.

11. If necessary, drag the PivotTable toolbar and Field List box so they do not cover any part of the PivotTable outline area.
    Notice that the PivotTable Field List box contains a list of all the data fields in the database, including Name, HW Sales, SW Sales, etc.

12. Select cell A18, which is outside the boundary of the PivotTable outline.
    Notice that PivotTable Field List disappears and that most of the buttons on the PivotTable toolbar are grayed out. You must select a cell within the PivotTable outline to display the available field names and toolbar buttons.

13. Select cell A4, within the PivotTable outline, to restore the PivotTable Field List.

14. Follow these steps to define the PivotTable:

Ⓐ **Drag and drop the Region field into the Row Fields area.**

Ⓑ **Drag and drop the SW Sales field into the Data Items area. Notice that the Data Items area shrinks to just the column necessary to hold the SW Sales summary.**

Ⓒ **Drag and drop the HW Sales field into the Data Items area of the PivotTable. Now the Data Items area enlarges to hold the new summary data.**

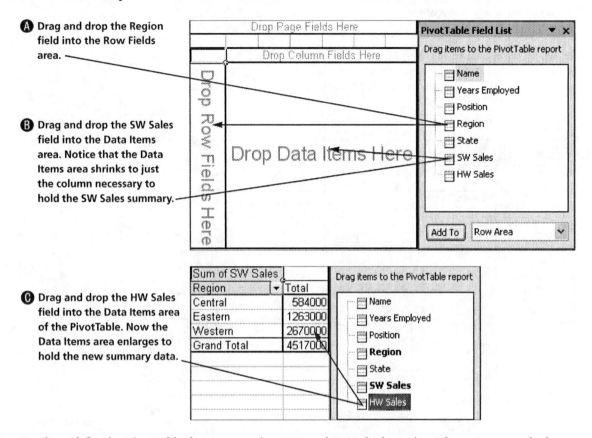

You have defined a PivotTable that summarizes HW and SW sales by region. The summary calculations are created for you automatically.

15. Examine the total SW and HW sales figures for the Central region and keep these figures in mind.

16. Display the Sales by Region worksheet. Compare the totals from the PivotTable with the Central region totals on this worksheet. They should be identical.

17. Display the PivotTable worksheet to view the PivotTable again.

Manipulating Fields on a PivotTable

You can add and subtract fields on a PivotTable by simply dragging and dropping. The Pivot-Table will automatically reconfigure to display the new data. One of the most powerful ways of manipulating data is to move a field from the row area to the column area or vice versa. This is called pivoting the field (thus the name PivotTable). You can also change the order of fields within the row and column areas. This rotates the display of the data field to give you an entirely different view of your data. The following example illustrates this.

You pivot the field by dragging from the row area to the column area and vice versa.

Region	Name	Data	Sales Rep	Senior Sales Rep	Telemarketer
				Position ▾	
Central	Cain, Mary	Sum of SW Sales		234,000	
		Sum of HW Sales		560000	
	Thomas, Will	Sum of SW Sales	230,000		
		Sum of HW Sales	120000		
	Wilson, Bernie	Sum of SW Sales	120,000		
		Sum of HW Sales	170000		
Central Sum of SW Sales			350,000	234,000	
Central Sum of HW Sales			290000	560000	
Eastern	Hubbs, Daniel	Sum of SW Sales			340,000
		Sum of HW Sales			230000
	Martinez, Carlos	Sum of SW Sales		450,000	
		Sum of HW Sales		450000	
	Smith, Michael	Sum of SW Sales			123,000
		Sum of HW Sales			230000
	Watson, Tom	Sum of SW Sales	230,000		
		Sum of HW Sales	340000		
	Williams, Michael	Sum of SW Sales	120,000		
		Sum of HW Sales	340000		
Eastern Sum of SW Sales			350,000	450,000	463,000
Eastern Sum of HW Sales			680000	450000	460000
Western	Alvizo, Alex	Sum of SW Sales		450,000	
		Sum of HW Sales		340000	
	Brown, Bill	Sum of SW Sales			546,000
		Sum of HW Sales			120000
	Cray, Zip	Sum of SW Sales			900,000
		Sum of HW Sales			780000
	Richards, Paul	Sum of SW Sales			234,000
		Sum of HW Sales			546000
	Smith, Bob	Sum of SW Sales	200,000		
		Sum of HW Sales	180000		
	Zain, Beth	Sum of SW Sales		340,000	
		Sum of HW Sales		800000	
Western Sum of SW Sales					
Western Sum of HW Sales					

Before pivoting: The SW and HW sales data are summarized in the rows. This makes it easy to compare the software to hardware sales by salesperson. The table after pivoting is shown below.

Region	Name	Sum of SW Sales			Sum of HW Sales		
		Sales Rep	Senior Sales Rep	Telemarketer	Sales Rep	Senior Sales Rep	Telemarketer
Central	Cain, Mary		234,000			560000	
	Thomas, Will	230,000			120000		
	Wilson, Bernie	120,000			170000		
Central Total		350,000	234,000		290000	560000	
Eastern	Hubbs, Daniel			340,000			230000
	Martinez, Carlos		450,000			450000	
	Smith, Michael			123,000			230000
	Watson, Tom	230,000			340000		
	Williams, Michael	120,000			340000		
Eastern Total		350,000	450,000	463,000	680000	450000	460000
Western	Alvizo, Alex		450,000			340000	
	Brown, Bill			546,000			120000
	Cray, Zip			900,000			780000
	Richards, Paul			234,000			546000
	Smith, Bob	200,000			180000		
	Zain, Beth		340,000			800000	
Western Total							

Suppressing the Display of Data Items

You can set the PivotTable to exclude specific items from the data summaries. Each field on the PivotTable has a drop-down list button. You can uncheck items in the drop-down list to suppress their display in the PivotTable.

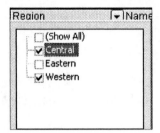

In this example, the display of Eastern region data will be suppressed from the PivotTable summaries.

Page Fields on a PivotTable

The page field area is at the top of the PivotTable outline. When you drop a field into this area, you can choose to display all of the items in this field or just a single type of item—such as a specific type of sales position. The page field area lets you control the display of data without adding columns to the PivotTable.

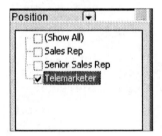

In this example, Allen chooses to display only Telemarketer sales data in the body of the PivotTable.

 Hands-On 6.2   Manipulate Fields on the PivotTable

In this exercise, you will redefine the PivotTable to create a different view of the data. The first change will be to summarize the data by state.

Add Fields to the PivotTable

1. Follow these steps to add the State field to the row data area:

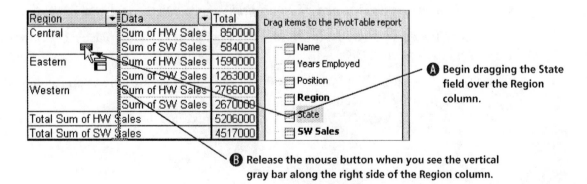

Ⓐ Begin dragging the State field over the Region column.

Ⓑ Release the mouse button when you see the vertical gray bar along the right side of the Region column.

The PivotTable automatically creates new rows and summaries for the State data. Imagine what you would have to do to create these summaries in a standard worksheet!

2. Taking care to see that the gray bar is displayed as shown in the following illustration, drag and drop the Name field over the Region field.

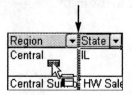

Notice that the data is now summarized by Region, Name, and State. This looks rather awkward since each salesperson only operates in one state. It would be more useful to view the data by Region, State, and Name. Let's reconfigure the PivotTable to do just that.

3. Follow these steps to move the Name field:

Ⓐ Drag the Name field to the right and over the State field.

Ⓑ Release the mouse button when you see the gray bar between the State and Data fields, as shown here.

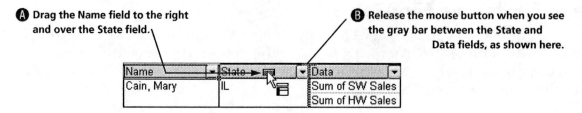

This PivotTable configuration displays the data much more logically.

Suppress the Display of Items in a PivotTable

4. Follow these steps to suppress the display of data for the Eastern region:

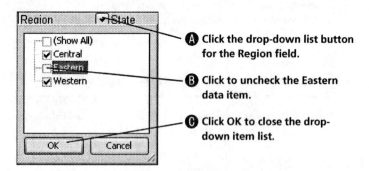

Ⓐ Click the drop-down list button for the Region field.

Ⓑ Click to uncheck the Eastern data item.

Ⓒ Click OK to close the drop-down item list.

Notice that no data is displayed for the Eastern region. You can use this method to switch the display of individual data items on and off for any field.

5. Click the drop-down list button for the Region field again, place a checkmark in the Show All box, and click OK.

6. Drag the Position field from the PivotTable Field List into the Drop Page Fields Here area at the top of the PivotTable.
Notice that the body of the table does not change—because the Position field is set to display (All).

7. Follow these steps to display only data for telemarketer positions:

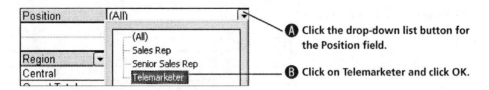

Ⓐ **Click the drop-down list button for the Position field.**

Ⓑ **Click on Telemarketer and click OK.**

Now only the names and data for telemarketers are displayed. Without the page field area, you would have needed to insert the Position column into the body of the table then switch off the display of the other two positions.

8. Click the Position field drop-down list button, choose Senior Sales Rep from the list, and click OK.
Now only data for senior sales representatives are displayed.

Remove a Field from the PivotTable

9. Follow these steps to remove the Region field from the PivotTable:

Ⓐ **Point at the Region heading until you see the four-pointed arrow then begin dragging the Region field off the PivotTable.**

Ⓑ **Release the mouse button when the field is outside the boundary of the PivotTable. You will see a delete symbol under the mouse pointer when the field is outside the PivotTable.**

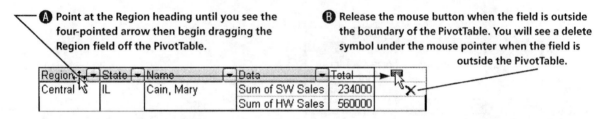

The Region-level summary items are removed from the table. Now the data is organized by State then by Name but the table only displays data for senior sales representatives.

10. Drag the State field off the PivotTable.

11. Drag the gray Position field heading (not its drop-down list) from the top of the PivotTable to the left side of the table, as shown at right.
Now the data is organized first by Position and then by Name. All data for the three position types is displayed.

12. Follow these steps to pivot the Data field from the rows area to the columns area:

Ⓐ **Begin dragging the Data field immediately to the right and over the Total cell.**

Ⓑ **Release the mouse button when you see the gray highlight around the border of the Total cell, as shown here.**

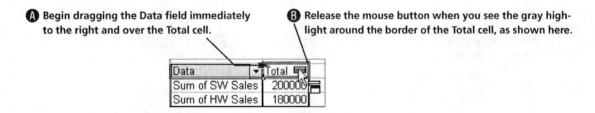

Now the SW and HW sales are arranged in columns rather than rows. This makes the data more readable.

13. Follow these steps to pivot the Position field from the Rows area to the Columns area:

🅐 **Begin dragging the Position field immediately under the Data field.**

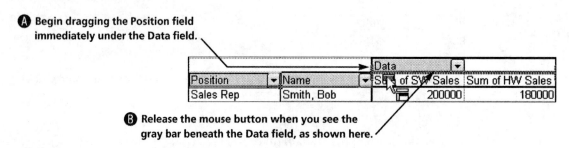

🅑 **Release the mouse button when you see the gray bar beneath the Data field, as shown here.**

Now you see the Position data in columns rather than rows. The Name field is automatically sorted alphabetically. The ability to pivot the position of a field is one of the most dynamic features of PivotTables.

14. Click the Undo 🔄 button to put the Position field back on the left. Then, taking care to see that the gray bar is displayed, drag and drop the Region field over the Position field.

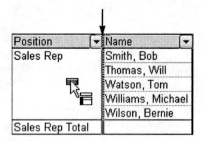

Notice that the data is now summarized by Position, Region, and Name. This is rather difficult to read because no formatting has been applied. In the next exercise, you will add a special pre-designed Auto-Format to make the PivotTable more readable.

15. Save 💾 the workbook.

PivotTable AutoFormat

You can use normal formatting commands to format cells in a PivotTable. There is also a special PivotTable AutoFormat command that works similar to the AutoFormat command for worksheets. Excel provides more than 20 AutoFormat styles that you can apply to PivotTables.

 Hands-On 6.3   AutoFormat the PivotTable

In this exercise, you will use the AutoFormat button on the PivotTable toolbar to display the AutoFormat dialog box. You will choose a suitable format for the PivotTable.

1. Select at least one cell in the PivotTable then choose Format→AutoFormat from the menu bar.
The AutoFormat dialog box displays formats designed especially for PivotTables.

2. Scroll up and down to view the available AutoFormats then choose the Table 10 format near the bottom of the list and click OK.

3. Click cell B6 to clear the selection so you can view the results of the AutoFormat more easily.

This format highlights the column headings and totals for greater readability.

4. Click the Format Report button on the PivotTable toolbar then choose Report 6 in the dialog box and click OK.

Notice that this AutoFormat pivoted the Position field back into the Rows field area at the left side of the PivotTable. An AutoFormat command can pivot fields to conform to the selected AutoFormat design.

Leave the PivotTable worksheet page open, as you will use it again in a moment.

Updating PivotTable Data

You can update a PivotTable to reflect any changes in the data used to create it. You edit the values in the data list used to create the PivotTable. For example, after sending out the PivotTable for review, Allen receives information that the SW Sales figure for Bernie Wilson is incorrect. Changing values in the original list does not automatically update the PivotTable. Allen must click the Refresh Data button on the PivotTable toolbar to prompt Excel to do the update.

You can also update the PivotTable when new rows are added. For example, both the Central and Eastern regions added new sales representatives last year. The new data can be added easily to the existing PivotTable using the PivotTable Wizard. Also, once data is summarized in a PivotTable, you can change the function or number format using the Field Settings command.

 Hands-On 6.4   Update a PivotTable

In this exercise, you will edit the value for Bernie Wilson's sales in the data list on the Sales Database worksheet then use the Refresh Data command to update the PivotTable. You will also add two new rows to the data list and expand the data list range of the PivotTable using the PivotTable Wizard. Later in the lesson, you will use the PivotTable Field dialog box to recalculate the sales figures as averages and change number formats.

Refresh PivotTable Data

1. Display the PivotTable worksheet and examine the summarized figures in the SW Sales column.

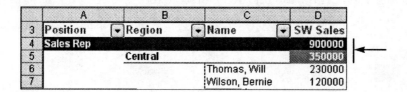

Notice that the current SW sales for the Central region is $350,000 and the sales representative total is $900,000.

2. Click the Sales Database sheet tab.

3. Change the value in cell F7 to **220000** and display the PivotTable worksheet again.
   Notice that the SW Sales totals have not yet changed in the PivotTable.

4. Click the Refresh Data 🔳 button on the PivotTable toolbar.
   Notice that the PivotTable is now updated and reflects the change made to Bernie Wilson's sales figure in the data sheet.

	A	B	C	D
3	Position ▾	Region ▾	Name ▾	SW Sales
4	Sales Rep			1000000
5		Central		450000
6			Thomas, Will	230000
7			Wilson, Bernie	220000

Expand the Range in a PivotTable

5. Display the Sales Database worksheet and change F7 back to **120000**.

6. Select rows 20 and 21 by dragging the mouse over the row headings.

7. Right-click row heading 20 and choose Insert from the context menu.

8. Follow these steps to add new rows of data to the list:
   Remember to use AutoComplete whenever you can to quickly enter repeated data in a column.

Ⓐ Enter this data in the range A19:G20.

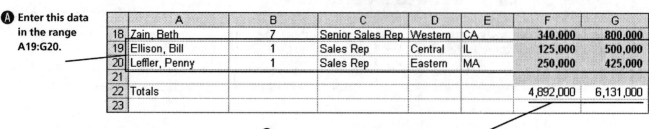

	A	B	C	D	E	F	G
18	Zain, Beth	7	Senior Sales Rep	Western	CA	340,000	800,000
19	Ellison, Bill	1	Sales Rep	Central	IL	125,000	500,000
20	Leffler, Penny	1	Sales Rep	Eastern	MA	250,000	425,000
21							
22	Totals					4,892,000	6,131,000
23							

Ⓑ Notice that the totals in the Sales Database update automatically.

9. Display the PivotTable worksheet.
   Note that since the original range did not include the two new rows you just added to the data list, the PivotTable has not been updated.

10. Click in any cell within the PivotTable and click the PivotTable button on the PivotTable toolbar.

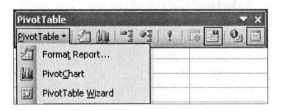

   A drop-down list displays. Take a moment to examine the options in the list.

11. Choose PivotTable Wizard from the drop-down list.
    With the PivotTable Wizard open, you can change any of the options you originally set for the PivotTable.

12. Leave the default choice at Existing Worksheet in Step 3 of the wizard and click Back.
    Note that the marquee surrounds the original database range. You need to change this range now to include the two new rows of data by dragging over the entire range.

13. Click and drag over the range A4:G20 to select it for the PivotTable.
    The marquee now surrounds the expanded range.

14. Click Finish.
    Since no other options are being changed at this time, you don't have to click Next to advance the wizard. Also, notice that by expanding the database range, the PivotTable updated automatically; therefore, you don't need to click the Refresh Data button on the PivotTable toolbar.

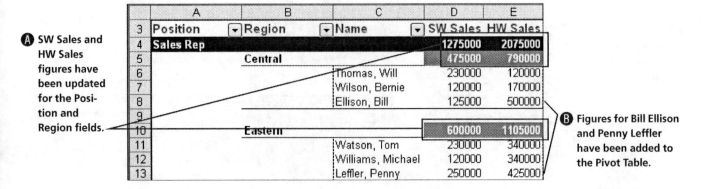

A SW Sales and HW Sales figures have been updated for the Position and Region fields.

B Figures for Bill Ellison and Penny Leffler have been added to the Pivot Table.

15. Take a few minutes to examine the updated PivotTable, then save the workbook and continue with step 16.

Change Field Settings for Calculated Fields

16. Examine the HW Sales totals for Regions and Positions before you change them.

17. Click cell E15 then click the Field Settings button on the PivotTable toolbar.

⚠️TIP! *You can also display the Field Settings dialog box by right-clicking any cell within the PivotTable that contains data and choosing Field Settings from the pop-up menu.*

The PivotTable Field dialog box appears. You will use this box again in just a minute to change the number format of the HW Sales field.

18. Follow these steps to change the function from SUM to AVERAGE for the HW Sales:

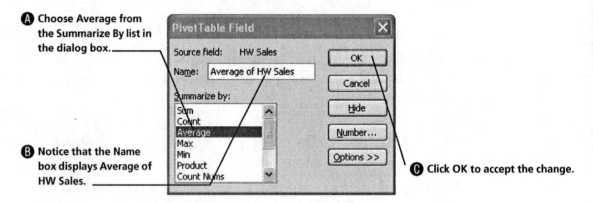

Ⓐ Choose Average from the Summarize By list in the dialog box.

Ⓑ Notice that the Name box displays Average of HW Sales.

Ⓒ Click OK to accept the change.

Notice the new heading in column E, Average of HW Sales, and the new figures.

19. Click the Field Settings button again on the PivotTable toolbar and click the Number button.

20. Follow these steps to change the format of the HW Sales to Currency with no decimals:

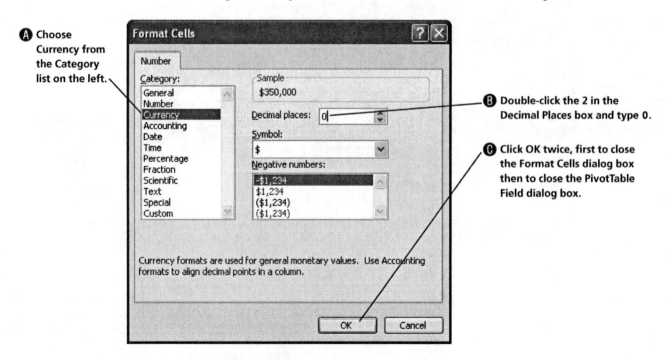

Ⓐ Choose Currency from the Category list on the left.

Ⓑ Double-click the 2 in the Decimal Places box and type 0.

Ⓒ Click OK twice, first to close the Format Cells dialog box then to close the PivotTable Field dialog box.

21. Using the same method, change the HW Sales totals back to the Sum function.

22. Reformat the SW Sales field to Currency Style with no decimals.

23. Drag the Region field off the PivotTable.
The final PivotTable should match the following illustration.

	A	B	C	D
3	Position ▼	Name ▼	SW Sales	HW Sales
4	**Sales Rep**		**$1,275,000**	**$2,075,000**
5		Smith, Bob	$200,000	$180,000
6		Thomas, Will	$230,000	$120,000
7		Watson, Tom	$230,000	$340,000
8		Williams, Michael	$120,000	$340,000
9		Wilson, Bernie	$120,000	$170,000
10		Ellison, Bill	$125,000	$500,000
11		Leffler, Penny	$250,000	$425,000
12				
13	**Senior Sales Rep**		**$1,474,000**	**$2,150,000**
14		Alvizo, Alex	$450,000	$340,000
15		Cain, Mary	$234,000	$560,000
16		Martinez, Carlos	$450,000	$450,000
17		Zain, Beth	$340,000	$800,000
18				
19	**Telemarketer**		**$2,143,000**	**$1,906,000**
20		Brown, Bill	$546,000	$120,000
21		Cray, Zip	$900,000	$780,000
22		Hubbs, Daniel	$340,000	$230,000
23		Richards, Paul	$234,000	$546,000
24		Smith, Michael	$123,000	$230,000
25				
26	**Grand Total**		**$4,892,000**	**$6,131,000**

Working with PivotCharts

A PivotChart lets you summarize data in a chart with the same methods you use in a PivotTable. To create a PivotChart, you can either chart a PivotTable directly or create one from scratch using the same wizard that helps you create PivotTables. Once you have created a PivotChart you can use the same techniques to position and pivot fields that you use on PivotTables.

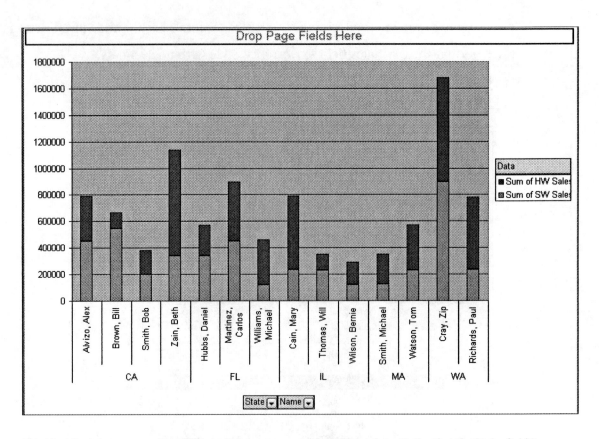

This PivotChart lets you use PivotTable techniques to organize the chart data. Notice that the Name field items are arranged by state.

Formatting PivotCharts

You use the same commands and wizards to format PivotCharts that you use with normal Excel charts. You choose from the same variety of chart styles, including bar, column, and line. You format chart objects just as you would on a normal Excel chart.

QR

QUICK REFERENCE: CREATING A PIVOTCHART

Task	Procedure
Create a PivotChart from an Excel database	■ Select any cell in the database.
	■ Choose Data→PivotTable and PivotChart Report from the menu bar.
	■ Choose the Microsoft Office Excel List or Database and PivotChart Report in Step 1 of the wizard and click Next.
	■ Choose Database in Step 2 of the wizard and click Next.
	■ Choose whether to create the PivotChart on a new or existing worksheet and click Finish.
Create a PivotChart from an existing PivotTable	■ Select any cell in the PivotTable.
	■ Click the Chart Wizard button on the PivotTable toolbar.

Hands-On 6.5   Create a PivotChart

In this exercise, you will create a PivotChart from your PivotTable. In a Skill Builder exercise at the end of this lesson you will create a PivotChart from a database.

1. Select any cell within the PivotTable and click the Chart Wizard button on the PivotTable toolbar.

   A new column chart worksheet is created immediately from your present PivotTable data. Notice that the Names data is arranged by position, just as it was in the PivotTable.

2. Change the name of the Chart 1 worksheet tab to **PivotChart**.

   Once you have created the PivotChart, you can add and delete fields just as you did with the PivotTable. You can also pivot fields between the lower (rows) area and the right (columns) area.

3. Follow these steps to add a new field to the PivotChart:

   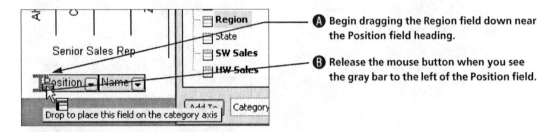

   A Begin dragging the Region field down near the Position field heading.

   B Release the mouse button when you see the gray bar to the left of the Position field.

   Now the column chart is further arranged by Region. This enables you to visually analyze the productivity of sales staff within each region.

4. Drag the Position field directly to the left so it is positioned to the left of the Region field, as shown here.

   Now you can compare the performance of sales staff between various regions.

5. Click the Chart Wizard ▥ button on the PivotTable toolbar. Choose the Line chart type, then choose the top-left subtype and click Finish.

6. The chart is reconfigured to the new chart type. You can use normal chart formatting commands on any PivotChart.

7. Save ▥ the workbook then close it.

Using Interactive PivotTables on the Web

You can save a PivotTable as a Web page just as you can with normal Excel worksheets. You can also publish the PivotTable as an interactive Web page. Interactivity allows users to manipulate and pivot the fields when viewing the PivotTable in their Web browsers. Fields can be added, moved, and removed in the Web browser just as they can on normal PivotTable worksheets. You can also save the PivotTable without interactivity. This option displays the Pivot-Table with a static view that users cannot manipulate in their Web browser.

 NOTE! *Various types of formatting may be lost when you save a worksheet as an interactive Web page.*

QUICK REFERENCE: SAVING A PIVOTTABLE AS A WEB PAGE WITH INTERACTIVITY	
Task	**Procedure**
Save a PivotTable as a Web page with interactivity	■ Display the worksheet with the PivotTable. Make sure the PivotTable fields are configured as you wish them to display in a Web browser.
	■ Choose File→Save as Web Page from the menu bar.
	■ Click the Publish button.
	■ Choose the worksheet with the PivotTable, and then select PivotTable in the Item to Publish section of the dialog box.
	■ Place a checkmark in the Add Interactivity With option box and make sure PivotTable Functionality is selected in the adjacent drop-down list.
	■ If desired, change the page title or filename, and then click Publish.

Creating Trendlines

A trendline is a tool for data analysis and prediction. Trendlines visually display the trends in your data. There are several types of trendlines available, each suited to the display of particular types of data. For example, a linear trendline is a best-fit line that works best with data that follow a linear path. A moving average trendline smoothes out fluctuations in data by averaging two or more adjacent data points for each trendline data point.

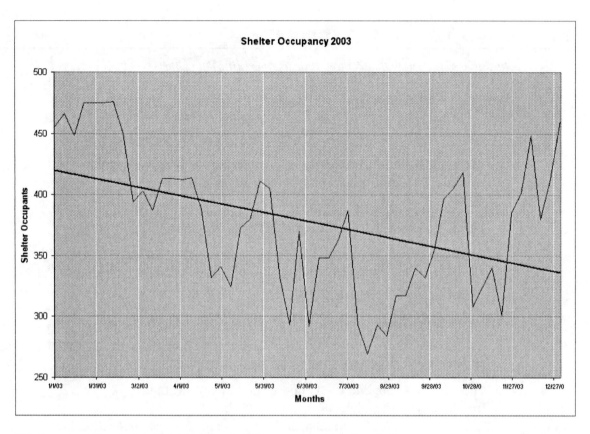

Shelter Occupancy 2003

This linear trendline depicts the overall trend of occupancy at a homeless shelter.

 !TIP! *You cannot add a trendline to certain types of charts, such as 3D, pie, and area charts.*

QUICK REFERENCE: CREATING A TRENDLINE	
Task	**Procedure**
Add a trendline to a chart	■ Display the chart to which you wish to add a trendline.
	■ Choose Chart→Add Trendline from the menu bar.
	■ Choose a trendline type, select a data series (if more than one), and click OK.
Edit a trendline	■ Choose Chart→Add Trendline from the menu bar.
	■ Choose the data series (if applicable) then edit the trendline type and options as desired.

🖱 Hands-On 6.6   Add a Trendline

In this exercise, you will add a trendline to an existing data chart.

Insert a Trendline

1. Open the 2003 Occupancy Trend workbook.
   This workbook summarizes weekly occupancy figures for a homeless shelter.

2. Take a moment to scan the occupancy data then display the 2003 Trends worksheet.
   This chart only displays data for the Week and Occupants columns.

3. Choose Chart→Add Trendline from the menu bar.
   This dialog box displays the various trendline types available.

4. Leave the trendline type on the default selection of Linear and click OK.
   The new trendline appears. This best-fit line indicates that overall occupancy at the shelter is gradually falling.

Edit the Trendline

5. Right-click the Trendline (not the data line) as shown at right and choose Format Trendline from the context menu.

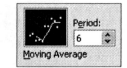

6. Click the Type tab, and then choose the Moving Average trendline type and click OK.
   This type of trendline follows data fluctuations. In the next step, you will set more data points to be averaged, which will smooth out this trendline.

7. Right-click the Trendline (not the data line) and choose Format Trendline from the context menu.

8. Change the Period box from 2 to 6 as shown at right and click OK.
   The trendline smoothes out to reflect the greater number of data points being averaged for each point on the trendline. Notice that the trendline no longer begins near the left side of the chart—reflecting the need to average the first six data points before drawing the first trendline point.

9. Save and close the workbook.

Working with Styles

A style is cell formatting to which you give a name. Once you define a style, you can apply its formatting to any cell with just a couple of clicks. Some styles may be very simple, such as changing the color of a cell's contents. Other styles may combine changes in the font, number format, borders, and shading. To apply a style, select the range of cell(s) to be formatted and choose a style from the style box, which you will learn how to add, on the toolbar or use Format→Style to choose a style from a dialog box.

The Benefits of Styles

Using styles offers two tremendous advantages compared to manual formatting methods:

- Styles make your formatting more consistent—When you use a style you no longer need to remember the format settings used for specific types of cells, such as headings and subtotals. You simply apply the appropriate style. If you change your mind later, you can edit the style and the changes will be applied to every cell in the workbook to which the style was applied previously.

- Styles are convenient—Especially when you must make several formatting changes in a cell, applying a style is faster than manually making the formatting edits. It is even faster than using the format painter. Using styles can spare you the tedium of repeatedly giving the same formatting commands in various cells.

Creating Styles

To create a style you can use one of two methods:

- Create by Example—With this method, you manually apply all desired formatting commands to one cell then assign a style name to the formatting. This is the easiest method of creating new styles.

- Create by Definition—With this method, you open the Style dialog box and choose the format settings you wish to assign to the style.

The Style Box

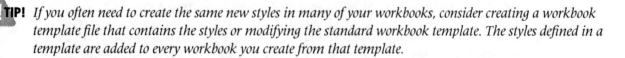 Excel's toolbar can contain a style box that lists all available styles. The style box is useful for defining styles by example. Unfortunately, Excel's default Formatting toolbar does not contain the Style box but it is easy to add it to the toolbar yourself. The first part of Hands-On 6.7 will show you how to do this.

The Style List

Every workbook has its own style list. The list includes styles in the template from which you created the workbook and any additional styles you create in that workbook. The styles you edit or create in one workbook will not appear in other workbooks. However, you can merge (i.e., copy) styles into a workbook from other open workbooks with the Merge button in the Style dialog box.

!TIP! *If you often need to create the same new styles in many of your workbooks, consider creating a workbook template file that contains the styles or modifying the standard workbook template. The styles defined in a template are added to every workbook you create from that template.*

Task	Procedure
Add the Style box to the Formatting toolbar	■ Right-click on any toolbar and choose Customize from the context menu.
	■ Display the Commands tab.
	■ Choose the Format Category on the left side of the dialog box.
	■ Drag the [Normal ▼] drop-down list box from the Customize dialog box onto the Formatting toolbar—just to the left of the Font Style box.
	■ Click the Close button on the Customize dialog box.
Create a new style by example	■ Select a cell in the workbook.
	■ Apply any custom formatting to the cell you wish to incorporate in the new style.
	■ Click in the Style box on the toolbar, type a name for the style, and tap [Enter]. Or, choose Format→Style from the menu bar, type the new style name in the dialog box, and click OK.
Edit a style by example	■ Select a cell on the worksheet to which you have already applied the style you wish to edit.
	■ Manually format the cell with the desired changes for the style.
	■ Click the drop-down list [▼] button (not the style name) on the Style box and choose the same style name.
	■ Choose Yes when Excel asks if you wish to redefine the style based on your selection.

Hands-On 6.7   Define and Edit Styles by Example

In this exercise, you will create a new style for column headings and apply it to all column headings. You will also edit the style and see that all cells originally formatted with the style update automatically.

Make Sure the Styles Box Is on the Formatting Toolbar

Having the Style box on the Formatting toolbar makes defining styles by example much more convenient. Since the Style box is not part of Excel's default Formatting toolbar, you may need to add it.

1. Open the 2004 Sales workbook, display the Sales Database worksheet, and select cell A4.

2. Examine the Formatting toolbar. If you see a box on the toolbar with the name Normal, the Style box is already installed on the toolbar. Skip to step 6.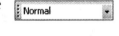

3. Right-click on any toolbar and choose Customize from the context menu.

4. Follow these steps to add the Style box to the Formatting toolbar:

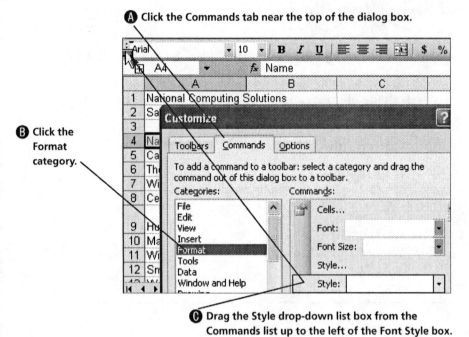

A Click the Commands tab near the top of the dialog box.

B Click the Format category.

C Drag the Style drop-down list box from the Commands list up to the left of the Font Style box.

5. Close the Customize dialog box.

Define a Style by Example

Now you will define a style for use with column headings.

6. Make sure cell A4 is still selected.

7. Set the Font Color to a light shade of yellow and set the Fill Color to a dark shade of blue.
These formats will define your style. Now you will use these formats to define a style named Heading.

8. Click in the Style box on the toolbar, type **Heading** as the name for the new style, and tap Enter.
That's all there is to it! You have created a new style by example. Now let's apply the style to other cells.

9. Select the range B4:G4, click the Style box drop-down list [▾] button, and choose Heading from the list.
The formatting of your new style is immediately applied to the cells.

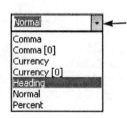

10. Display the Sales by Region worksheet and select the range A4:H4.

11. Click the drop-down list [▾] button on the Style box and choose Heading.
Once you define a style, it is available to use on any worksheet in the workbook.

Edit a Style by Example

You will now edit the style by example and review the results.

12. Select cell A4.

    When you edit a style by example, you must always begin by selecting a cell to which the style has already been applied.

13. Set the Font Color to a dark shade of green and set the Fill Color to a light shade of green.

14. Choose Heading from the Style list on the toolbar.

    Excel will ask if you wish to redefine the Heading style to match the changes you made in cell A4.

15. Click Yes to redefine the style by example.

    Notice that all cells with the Heading style have changed to match the new style definition. Styles can save you time when you need to change a worksheet's formatting.

16. Display the Sales Database worksheet.

    Perhaps you saw this coming! Your new style definition has been applied to this worksheet as well. Styles are a very powerful formatting tool.

The Style Dialog Box

The Style dialog box contains a list of all available styles and command buttons to add, modify, and delete styles. For example, you use the Delete button in the Style dialog box to delete unneeded styles. You can also use the Style dialog box to copy styles from one open workbook to another and include or exclude various types of formatting from a style definition. A portion of a typical Style dialog box is displayed below.

Only formats that are checked are applied by the style. In this example, Alignment is unchecked so the current cell alignment is retained when the style is applied.

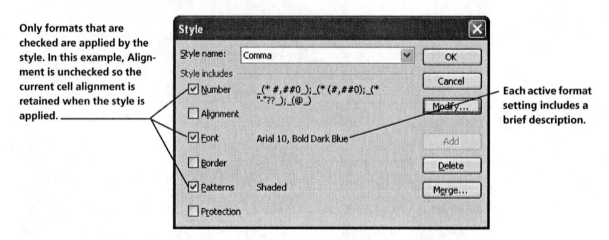

Each active format setting includes a brief description.

Overriding a Style

You can always change the formatting of a cell with a style. This is called overriding the style. When you override a style, the change will remain, even if the style is redefined later.

 TIP! *To end an override, reapply the style to the cell(s) and choose No when asked if you wish to redefine the style.*

NOTE!

You cannot delete the Normal style.

Hands-On 6.8   Edit a Style by Definition

In most cases you will define styles by example. However, you can also accomplish the same tasks with the Style dialog box. In this exercise, you will edit a style for numeric values and override the style setting in a range of cells.

1. Select cell F5 on the Sales Database worksheet.

2. Choose Format→Style from the menu bar.
   Notice that this cell already has a style assigned to it (Comma). At present, this style includes number formatting. Comma Style is one of the styles built into Excel and it is available in all new workbooks.

3. Place checkmarks in the Font and Patterns options boxes, if necessary.
   The present setting for these types of formatting appear to the right of the checkboxes. These checked format types are now part of the style definition.

4. Click the Modify button.
   The Format Cells dialog box appears. It is the same one displayed when you choose Format→Cells from the menu bar.

5. Display the Font tab, then set the font color to dark blue and the font style to bold.

6. Display the Patterns tab and choose a shade of light blue for the cell shading.

7. Click OK to close the Format Cells dialog box. Examine the descriptions beside the Font and Patterns format settings you just changed.
   The descriptions now match the new settings.

8. Click OK to close the Style dialog box.
   Since most cells in the SW and HW Sales columns use the Comma Style, the formatting immediately changes to reflect the new style definition. The changes to the Comma Style will only affect this workbook. They will not affect other workbooks or new workbooks you create later.

Override a Style

9. Display the Sales by Region worksheet.
   The style change was applied to this worksheet as well.

10. Select the range F8:H8 then use the Fill Color button on the toolbar to set the fill for these cells to a shade of yellow.
    The fill color for the Comma Style has been overridden in cells F4:G4.

11. Set the fill color for cell G5 to a light shade of green.

12. Choose Comma in the Style box and choose Yes when asked to confirm that you wish to redefine the style.
    Notice that cells F8:H8, where you overrode the style, were not affected by the style change. Your formatting override will stay in effect until the style is applied to these cells again. Let's do that now.

13. Select the range F8:H8 and choose Comma in the Style box.
    Excel will ask again if you wish to redefine the style based on the example. In this case, you don't want to redefine the style—you want to reapply the style to these cells and remove the override.

14. Choose No to reapply the style to the selected cells.
    The override is canceled and the cells will conform to the Comma Style whenever it is changed in the future.

15. Save ⊞ the workbook.

Working with Outlines and Grouping

Excel's Outline feature lets you control the display of detail data in worksheets. This helps you see the big picture while still being able to view the details when necessary. If your worksheet contains SUM formulas, Excel can automatically apply an outline to the data. For detail areas without summary formulas, you can manually group rows and columns of cells.

How Outlines Work

When you create an outline for a worksheet, Excel groups the data into detail rows and columns. This structure is displayed visually along the top and left border of the worksheet. The outline area also contains plus (+) and minus (−) symbols you can click to expand and collapse your view of the data. The following example shows an outlined worksheet.

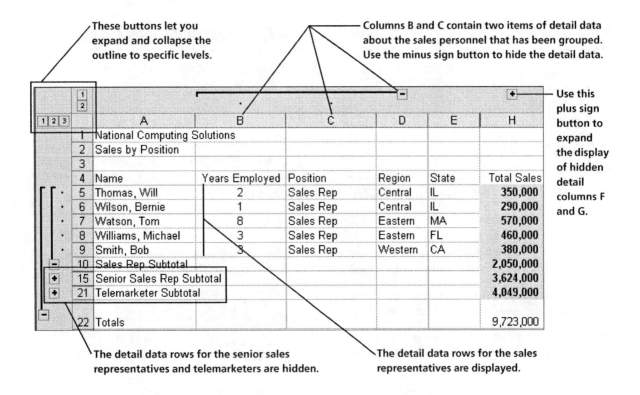

These buttons let you expand and collapse the outline to specific levels.

Columns B and C contain two items of detail data about the sales personnel that has been grouped. Use the minus sign button to hide the detail data.

Use this plus sign button to expand the display of hidden detail columns F and G.

The detail data rows for the senior sales representatives and telemarketers are hidden.

The detail data rows for the sales representatives are displayed.

Auto Outline

Excel can analyze and apply an outline to most worksheets automatically. The key to smooth automatic outlining is to arrange the detail and summary data consistently. For example, if the data is laid out in columns, make sure all detail data appears to the right or left of the summary formulas. The more hierarchical your layout, the more effective the resulting outline will be. Excel will try to outline all data related to summary formulas in the worksheet. If you are not satisfied with the results of the Auto Outline command, you can group rows and columns manually.

QUICK REFERENCE: AUTO OUTLINING A WORKSHEET

Task	Procedure
Apply an automatic outline	■ Make sure the detail rows or columns are immediately to the left or above the cells with formulas that summarize the detail data.
	■ Select the portion of the worksheet to be outlined or select a single cell to outline the entire worksheet.
	■ Choose Data→Group and Outline→Auto Outline from the menu bar.
Clear the outline from a worksheet	■ Choose Data→Group and Outline→Clear Outline from the menu bar.

TIP! *You can adjust the relative position of summary formulas to detail data with the Data→Group and Outline→Settings command.*

Hands-On 6.9   Automatically Outline a Worksheet

In this exercise, you will use the Auto Outline command to outline a worksheet. Then you will expand and collapse the outline.

1. Display the Sales by Position worksheet.

2. Choose Data→Group and Outline→Auto Outline from the menu bar.
   Excel will automatically group the rows and columns of the table. Notice that the rows are divided into three groups at Level 2 and one larger group at Level 1. There is just one group formed for the columns. Excel reviewed the formulas on the worksheet to arrive at these groupings.

3. Follow these steps to collapse the display of detail data:

   Ⓐ Click the Level 1 button for the column group. Notice that the SW and HW sales columns collapse, leaving only the Total Sales summary column in view.

   Ⓑ Click the Level 1 button for the row groups. This leaves only a single figure for the grand total sales.

   Ⓒ Click the Level 2 button for the row groups. Now you can see subtotals for the three types of sales positions.

		A
1		National Computing S
2		Sales by Position

   Notice the plus and minus buttons in the outline area. An outline with a minus button is currently displaying its detail data. An outline with a plus button has details that are not displayed.

4. Follow these steps to collapse and expand the row detail data:

   Ⓐ Click the plus button for the Sales Rep Subtotal row. This expands the detail display of individual sales reps.

   Ⓑ Click the plus button for the Telemarketer Subtotal row. Now the details for this group are displayed.

		Name	Years
+	4	Name	Years
+	10	Sales Rep Subtotal	
+	15	Senior Sales Rep Subtotal	
−	21	Telemarketer Subtotal	
	22	Totals	

5. Click the Level 2 button for the row groups.
   The expanded Level 3 rows for the Level 2 groups are immediately collapsed again. Now only the Level 2 rows are visible.

6. Click the Level 3 button for the row groups.
   This command reveals all detail rows grouped at the lowest level of the outline. You can independently expand and collapse individual groups with the plus and minus buttons. The Level 1, 2, 3 buttons save you the time of clicking the plus and minus buttons for the individual groups at each level.

Creating Groups Manually

When you have non-numeric detail data or when Excel simply does not outline the worksheet as you desire, you can group rows and columns manually. You simply select the rows or columns to be grouped and choose Data→Group and Outline→Group from the menu bar. The selected rows or columns will be grouped in the outline or added to an existing adjacent group. You use a similar procedure to manually ungroup rows and columns. If desired, you can even ungroup rows and columns originally grouped by Excel's Auto Outline command.

QUICK REFERENCE: CREATING GROUPS MANUALLY

Task	Procedure
Manually group rows or columns	■ Select the detail row(s) or column(s) to be grouped. ■ Choose Data→Group and Outline→Group from the menu bar.
Manually ungroup rows or columns	■ Select the rows or columns to be ungrouped. ■ Choose Data→Group and Outline→Ungroup from the menu bar.

 Hands-On 6.10   **Create Groups Manually**

In this exercise, you will create a new group manually. This group was not created by the Auto Outline command because there were no summary formulas for the detail data.

Add a Group to the Auto Outline

1. Follow these steps to create a group for the detail sales staff data:

Ⓐ Select columns B and C by dragging the column headings.

Ⓑ Choose Data→Group and Outline→Group from the menu bar.

Ⓒ Click the new group's minus button to collapse the detail columns. Now the Years Employed and Position details about the salespersons are hidden, allowing you to concentrate on the data in other columns.

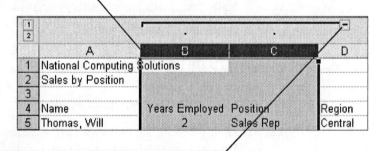

Clear the Outline

2. Click the Level 2 button to expand the column groups. Columns B, C, F, and G should now be visible.
In the next step, you will clear the auto outline. It is always a good idea to display all hidden detail rows and columns before you clear an outline.

3. Select cell A1.
If you have selected a range of cells, the Clear Outline command will only affect outline levels that lie within the selected cells. Any cells outside the selection will not be ungrouped.

4. Choose Data→Group and Outline→Clear Outline from the menu bar.
All outline groups on the worksheet are cleared, even the group you created manually in step 1.

Create an Outline Manually

5. Select columns B–E.

6. Choose Data→Group and Outline→Group from the menu bar.
The new group is created. Although Auto Outline is handy for certain types of worksheets with summary formulas, you can easily create groups manually.

7. Click the minus button for the newly created group to collapse its data.

8. Select rows 5–9 by dragging the mouse over the row headings at the left edge of the worksheet.
These are the detail rows for the Sales Rep subtotal. Now you will create a group out of these detail rows that you can collapse and expand.

9. Choose Data→Group and Outline→Group from the menu bar and click the minus button to collapse the new group.

Use the Ungroup Command

10. Click the plus buttons for both groups to expand the detail rows and columns.
You could also have clicked the Level 2 buttons for the row and column groups at the top-left corner of the worksheet.

11. If necessary, select rows 5–9, then choose Data→Group and Outline→Ungroup from the menu bar.
The selected rows are ungrouped manually.

12. Select any cell in the worksheet to deselect rows 5–9 then choose Data→Group and Outline→Clear Outline from the menu bar.
The column group is removed as well. This command can remove both auto outline and manually created groups.

13. Save the workbook then close the Excel window.

 **Concepts Review**

True/False Questions

1. A PivotTable automatically creates summary formulas for your data. TRUE FALSE

2. Changing the order of the fields in the row or column areas of a PivotTable does not affect data display. TRUE FALSE

3. A PivotChart does not allow you to rearrange the data fields. TRUE FALSE

4. A style is created automatically whenever you change the formatting of a cell. TRUE FALSE

5. Styles help you format worksheets consistently. TRUE FALSE

6. You cannot outline a worksheet manually. TRUE FALSE

7. The Auto Outline command only groups cells with label data. TRUE FALSE

8. The Clear Outline command only removes groups created with the Data→Group and Outline→Auto Outline commands. TRUE FALSE

9. A trendline indicates the general direction of a data series. TRUE FALSE

10. A PivotTable field corresponds to a column in the data table on which it is based. TRUE FALSE

Multiple Choice Questions

1. What happens on a PivotTable when you pivot a field from the rows to the columns area?

   a. Nothing happens. Only numeric data fields can be placed in the row and columns areas.

   b. The field exchanges positions with a field that is already positioned in the columns area.

   c. The data for the field is summarized in columns rather than rows.

   d. You cannot pivot a field directly between rows and columns; you must remove it from the PivotTable then add the field to the column fields area.

2. How do you change the chart type of a PivotChart?

   a. You can only use the chart types designed specifically for PivotCharts.

   b. You use the same chart type commands you use for normal charts.

   c. You arrange the fields on the PivotTable then issue the PivotChart command.

   d. You cannot change the chart type of a PivotChart. You must use the default format.

3. To create a style by example, which procedure works best?

   a. Use the Format→Styles command then define the style and click OK.

   b. Type a new name for the style in the Style box on the toolbar then assign formatting for the style.

   c. Click the style name in the Style box then click Yes to redefine the style.

   d. Manually format a cell then type a name for the style in the Style box on the toolbar.

   e. None of the above

4. What happens when you give the Auto Outline command?

   a. Only rows and columns with summary formulas are grouped.

   b. Excel creates groups for all types of detail data on the worksheet.

   c. You must select the rows or columns to be grouped then give the Group command.

   d. Excel creates an outline based on your entries in a dialog box.

Skill Builders

Skill Builder 6.1   Create a PivotTable

In this exercise, you will create a PivotTable from another database. You will practice placing and pivoting fields to change your view of the data.

1. Start Excel then open the Jan Sales PivotTable workbook.
   This workbook displays one month's activity at Acme Auto Sales. Before you create a PivotTable, take a moment to look over the layout of the data fields and records. For example, because there is just one field for numeric data in this database, you will want to place the Price field in the Data area of the PivotTable.

2. Select cell A4.
   This tells Excel that it should use the database fields when you create the PivotTable.

3. Choose Data→PivotTable and PivotChart Report from the menu bar then click Finish to use the default settings in the wizard.

4. Rename the Sheet 1 worksheet tab **PivotTable**.

5. Drag the Sold By field into the row fields area along the left side of the PivotTable.
   Since there is no data to display for the field yet, the PivotTable just shows the location of this field.

6. Drag the Price field into the Data area of the PivotTable.
   The PivotTable displays the total sales for each salesperson. Since you might want to know which type of car each salesperson sold this month you will place a new field in the row fields area.

7. Follow these steps to add the Type field to the row field area of the PivotTable:

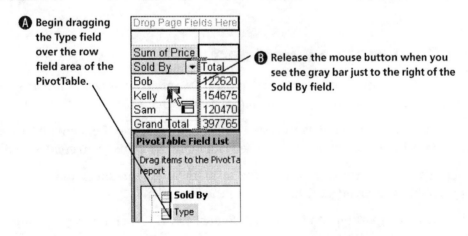

Ⓐ Begin dragging the Type field over the row field area of the PivotTable.

Ⓑ Release the mouse button when you see the gray bar just to the right of the Sold By field.

The PivotTable expands to display the sales of the various types of vehicles sold by each salesperson. It might also be interesting to summarize how the revenue at the dealership breaks down by vehicle type so in the next step you will pivot the Type field from the row field area to the column fields area.

8. Drag the Type field to the column field area (where you see the word Total) as shown at right.
   Now the Grand Total line at the bottom of the PivotTable displays the revenue for each type of car.

9. Drag the New/Used field into the left side of the row fields area of the PivotTable (just to the left of where the Sold By field is located now).

10. Pivot the New/Used field into the column field area of the PivotTable (where the Type field is located now).

Set the PivotTable Options

There is an Options dialog box for PivotTables. It lets you control several aspects of the way your PivotTable displays data.

11. Click the PivotTable button on the PivotTable toolbar and choose Table Options from the drop-down menu.

12. Uncheck the Grand Totals for Columns and Grand Totals for Rows options and click OK.
The grand totals on the bottom row and right column are removed from the table.

13. Click the Undo 🔄 button on the Excel toolbar to restore the grand totals.

14. Use the Field Settings dialog box to change the function to the Average of Prices and format the numbers as currency with no decimals.

15. Experiment with other fields on the PivotTable and practice pivoting fields between the row and column field areas. You can also remove fields from the PivotTable.

16. When you are finished, save 💾 the workbook.

Skill Builder 6.2   Create a PivotChart

In this exercise, you will create a PivotChart to display the same data you used in Jan Sales PivotTable. You will practice placing and pivoting fields to change the PivotChart's display of this data.

1. The Jan Sales PivotTable workbook should be open. Save the file with the new name **Jan Sales PivotChart** then delete the PivotTable worksheet you created in Skill Builder 6.1.

2. Select any cell in the database on the January Sales worksheet and choose Data→ PivotTable and PivotChart Report from the menu bar.

3. Change the report type to PivotChart Report (with PivotTable Report) and click Next.

4. Click Next again to accept the database as the data range for the PivotChart.

5. Click Yes if you were asked to use the same source data and reduce the size of the workbook file.

6. Choose the New Worksheet option and click Finish.
Notice that two new worksheets were created—a Chart1 sheet and a Sheet1 sheet. Sheet1 contains another PivotTable. This new PivotTable will match the field locations you set in the PivotChart.

7. Drag and drop the Sold By field into the Category fields area at the bottom of the chart.

8. Drag and drop the Price field into the Data Items area at the center of the chart.
   The PivotChart will display a summary of the total sales for each salesperson.

9. Drag and drop the New/Used field into the Series fields area on the right side of the chart.
   It looks like Bob brought in the highest used car revenue while Kelly was the leader in overall revenue.

10. Drag and drop the Type field into the series field area on the right side of the chart (above or below the New/Used field).
    This produces a confusing array of data. Let's pivot a field and see if that helps.

11. Drag the New/Used field just to the left of the Sold By field in the Categories area at the bottom of the chart.
    This makes a more informative display. Now you can see the breakdown of vehicle types more clearly. You can also compare the sales of new and used cars.

12. Now drag the New/Used field to the right of the Sold By field.
    Now you can easily compare the performance of individual salespersons. The ability to pivot the data in the various areas is a key feature of PivotCharts.

13. Experiment with other fields on the PivotChart and practice pivoting fields between the series and category areas. You can also remove fields from the PivotChart.

14. Display the Sheet1 worksheet and review the figures in the PivotTable.
    Notice that the configuration of the fields in this PivotTable matches their locations in the PivotChart. For example, the new and used car sales of each salesperson are totaled, just as they are in the PivotChart.

15. Save and close the workbook when you are finished.

Skill Builder 6.3   Work with Trendlines

In this exercise, you will add a trendline to the data on an existing chart.

1. Open the Shelter Occupancy workbook. Take a moment to review the data.
   This database depicts the weekly occupancy of a homeless shelter over the course of three years.

2. Display the Occupancy Chart worksheet.
   This chart displays the three years of data. Notice that the data fluctuates by season and year.

3. Choose Chart→Add Trendline from the menu bar. Choose the Linear trendline type and click OK.
   This best-fit line clearly shows that overall occupancy at the shelter has fallen over the three years. Now let's see how a linear trendline might predict future occupancy.

4. Taking care to place the tip of the mouse pointer on the trendline (not the data line), right-click and choose Format Trendline from the context menu.

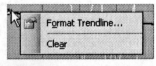

5. Display the Options tab, enter **120** in the Forecast Forward box, and click OK.

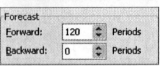

Each period represents one day. Notice that the Dates scale at the bottom of the chart has extended well past March 2004—a four-month forecast. This trendline predicts that occupancy will continue to fall. However, since the data has seasonal fluctuations, a linear trendline may not give the most accurate forecast. Let's try a different style trendline.

Change the Trendline Type

6. Right-click on the trendline and choose Format Trendline from the context menu.

7. Display the Type tab, choose the Polynomial trendline type, and click OK.
The polynomial trendline can follow the fluctuations better than the linear type. In this case, it follows the overall dip and rise of the three-year pattern. This trendline predicts that occupancy will rise over the next four months—the opposite of the linear trendline forecast.

8. Right-click on the trendline and choose Format Trendline from the context menu.

9. Use the spinner bar to set the Order for the trendline to 4 as shown at right, then click OK.

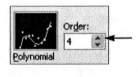

Now the rise of the forecast is not quite as steep, but it still does not match the general trend. Notice the three dips in the data for each summer. Now you will set the order of the trendline to match the number of dips.

10. Right-click and format the trendline again. Set the order from 4 to 3. Display the Patterns tab, set the Color to a medium shade of blue, and click OK.
This trendline appears to match the fluctuations in the data better than any of the others we've viewed so far. Now let's compare it to the linear trendline.

Add Another Trendline

11. Choose Chart→Add Trendline from the menu bar. Choose the Linear trendline type, display the Options tab, set it to forecast **120** days, and click OK.
You can display more than one trendline on a chart. As you can see, the polynomial trendline forecasts less of a drop in occupancy than the linear type. One way to compare the accuracy of a trendline is to display its R-squared value. The closer a trendline's R-squared value is to 1, the better it fits the data.

12. Right-click the linear trendline, display the Options tab, place a checkmark in the Display R-squared Value on Chart option (near the bottom of the dialog box), and click OK.
The R-squared value displays on the right side of the trendline. It should read $R^2 = 0.0721$.

13. Display the R-squared value for the polynomial trendline.
This trendline displays $R^2=0.2478$. Since its value is closer to 1, this trendline represents a more accurate forecast than the linear type. An ideal trendline will have an R^2 value very close to 1.

 TIP! *You can learn more about trendlines in Excel's online help. Type **trendline** in the Type a Question for Help box and choose the About Forecasting and Showing Trends in Charts topic.*

14. Right-click on the linear trendline and choose Clear from the context menu.
This deletes the trendline.

15. Save and close the workbook.

Skill Builder 6.4   Create and Apply Styles

In this exercise, you will create styles by example for numeric fields and dates.

1. Open the Jan Sales PivotTable workbook and display the January Sales worksheet.

Create and Edit a Style for Numeric Values

2. Select cell E5 and click the Currency Style $ button on the toolbar.
Excel formats the cell with a dollar sign ($) and adds two decimal places. Notice that the Currency style is displayed in the Style box. This built-in style came from the standard Excel workbook template. Rather than alter this built-in style, you will create a new style.

3. Click in the Style box on the toolbar, type **Price** as the new style name, and tap ⌷Enter⌷.
The new style name is now displayed in the Style box.

4. Select the range E6:E27 and choose Price in the Style box.
Now all of the cells have the dollar sign and decimal places. Since you don't really need the decimals, let's edit the style by example to remove them.

5. Select cell E27 and click the Decrease Decimal button twice to eliminate the unnecessary decimal places.

6. Choose Price again from the Style list.
Excel will ask if you want to redefine the Price style to match the formatting in the selection.

7. Choose Yes to redefine the style based on the selection.
Notice that all cells formatted with the Price style immediately lost their decimals. Using styles helps you create consistent formatting throughout a workbook. Styles also can save time by allowing you to update the formats of cells to which the styles have been applied with ease.

Create and Use a Style for Dates

8. Select cell F5.

9. Choose Format→Cells from the menu bar and display the Number tab. Choose the Date Category, choose the 3/14 date style from the Type list, and click OK.

10. Click in the Style box on the toolbar, type **Date** as the new style name, and tap Enter.

11. Select the range F6:F24 and choose Date from the Style box.
The date format in the selected cells immediately changes to the new style.

12. Select one of the date cells and choose Format→Cells from the menu bar. Change the date format of the cell then redefine the Date style by example.
All date cells should change to reflect the style change.

13. Feel free to practice creating styles for other cells on the worksheet. For example, you might want to create a style for the column headings, including bold type, font color, and cell border settings.

14. Save ⊟ the workbook when you are finished.

Skill Builder 6.5   Outline a Worksheet

In this exercise, you will use the Auto Outline command to manually group and ungroup columns.

1. Display the January Sales worksheet in the Jan Sales PivotTable workbook.

Auto Outline the Worksheet

2. Select cell E26 and examine its formula.
This cell contains the only summary formula in the worksheet.

3. Choose Data→Group and Outline→Auto Outline from the menu bar.
Excel automatically outlines the detail rows of the worksheet above the Total Sales row. None of the columns were outlined because there are no summary formulas to summarize column data.

4. Click the Level 1 button near the upper-left corner of the worksheet to collapse the display of the detail data rows.
Now only the summary data is visible.

5. Click the plus button on the left side of the worksheet to expand the view of the detail rows.

Manually Group Columns

The columns do not contain summary formulas.

6. Drag on the column headings to select columns C through E then choose Data→Group and Outline→Group from the menu bar.

7. Click the minus button near the top of the worksheet to collapse the detail data columns then click the plus button to expand the detail data columns.

8. Click the column B heading to select the column and choose Data→Group and Outline→ Group from the menu bar.

9. Click the plus button on the top of the worksheet window.
   Notice that column B has been added to the group you created in step 6. If a column lies directly to the left of a group, Excel will add it to the existing group. The same thing happens if you select a row immediately above an existing group.

10. Choose Data→Group and Outline→Settings from the menu bar.
    The Settings dialog box displays options for the placement of summary rows and columns. As you can see, the default is summary columns positioned to the right of detail columns. If your worksheet is laid out differently, you can adjust these options so the Auto Outline and Group commands function accordingly.

11. Click Cancel to close the Settings dialog box.

Ungroup the Worksheet

12. Drag the column headings to select columns B through E and choose Data→Group and Outline→Ungroup from the menu bar.
    The group is removed. You can manually ungroup columns and rows, including groups created by the Auto Outline command.

13. Click the Undo 🔄 button on the Excel toolbar to restore the group.

14. Select any cell in the worksheet to deselect the columns.

15. Choose Data→Group and Outline→Clear Outline from the menu bar.

16. Feel free to experiment with manually grouping rows and columns.

17. Save and close the workbook when you are finished.

Assessments

Assessment 6.1   Create a PivotTable

In this exercise, you will create a PivotTable to calculate the cost of care and shelter for healthy and sick animals summarized by animal type and age.

1. Open the March Expenses workbook.
   This database records expenses at the Capitol City Animal Shelter.

2. Examine the March Expense Report worksheet before creating the PivotTable. Be sure to identify the data fields in the database.

3. Create a PivotTable on a new worksheet.

4. Drag fields onto the PivotTable to display the data as described here:
   - The data should summarize the total cost of care and shelter.
   - The columns should compare the cost of caring for healthy and sick animals.
   - The rows should summarize the data by cats/dogs, then by age.

5. Practice changing the Field Settings and experimenting with different AutoFormats.

6. Save the workbook as **March Exp PivotTable** but leave it open for the next exercise.
   When you finish, your PivotTable should match this figure—with Field buttons.

		Healthy	Sick	Grand Total
Cat	Adult	$205.00		$ 205.00
	Pup/Kitten	$ 67.75	$102.00	$ 169.75
Cat Total		$272.75	$102.00	$ 374.75
Dog	Adult	$369.75	$ 55.25	$ 425.00
	Pup/Kitten	$146.50	$282.00	$ 428.50
Dog Total		$516.25	$337.25	$ 853.50
Grand Total		$789.00	$439.25	$ 1,228.25

The blank cells in this figure will normally display field names. They have been deliberately removed from this figure since they would display a significant part of the answer.

Assessment 6.2   Create a PivotChart

In this exercise, you will create a PivotChart that displays the cost of care and shelter for sick and healthy animals summarized by animal type and age. The chart will be a stacked 2-D column chart.

1. Examine the March Expense Report worksheet in the March Exp PivotTable workbook. Look over the data before you create the PivotChart. Be sure to identify the data fields in the database.

2. Create a PivotChart on a new worksheet.

3. Drag fields onto the PivotChart to display the data as described below:

    ■ The data bars should summarize the total cost of care and shelter.

    ■ The data bars should display the costs of care for sick and healthy animals.

    ■ The data should be broken down by the costs for cats/ dogs and compare the costs between kittens/pups and adults.

4. Save the workbook as **March Exp PivotChart** but leave it open for the next exercise. *When you finish, your PivotChart should match this figure—with Field buttons.*

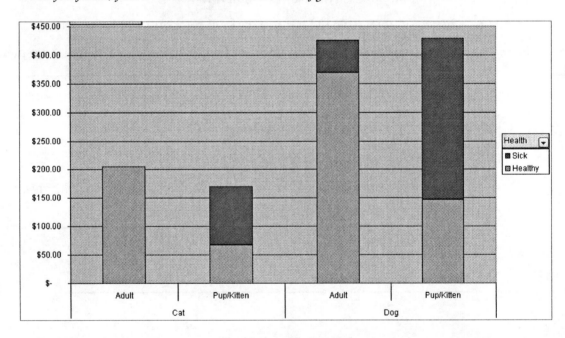

Assessment 6.3   Apply Styles to a Worksheet

In this exercise, you will create and apply a style for the column headings and subtotals.

1. Display the March Expense Summary worksheet in the March Exp PivotChart workbook.

2. Create a style for the column headings according to the following specifications:
   - The style name should be **column head**.
   - The font style should be bold and the font color should be a shade of blue.
   - There should be a border on the bottom of the cell.

3. Apply the column head style to all column headings.

4. Create a style for the subtotal row headings according to the following specifications:
   - The style name should be **subtotals**.
   - The font style should be bold and the font color should be a shade of red.
   - There should be a light fill color on the cell that makes the font easy to read.

5. Apply the subtotals style to all subtotal rows.

6. Edit the subtotal style to feature a dark fill color and a light text color.

7. Save the workbook as **March Exp Styles** but leave it open for Assessment 6.5.

Assessment 6.4   Create a Trendline

In this exercise, you will add a trendline to a line chart.

1. Open the Projected Revenues workbook and display the Financial Projections worksheet.

2. Add a linear trendline to the chart.

3. Print the chart.

4. Close the workbook.

Assessment 6.5　Outline a Worksheet

In this exercise, you will group the March expenses by cost, age, and health of the animals. You will also display subtotals.

1. Display the March Expense Summary worksheet in the March Exp Styles workbook.

2. Use any methods to group the worksheet according to the following:

   ■ The details of shelter cost and veterinary care

   ■ The details of age and health

   ■ The detail rows for all subtotals

   ■ The subtotal rows

TIP!

You may need to ungroup the Date Arrived column.

Your outline should match this figure.

	A	B	C	D	E	F	G
1	**Capitol City Animal Shelter**						
2	March Expense Summary						
3							
4	Animal	Age	Health	Date Arrived	Shelter Cost	Veterinary Care	Total Costs
5	Cat	Adult	Healthy	1-Mar	$ 82.50	$ 10.00	$ 92.50
6	Cat	Adult	Healthy	9-Mar	$ 60.50	$ 10.00	$ 70.50
7	Cat	Adult	Healthy	24-Mar	$ 19.25	$ 10.00	$ 29.25
8	Cat	Adult	Healthy	30-Mar	$ 2.75	$ 10.00	$ 12.75
9	Cat Subtotal				$ 165.00	$ 40.00	$ 205.00
10	Cat	Pup/Kitten	Sick	3-Mar	$ 77.00	$ 25.00	$ 102.00
11	Cat	Pup/Kitten	Healthy	10-Mar	$ 57.75	$ 10.00	$ 67.75
12	Kitten Subtotal				$ 134.75	$ 35.00	$ 169.75
13	Dog	Adult	Healthy	2-Mar	$ 79.75	$ 10.00	$ 89.75
14	Dog	Adult	Healthy	8-Mar	$ 63.25	$ 10.00	$ 73.25
15	Dog	Adult	Healthy	9-Mar	$ 60.50	$ 10.00	$ 70.50
16	Dog	Adult	Healthy	11-Mar	$ 55.00	$ 10.00	$ 65.00
17	Dog	Adult	Sick	20-Mar	$ 30.25	$ 25.00	$ 55.25
18	Dog	Adult	Healthy	20-Mar	$ 30.25	$ 10.00	$ 40.25
19	Dog	Adult	Healthy	28-Mar	$ 8.25	$ 10.00	$ 18.25
20	Dog	Adult	Healthy	30-Mar	$ 2.75	$ 10.00	$ 12.75
21	Dog Subtotal				$ 330.00	$ 95.00	$ 425.00
22	Dog	Pup/Kitten	Sick	3-Mar	$ 77.00	$ 75.00	$ 152.00
23	Dog	Pup/Kitten	Healthy	3-Mar	$ 77.00	$ 10.00	$ 87.00
24	Dog	Pup/Kitten	Healthy	13-Mar	$ 49.50	$ 10.00	$ 59.50
25	Dog	Pup/Kitten	Sick	15-Mar	$ 44.00	$ 25.00	$ 69.00
26	Dog	Pup/Kitten	Sick	27-Mar	$ 11.00	$ 50.00	$ 61.00
27	Pup Subtotal				$ 258.50	$ 170.00	$ 428.50
28	Total Costs				$ 888.25	$ 340.00	$ 1,228.25

3. Edit the Subtotal style, setting the font color to Automatic and the fill color to No Fill.

4. When you finish, save the workbook as **March Exp Outline** then close it.

Critical Thinking

Critical Thinking 6.1   On Your Own

Linda Johnson decides to use the database you developed in the Suppliers workbook (Lesson 5, Introducing Databases) to keep track of her monthly purchases. She asks you to add new columns to the Subtotals worksheet that calculate the quantity ordered and the wholesale price paid for each purchase.

■ Add a column to the database named **Quantity**.

■ Add a column to the database named **Wholesale Value**. The rows in this column should calculate the wholesale price multiplied by the quantity.

■ Use the data form dialog box to insert the quantities of each product to be ordered according to the following table:

Product	Quantity
Rakes	12
Roto Tiller	4
Seeds	144
Shovels	12
Stakes	144
Azalias	48
Books	12
Bricks	200
Fake Plants	6
Ferns	48
Fertilizer	36
Hoses	24
Miracle Grow	48
Orchids	48
Planters	72
Pots	72
Potting Soil	24
Spades	12
Stones	24
Watering Buckets	18

■ Save the workbook as **Quantities** then close it.

Critical Thinking 6.2 On Your Own

Linda Johnson was pleased with the database you developed in the Suppliers workbook and the summary worksheets you designed in the Suppliers Filtered workbook. She wants to know if PivotTables can display these summaries, too. She asks you to design a PivotTable and a PivotChart from the database.

Task A: Create a PivotTable

You have 10–15 minutes to complete Task A.

- Create a PivotTable on a new worksheet from the database on the Subtotals worksheet in the Suppliers Filtered (Lesson 5, Introducing Databases) workbook.

 TIP! *Before you can create a PivotTable or PivotChart from the database in Suppliers Filtered, you must remove the subtotals from the database.*

- Add fields to the PivotTable to display a summary of the Wholesale Value of each product ordered organized by Category ID.

- Add a field to the PivotTable that displays the summary broken down by Supplier.

- Edit the PivotTable so the Garden category is excluded from the summary. When you are finished, your PivotTable should look similar to the following example.

			Total
Home	Bay Area Garden Supply	Spades	$3.75
	Bay Area Garden Supply Total		$3.75
	Bright Flowers Supplies	Azalias	$2.07
		Fake Plants	$41.85
		Ferns	$1.05
		Fertilizer	$7.05
		Orchids	$5.85
		Planters	$23.85
		Potting Soil	$11.85
		Watering Buckets	$6.30
	Bright Flowers Supplies Total		$99.87
	Home and Garden Warehouse	Books	$8.85
		Bricks	$2.25
		Hoses	$13.50
		Miracle Grow	$7.95
		Pots	$7.05
		Stones	$7.05

- Take a few minutes to try other configurations of the PivotTable. See if there are any other useful ways to display the data.

- When you are finished, save the workbook as **Wholesale PivotTable** and go on to Task B.

Task B: Create a PivotChart

You have 10–15 minutes to complete Task B.

■ Create a PivotChart on a new worksheet from the database on the Subtotals worksheet.

■ Add fields to the PivotChart to display summary of the wholesale value of products purchased broken down by Category ID.

■ Add a field to the PivotChart to display the summary broken down by Supplier.

■ Add a field to the PivotChart to display the summary broken down by Product. When you are finished, your PivotTable should look similar to the following example.

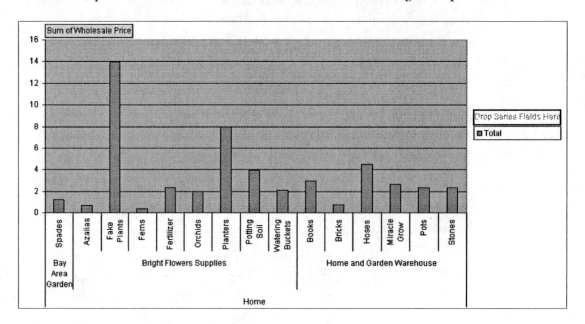

■ Format the number columns with the style of your choice.

■ When you are finished, save the workbook as **Wholesale PivotChart** then close it.

Critical Thinking 6.3   On Your Own

Ned Armstrong is happy with the database you created in the Customer Returns workbook in Lesson 5, Introducing Databases, to analyze book returns, but he wants to know if you can streamline the look of the worksheet. Sometimes there is more data visible than he needs. Ned asks you to set up the worksheet so he can focus only on the Return Date, Title, and Refund Amount columns. Group the worksheet so Ned can suppress the display of the other columns on the worksheet. When you are finished, save the workbook as **Returns Outline** then close it.

APPENDIX

Using File Storage Media

You may wish to use storage media besides the floppy disk referred to in most of the lessons. This appendix contains instructions for downloading and unzipping the exercise files used with this book, and an overview for using this book with various file storage media.

In This Appendix

The following topics are addressed in this appendix:

Downloading the Student Exercise Files

The files needed to complete certain Hands-On, Skill Builder, Assessment, and Critical Thinking exercises are available for download at the Labyrinth Website. Use the following instructions to copy the files to your computer and prepare them for use with this book.

Hands-On A.1   Download and Unzip Files

Follow these steps to download a copy of the student files necessary for this book:

1. Launch Internet Explorer.

2. Enter **labpub.com/students/fdbc2003.asp** in the browser's address bar and tap Enter.
   A list of books in the applicable series appears. If you don't see the title of your book in the list, use the links on the left side of the Web page to display the list of books for your series.

3. Click the link for your book title.
   A prompt to open or save a file containing the student exercise files appears.

4. Click the Save button.

5. Choose your file storage location and click Save.
   After a pause, the exercise files will begin downloading to your computer. Continue with the next step after the download is complete.

6. Click the Open button on the Download Complete dialog box. Or, open your file storage location and double-click the newly downloaded file if the dialog box closed automatically.

7. Click OK, and then follow the step for your file storage location:
   - **Floppy Disk:** Click the Browse button, choose the $3\frac{1}{2}$ Floppy A: drive, click OK, and then click the Unzip button.
   - **USB Flash Drive:** Click the Browse button, navigate to your USB flash drive, click OK, and then click the Unzip button.
   - **My Documents Folder:** Click the Browse button, navigate to the My Documents folder, click OK, and then click the Unzip button.
   - **Network Drive Folder:** Click the Browse button, navigate to your assigned folder on the network drive, click OK, and then click the Unzip button.

8. Click the Close button after the files have unzipped.

Working with File Storage Locations

New technologies continue to expand the variety of available computer storage media. The 3½ inch floppy disk has been around since about 1983. That's incredibly ancient in the fast-moving field of computers. It's easy to use other storage media with this book. Potential alternative storage locations include:

- The My Documents folder

- A USB flash drive

- A folder on your local hard drive

- A folder on a network drive

Using Alternative File Storage Locations

Depending on the file storage media you select, some steps you perform in the exercises will differ from what you see illustrated. However, with a little practice you should find it easy to interpret the instructions for use with your file storage media.

Example: Using a USB Flash Drive

You are performing an exercise in which you create and save a new file. If you are using a USB flash drive, simply substitute the drive letter for your flash drive for the 3½ Floppy (A:) drive shown in the figure instruction.

The storage location as it appears in the book

The storage location as you perform it on the screen

Using a Floppy Disk

If you use a floppy disk to store your exercise files, you should be aware of space limitations. This section explains how to keep track of the available space on a floppy diskette, and how to delete unnecessary files to conserve space.

Storage Limitations of Floppy Disks

As you work through the exercises in this book, you will create numerous files that are to be saved to a storage location. A floppy diskette may not have enough storage capacity to hold all files created during the course (particularly if you perform all of the Skill Builder and Critical Thinking exercises). Thus, you may want to use an alternate storage location for all files accessed and created during the course.

Checking Available Space on a Floppy Disk

If you choose to use a floppy disk as your storage location, you may reach a point at which the disk fills up and no additional files can be stored on it. However, if you regularly check the available space on your floppy disk, this problem should not arise.

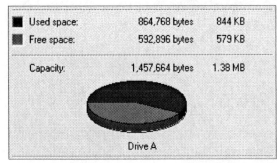

Windows can display a pie chart of the available space on your floppy disk.

Freeing Up Space on the Floppy Disk

If your floppy disk runs short of space, you will need to selectively delete files from it. You should delete files from lessons already completed, freeing up space for exercises in the current lesson.

 TIP! *Use the following procedure to check your available floppy disk space before you begin work on a new lesson. If you have less than 100 KB remaining on the disk, delete some files to free up space.*

Hands-On A.2   Check Free Space on a Floppy Disk

1. Open a My Computer window.

2. Right-click the 3½ Floppy (A:) drive and choose Properties from the context menu.
   Windows displays a pie chart with details on the used and available space on the floppy disk.

3. Examine the Free Space information and click OK.

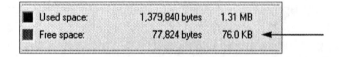

■ Used space:	1,379,840 bytes	1.31 MB
■ Free space:	77,824 bytes	76.0 KB ◄———

4. Follow the step for the amount of disk space remaining:
   - Close ☒ the Properties window. Close the My Computer window if there is more than 100 KB of space remaining on the disk. Skip the remaining steps in this procedure. You are finished and ready to proceed with the next lesson.
   - Close ☒ the Properties window. Continue with the remaining steps in this exercise if there is less than 100 KB of space remaining on your floppy disk.

Delete Unnecessary Files

5. Double-click to open the 3½ Floppy (A:) drive.

6. Choose View→List from the menu bar.
   The My Computer window displays your files as a compact list.

7. While holding down the Ctrl key, select files for lessons that preceded the one you are working on now and tap the Delete key on the keyboard. Choose Yes if you are asked to confirm the deletion of these files.
   Windows deletes the selected files.

8. Close ☒ the My Computer window.
   You now have plenty of space for your work in the next lesson.

TIP! *If you accidentally delete an exercise file needed for a later lesson, don't worry. You can repeat the procedure outlined in Hands-On A.1 to download and unzip the student exercise files as many times as necessary.*

■

Using a USB Flash Drive

A USB flash drive stores your data on a flash memory chip. You simply plug it into a USB port on any computer and Windows immediately recognizes it as an additional disk drive. USB flash drives typically are able store 32 megabytes (MB) or more of your data files. Large capacity USB flash drives can store 512 MB or more.

Most USB flash drives are about the size of your thumb and plug into any available USB port on your computer.

USB Flash Drive Letter

When you plug in a USB flash drive to a Windows computer, Windows automatically assigns it the next available drive letter. Windows uses drive letters to identify each drive connected to the computer. For example, the primary part of the hard drive is always identified as the C: drive. The CD/DVD drive is typically the D: or E: drive.

This USB flash drive is the F: drive.

Devices with Removable Storage

3½ Floppy (A:)   DVD/CD-RW Drive (E:)   Removable Disk (F:)

TIP! *Your USB flash drive may receive a different drive letter on different computers. This does not affect any files stored on the drive.*

Hands-On A.3   Rename Your USB Flash Drive

You may find it convenient to rename your USB flash drive to make it easier to recognize when you save or open files.

 TIP! *Some Windows systems may not give you renaming privileges for drives.*

1. Plug the USB flash drive into an available USB port.

2. Open a My Computer window.

3. Right-click your USB flash drive and choose Rename from the context menu.

 NOTE! *In the next step, Windows may display a prompt that you cannot rename this flash drive. You have not done anything wrong! You can use the drive with its current name. You may also want to try renaming it later using a different login.*

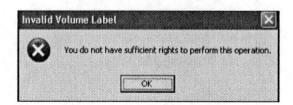

4. Type **FlashDrive** as the new drive name and tap [Enter]. Click OK if you receive a prompt that you do not have sufficient rights to perform this operation.
If you were unable to rename the flash drive, don't worry. Renaming the flash drive is a convenience for recognition and has no other effect.

Using the My Documents Folder

Windows creates a unique My Documents folder for each login. This folder resides on the main system drive (usually the C: drive). The Office 2003 application programs provide a My Documents button in their Open and Save As dialog boxes to make navigation to this folder convenient.

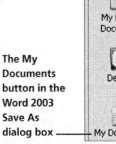

The My Documents button in the Word 2003 Save As dialog box

Using a Network Drive Folder

You may use a system connected to a network. There may be a folder on a network server computer in another location that is dedicated to storing your work. Usually, you will find this folder within the My Network Places folder of your computer. The Office 2003 application programs provide a My Network Places button in their Open and Save As dialog boxes to make navigation to this folder convenient. You may have to navigate deeper into the folder to locate your personal network drive folder.

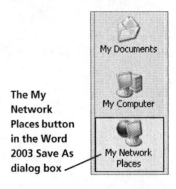

The My Network Places button in the Word 2003 Save As dialog box

Index

Numerics
3-D selecting/formatting of worksheets, 84–87

A
Analysis ToolPak, 112–113
AutoFilter, 132
AutoFormat, 162
automatic outlining, 179–180
AutoShapes, 41, 43–45
averaging function, databases, 135, 136

B
breaks, manual page, 18–20

C
calculations, database functions, 135, 136, 137
cells
    linking among worksheets, 64–67, 74–78
    locking/unlocking, 82–83
    naming, 72–79
    styles for, 172–178
charts (PivotCharts), 167–169
clip art, 34–36
Clip Art task pane, 34–36
columns and rows
    freezing header, 7–8
    sorting, 4–6, 130
    Subtotal tool, 130
    title, 16, 17, 78–79, 124
constraining objects, 45
contrast and brightness in images, 38–39
copying and moving worksheets, 68–72
criteria
    criteria ranges for database functions, 135–137
    data filtering, 132–134
    searching databases, 128–129
cropping graphic images, 37–38

D
data analysis tools
    Analysis ToolPak, 112–113
    Goal Seek, 108–109
    Solver, 110–111
databases
    creating, 124–126
    data forms, 126–129
    filtering techniques, 132–134
    functions for, 135–137
    queries, 138–139
    Subtotal tool, 129–132
DAVERAGE function, 135, 136, 137
default settings, number of sheets, 64–65
deleting
    cell names, 75–76
    files on floppy disks, 204
deposits, tracking (FV function), 104
digital signatures/certificates, 85–87
drawing objects, 39–48
Drawing toolbar, 39, 42–43
DSUM function, 135, 136, 137

E
editing
    cell names, 75–76
    styles, 174–176, 177
exercise files, storing, 202
extracting data from databases, 132–134

F
fields, definition of database, 124
filtering, data, 132–134
finding database records, 128–129
floppy disk storage option, 203–204
Format Painter, 70–72
formatting
    copying formats, 70–72
    drawing objects, 42–43
    PivotTables, 162–163
    styles, 172–178
forms, data, 126–129

formulas
    database functions, 135–137
    linking, 65, 74–78
freezing header columns/rows, 7–8
functions
    database, 135–137
    PMT and FV, 104–107
FV (Future Value) function, 104–107

G

Goal Seek, 108–109
graphic images
    clip art, 34–36
    contrast and brightness in, 38–39
    cropping and scaling, 37–38
    drawing objects, 39–48
    manipulating, 36–37
grouping data, 178–182

H

headers and footers, 12, 13–16
heading columns/rows, freezing, 7–8
highlighting (selecting) worksheets, 69, 84

I

installation
    data analysis tools, 110
    Query feature, 138, 139

K

keyboard shortcut commands, selecting worksheets,
    69

L

layering objects, 46, 47
linear trendline, 170
linking cells among worksheets, 65–67, 74–78
loan calculating function (PMT), 104
locking/unlocking cells, 82–83

M

manual page breaks, 18–20
margin settings, 12
moving and copying worksheets, 68–72
moving average trendline, 170
moving objects, 36–37

multiple column sorting, 6
multiple-sheet workbooks
    3-D selecting/formatting, 84–87
    copying individual sheets, 68–72
    default number of sheets, 64–65
    linking cells in, 65–67
    named ranges, 72–79
    printing, 88
    protection options, 80–83
My Documents folder, 207
My Network Places, 207

N

Name list for cell names, 74
naming cells, 72–79
network drive folder, 207
New Workbook task pane, 32

O

objects
    (see also graphic images)
    drawing, 39–48
    moving, 36–37
orientation, page, 10
Outline bar in databases, 132
Outline feature, 178–180, 181
overriding styles, 176

P

Page Break Preview, 19–20
page breaks, 18–20
page field area of PivotTable, 159
Page Setup dialog box, 10–20, 88
passwords and workbook protection, 80
pictures (see graphic images)
PivotCharts, 167–169
PivotTables, 152–167, 170
PMT (Payment) function, 104–107
printing
    multiple worksheets, 88
    settings for, 10–20
protection options, 80–83, 84–87

Q

Query feature for databases, 138–139

ISBN 1-59136-037-4